CAMBRIDGE STUDIES IN CRIMINOLOGY

CAMBRIDGE STUDIES IN CRIMINOLOGY XXXIX

General Editor: Sir Leon Radzinowicz

Juvenile Justice?

The practice of social welfare

THE HEINEMANN LIBRARY OF CRIMINOLOGY
AND PENAL REFORM

Juvenile Justice?

The practice of social welfare

Allison Morris

and

Mary McIsaac

HEINEMANN

LONDON

Heinemann Educational Books Ltd
LONDON EDINBURGH MELBOURNE AUCKLAND TORONTO
HONG KONG SINGAPORE KUALA LUMPUR NEW DELHI
NAIROBI JOHANNESBURG LUSAKA IBADAN
KINGSTON

ISBN 0 435 82601 8

First published 1978

Publisher's note: This series is continuous with the Cambridge
Studies in Criminology, Volumes I to XIX, published by
Macmillan & Co., London

Published by
Heinemann Educational Books Ltd
48 Charles Street, London W1X 8AH
Photoset and printed by Interprint (Malta) Ltd

CONTENTS

Preface

Interest in juvenile justice has been a continuing feature of work carried out by members of the Department of Criminology, University of Edinburgh. When Part III of the Social Work (Scotland) Act 1968 was about to be implemented, Professor G. H. Gordon, then Professor of Criminal Law and Criminology, who had earlier been responsible for an investigation into the operation of juvenile courts in two areas of Scotland, undertook responsibility for research into the development of the new children's hearings. This work began in the autumn of 1971 and was originally envisaged as a direct sequel to that carried out by Judy Duncan and Alison Arnott on children dealt with in Scottish juvenile courts in 1967, and although our own study subsequently spread in a number of different directions, we are very grateful for the groundwork which their report provided.

Professor Gordon moved to the Chair of Scots Law in 1973 but maintained his interest in juvenile justice and continued his encouragement and support in the later stages of the research, always acting as a ready, keen and perceptive critic when the ideas in this book were under discussion. Professor F. H. McClintock inherited overall responsibility for the project on his appointment as Professor of Criminology and Director of the School of Criminology and Forensic Studies and we are grateful for his continuing and wholehearted support, as well as for Professor Nigel Walker's ready agreement to the continuation of Allison Morris's collaboration in the research after she moved to the Institute of Criminology in Cambridge. Many people gave us the benefit of their experience by helpful advice in the early stages of the project, not least the members of Children's Panels Advisory Committees and of the children's panels of the two areas concerned who agreed to the work being carried out. But our main thanks must go to the reporters themselves and their staffs, who found time in the midst of awkward teething troubles arising out of the new administrative measures to allow and indeed encourage us to haunt vacant corners in their offices to collect our data; far from being charitably tolerated, we were actively welcomed. An invitation to join discussions and freedom to ask innumerable questions enabled us to acquire an understanding of the system which was invaluable. Police officials too, although faced with similar problems of working space and heavy work loads, made us feel at home in their offices and gave us access to their records. We also had many discussions with individuals in other allied services: social work, education, medicine and courts; all of whom shared with us their own interest in the new and developing system.

This research was financed by Scottish Home and Health Department, as was the earlier project on juvenile courts, and we would like to record our thanks not only for the funds which made the work possible but also for the unfailing help given and interest shown by many officials in Scottish Home and Health Department and in Social Work Services Group over the years.

Our thanks for help with data collection go to James Gallacher who was one of our team through the initial planning stages until summer 1973, and to Rosalind Goulstone who joined us from October 1973 to December 1974; and for typing the many successive drafts to several willing secretaries in Edinburgh and Cambridge. Among the many friends and colleagues to whom we turned for support and advice we would like to mention especially Dr Ann Smith in Edinburgh, who read successive versions of our manuscript with infinite patience and gave gentle but invaluable advice, and Henri Giller in Cambridge who pursued obscure footnotes and prepared the index. Sir Leon Radzinowicz it was who urged us on to publication, stimulating the energy and resolution necessary for success.

For the opinions expressed, the interpretations placed on the data, the comments made on the new system, we take full responsibility. We hope that the many who helped us will give us their understanding if not their complete agreement.

MARY McISAAC and ALLISON MORRIS
Cambridge and Edinburgh
January 1978

Prologue

Crime is increasingly viewed as a problem associated with youth. It is not surprising, therefore, that the juvenile justice systems which emerged in many countries at the end of the last century are also increasingly being questioned. Directions for the future are not clear; juvenile justice policy is in a state of flux.

In England, for example, the Children and Young Persons Act 1969 endorsed a treatment or social welfare approach towards children who offend. In a review of the operation of that Act a sub-committee of the House of Commons Expenditure Committee questioned whether such an approach was likely to influence juvenile offending or recidivism rates and suggested a new direction: 'that of satisfying society's wish to punish an offender and preventing him for a time from committing further offences at a reasonable cost and in the most humane way'.[1] The White Paper containing the Government's observations on the sub-committee's report moved in both these directions at once—it endorsed a social welfare approach but questioned its relevance in relation to *some* children who offend. The observations begin in a vein which is consistent with the philosophy of the 1969 Act. The White Paper states that 'the framework provided by the Act for dealing constructively and humanely with children in trouble remains a fundamentally sound one.' However, also in the introduction, there are statements which question this:

> The Government fully recognise and share the widespread anxiety that is felt, especially by magistrates, about the continuing problem of how to cope with a small minority, among delinquent children, of serious and persistent offenders. It is in this area that present measures under the Act are felt to be falling short.[2]

In the United States, the failure of the juvenile court to fulfil its original goals, along with increased concern about the civil liberties of offenders, also led to much criticism during the 1960s and 1970s. A series of Supreme Court decisions,[3] beginning in 1966, introduced a number of due process procedures into the social-welfare oriented juvenile justice system there, but these decisions have had little impact in practice and are largely ignored.[4] The reasons underlying this seem to lie in a deep-seated adherence to social welfare concepts. The Supreme Court itself was reluctant to abandon these concepts entirely. In withholding the right to jury trial the court stated:

> If the jury trial were to be injected into the juvenile courts system as a matter of right, it would bring with it into that system the traditional delay, the formality, and the clamour of the adversary system and, possibly, the public trial ... if the formalities of the criminal adjudicative process are to be superimposed upon the juvenile court system, there is little need for its separate existence. Perhaps the ultimate disillusionment will come one day, but for the moment we are disinclined to give impetus to it.[5]

Furthermore, the decisions providing for due process in the juvenile courts apply only to the adjudicative phase of the hearing (they do not apply to the more crucial pre-judicial and dispositional phases) and many issues which are already decided for adults remain unanswered for juveniles.[6]

These uncertainties reflect to some extent the confusion and ambivalence which characterizes our thinking about children who offend. Indeed there is in modern society an ambivalence towards children in general. Children are loved yet hated; indulged yet resented; a resource to be cherished yet both feared and envied. They deprive us of our freedom, they are costly and as they grow older they often question our values, our taken for granted assumptions. Consequently much of our time (in the family and in the schoolroom) is aimed at socializing the young into accepting certain sets of values, certain positions in the social structure. Nevertheless, as Friedenberg writes, many adults 'seem to use the terms "teenagers" and "juvenile delinquents" as if they were synonymous; to them the youth problem is one of law enforcement or treatment for the emotionally disturbed.'[7] Whether this tells us something of the 'problems' of adolescents or of the nature of our society, Friedenberg leaves it to the reader to decide. Faced, however, with information that a third of detected robberies, half of detected burglaries and a quarter of detected thefts are committed by those under 17,[8] the appropriateness of our ambivalence is confirmed— young people *are* nasty, selfish and brutish.

This ambivalence is reflected in the structure of tribunals dealing with children who offend. These tribunals—whether courts or welfare boards—*profess* to pursue both social control and social welfare goals. Consequently they are repeatedly confronted with ambiguities and contradictions in their ideology, structure and operation. They must protect the community from children who offend, yet many of the children referred to them have committed trivial offences, what Lemert has referred to as 'mickey-mouse stuff'.[9] These tribunals also profess to provide treatment to suit the needs of the child, yet they are often isolated from community (e.g. child guidance or psychiatric) services, and many of the children referred to them are dealt with by nominal measures.[10]

A key factor in these internal contradictions is the *apparent* incompatibility between social control objectives and social welfare objectives. These orientations, as ideal types, call for different patterns of response and different organizational structures. A social control orientation views the delinquent as a conscious lawbreaker who endangers the community. Social control is traditionally achieved within a criminal justice framework: punishment appropriate to the seriousness of the offence so that decisions reflect fairness and equality. A social welfare orientation, on the other hand, views the delinquent as a victim of circumstances—social, psychological, biological, economic—which have led to the commission of the offence. The aim is to provide him with the resources to overcome these circumstances. Action is determined by the needs of the child not by the nature of the offence committed, and is taken, not on proof of guilt, but on proof of these adverse circumstances. When a single tribunal tries to implement both of these goals it is bound to be riddled with inconsistencies: what is in the best interest of the child may conflict with what is in the best interests of the community. A tribunal dealing with children who offend cannot pursue both goals in these terms, and this dilemma becomes magnified because different groups (social workers, schools, police, etc.) expect the tribunal to meet their expectations. These pressures create competitions between the conflicting demands.

Recently attempts have been made to resolve this dilemma by explicitly stating one goal—social welfare—as dominant. This book examines one such jurisdiction—the children's hearings in Scotland. In 1971 the Scots abolished their juvenile courts and replaced them with welfare tribunals. We examine the ideology and practice of social welfare within that juvenile justice system: how does it work? does it work? is it different from a juvenile court? is it better than a juvenile court? does the stated dominance of one goal prevent inter-organizational conflict? do the various groups involved in the operation of a new system change their working ideologies to fit the dominant conception? The relevance of these questions transcends a national boundary. For this reason we outline in Chapter I the similarities underlying the Scottish and English systems of dealing with children who offend. Social welfare has been a dominant trend in the twentieth century. Its relevance to offenders has been questioned, but its grip is strong. Treatment and rehabilitation remain the watch-words of modern penal policy and practice. Why does this remain so when we have little objective data on the effectiveness of treatment methods? Is it merely because we feel more comfortable with the language of social welfare?

Social welfare is a particular type of control strategy. Mechanisms of social control are the various means used by a society to bring its recalcitrant members back into line. It involves, amongst other aims, reinforcing the desire to conform, making clear what is socially appropriate behaviour, discouraging deviation by negative sanctions and rewarding conforming behaviour. A major function of social institutions such as the family, marriage and religion is to contain men, to limit their self-interest. But there are many forms of social control, for example, public opinion, education, custom and law. The twentieth century witnessed a shift from primary means of social control (e.g. the family, the neighbourhood, the community) to secondary means of social control (e.g. police, courts, psychiatrists, social workers) although these secondary agents have *made use of* the primary means.[11] The stress placed on the family in the aetiology and prevention of deviant behaviour is a recurrent theme in criminological literature. Treatment (a technique of social welfare) is directed towards producing change in the behaviour of an individual and, when it occurs against the wish of the delinquent, becomes a type of social control.

This phrase, 'social control', has earned a bad reputation or at least there is some intellectual or emotional distaste for it. The authors of a recent book on juvenile justice rejected the idea that 'child welfare services are little more than methods of controlling unruly children.'[12] The inter-relationship between social welfare and social control is complex: as we have said, many of the difficulties in the practice of juvenile justice policy have stemmed from a confusion of the two. It is rarely asked whether or not social control is in the delinquent's interest as well as society's, or whether actions for the welfare of the delinquent preclude the interests of society.

The official banishment of social control means no more than the concealment of this dilemma. The language of social welfare *sounds* humane and its emotional appeal is considerable. But in practice welfare ideologies are subsumed by the goal of social control. Social welfare is a euphemism for social control and techniques of social welfare are *potentially* superior forms of social control. The Scottish system provides an illustration of this process.

Chapter I outlines the principles of social welfare and their gradual evolution. The present situation can best be understood in terms of the historical process of compromise between conflicting aims. In Chapter II we examine the endorsement of social welfare principles in Scotland in 1968 and demonstrate the influence of the civil service as well as various pressure groups, of practitioners as well as policy-makers. We develop a critique of the assumptions underlying social welfare in Chapter III and in Chapter IV, V, VI and VII we consider how policy was put into practice and the operation of social welfare. Legislation provides a mere outline of what is intended, and how this is interpreted and implemented by those operating the system can be of key significance. We discuss the operation of the new system both nationally and with reference to two particular areas. Chapter VIII questions the desirability of social welfare principles in relation to children who offend, and in the epilogue we discuss some ideas for future policy.

Notes on Statistics

The data quoted in the text are based on research carried out during the years 1972 and 1973. As a result of local government reorganization in Scotland in mid 1975 (with consequent changes in area boundaries) and a change in the format of statistical returns made to central government, recent national figures are not strictly comparable with those for earlier years. The Scottish Criminal Statistics for 1975 (Cmnd. 5531 HMSO) were published, therefore, without any figures relating to juveniles, and the Scottish Social Work Statistics for 1975 (not yet published) present separate figures for the pre- and post-reorganization periods. The overall pattern of decision-making, however, so far as we can check, has not changed materially over the years. We have referred to the data in general terms in the text but detailed information from the computer analysis can be made available on request.

Social Welfare: its principles and evolution

Introduction

Until the nineteenth century children were treated as adults as soon as they were considered capable of doing without their mothers. They did not have distinctive clothing or books, but rather shared in the work and play of adults.[1] At common law the age of criminal responsibility was 7 years. In England (though not in Scotland)[2] children aged from 7 to 14 were presumed incapable of crime, but it was open to the prosecution to prove that such a child in fact knew that his conduct was wrong. Sparing the child from the penalties of law merely on account of age would have weakened the deterrent force of law. Accordingly, children accused of crimes were treated as adults at both trial and disposition stages—they could be executed, transported and imprisoned.[3]

So accustomed are we to such notions as the immaturity of children that these practices strike us with horror; but it is difficult to know how many of the differences we now assume to exist between children and adults are a function of the idea that such differences exist; and, by enforcing these ideas, we may well have produced, or at least reinforced, such differences. At any rate it was during the nineteenth century that children came to be regarded as other than miniature adults and that child offenders were considered other than miniature criminals. It is self-evident that social and legal changes are linked, and in order to outline these changes and the reasons underlying them it is first necessary to present a brief picture of the surrounding circumstances.

Life in general in the early nineteenth century was brutal. Both the birth and the death rates were high and in the early nineteenth century 40% of the population was under 15. The Industrial Revolution required a supply of cheap labour. Statesmen, administrators and employers alike all turned to the child: the child was a source of industrial wealth. Philanthropists like Defoe and Hanway saw the advantages of extending labour to women and children in the struggle against poverty, and large families could prevent starvation by relying on child labour. Child labour was universal and inescapable. The family was employed as a whole and worked together just as it had done in the past. Bargains were entered into for the labour of the whole family unit and this necessarily involved the child in the same hours of work as the father. The kinship system determined the training, earnings and discipline of the family; and although discipline was harsh, it was socially tolerable because it came from the child's father. There was no state protection against abuse: the child was regarded as the property of the father, and as such was 'protected' from state interference; but, more importantly, the state itself was reluctant to interfere because the child played an essential role in maintaining trade.

As the century advanced there was a growing feeling of revulsion against the working conditions of the child. There were many reports of children being maimed by machinery and suffering from new industrial diseases. But progress was slow. Real attacks on child labour did not occur until the breakdown of the kinship system which itself had resulted from technological advances. Parents and children no longer worked together—the 1833 Factories Act limited the working hours of children and, by snapping the link between the child's shift and that of the adult, broke the kinship system—and the harsh discipline once administered by the father was now exercised by the foreman. Depersonalization prompted statutory interference.

This general concern with the lot of child was reflected in society's dealings with child offenders. The dangers of holding children and adults together in the same institutions were frequently pointed out. The stigmatizing aspect of imprisonment was also recognized and attacks were made against the court process itself. Some modification of criminal court procedure for dealing with children took place about the middle of the nineteenth century and this took them out of the orbit of the severest punishments. For example, an Act of 1847 gave justices in England the power to try children under 14 summarily for simple larceny, and the Summary Jurisdiction Act 1879 expanded the jurisdiction of justices so that most children were thereafter tried by magistrates' courts rather than at higher courts.[4]

By 1880 in Scotland most children also appeared before some petty, usually a burgh or police, court.[5]

But the main improvement in the lot of juvenile offenders came through the development of separate institutions to which the court could commit them.[6] Early in the nineteenth century, after-care institutions for children released from gaol were opened by a number of voluntary organizations and later, during the 1840s, a number of separate reformatories for children, also financed by voluntary organizations, were opened.[7] The position of these schools, however, was a precarious one—they had little official standing and the courts had no power to commit children to them. They had to obtain children either by conditional pardon, or by hiring the children as labourers from the prisons. In 1854, the Reformatory Schools Act and the Reformatory Schools (Scotland) Act gave official approval to the system of reformatory and industrial schools and the courts then had power to commit juvenile offenders to them rather than to prison.[8] Shortly before, an Act of 1838 had established a separate prison for juvenile offenders at Parkhurst in England. The Act's purpose was to provide a prison in which 'young offenders may be detained and corrected and may receive such Instructions and be subject to such Discipline as shall appear most conducive to their reformation and to the repression of crime.'

The arguments in favour of separate institutions were that young offenders should not be contaminated by the old, that they were different in kind from the old, that their offences arose from mischief, ignorance and the poor quality of their upbringing, and that they, by their nature, were malleable and deserved special treatment. To some extent, this reform movement was the specific application to children of changes in general penological doctrine—attitudes towards the adult offender were also modified during the nineteenth century.[9] But it was more than this. The distinction between the child and the adult offender was sharpened. This firm change in official attitude can be seen by comparing the Report of the Royal Commission on Reformatory and Industrial Schools in 1884 with that of the Departmental Committee on Reformatory and Industrial Schools in 1896. The former stated that, in the operation of reformatory schools, the protection of society was more important than the interests of the child. The 1896 Report, on the other hand, felt that the child and his welfare were the most important factors.[10]

The end of the nineteenth and the beginning of the twentieth centuries saw the growth of considerable pressure for the creation of separate juvenile courts. Many different people and groups presented alternative models for dealing with child offenders and played important roles in placing before the public information about the successes of juvenile courts already established (e.g. in many American states, Canada and South Australia) and in urging the government to act. Benjamin Waugh, for example, argued as early as 1876 for a new and distinct tribunal of 'persons interested in children and possessing special practical knowledge of them',[11] and the Howard Association published pamphlets in 1904 and 1905[12] which claimed that in the juvenile court in the State of Colorado 95% of the cases placed on probation proved successful in that no further offences had been committed by the children. Perhaps more importantly, this pamphlet also showed how the State could save money by the establishment of separate courts for children and of a probation service—the saving to the State of Colorado was estimated to be £20,000 a year. Around this time resolutions calling for separate courts for children were being adopted at various conferences throughout Great Britain. In fact, by 1904, separate courts for children had already been established in some areas of Britain. Children's cases were taken separately from adult cases in the courts of Glasgow, Birmingham, Leeds, Bradford, London, Liverpool and Cardiff.

This pressure eventually led to the Children Act of 1908 which formally established a separate court for children. The implementation to this Act was said to represent a 'revolutionary change of attitude from the days when the young offender was regarded as a small adult fully responsible for his crime.'[13] But it was rather the result of a gradual process of reform. Separate courts were a logical progression from separate institutions—the same arguments supported both.

Other ideas were also at work in the creation of the juvenile courts. Classical criminology, associated in Britain primarily with John Howard and Jeremy Bentham, remained a dominant force there until the middle of the 19th century.[14] Central tenets were the role of free will, the function of punishment as a manipulator of this will and like penalties for like offences. Men were seen as choosing between the anticipated pleasures of criminal acts and the pains imposed by society upon such behaviour, and it was believed that a fixed schedule of penalties could affect this calculation.

The challenge to classical criminology came with the growing awareness of the multiplicity of the social causes of crime. A Royal

Commission inquiring into the causes of crime reported, in 1863, that 'the number of crimes committed is probably less affected by the system of punishment which may be in use than by various other circumstances, such as the greater or lesser welfare of the population, the demand for work etc.' Positivist criminology emerged from Europe about this time.[15] Within the framework of positivist criminology, determinism replaced free will and moral guilt: individuals exercised little control over the factors leading to their criminal behaviour. In this view, 'every event is caused. Human freedom is illusory.'[16] In time, the emphasis in the search for factors to explain criminal behaviour shifted from socio-economic and hereditary factors to the psychology of the individual offender. Criminals and the law-abiding differed in certain characteristics, but the characteristics assigned at any one time depended on the theories in fashion. Crime was a disease and, consequently and more importantly, was something that could be cured. The factors which caused crime could be controlled by others (though not by the individual offender). In determining penal measures, the offender's heredity, personality and environment were to be taken into account. The maxim was 'punishment should fit the individual, not the offence.' Persons without choice, it was argued, could not be seen as responsible for their behaviour, and so they could not be punished; rather, they required treatment. Positivism also justified intervention. Ideally, it involved indeterminate sentences (to fit the criminal, not the crime) and wide discretion in formulating programmes which might effectively curb and modify deviant behaviour.

Britain was not much involved in these debates but there was sufficient interest in the new theories of criminality to influence penal policy. As the new theories suggested that crime was the result of predisposition, or of deterministic forces either in society or in the individual himself, penal policy moved away from punishment and towards social defence, prevention and reformation. Those interested in child welfare were much influenced by these writings and subscribed whole-heartedly to the positivist image of man: this emphasized the primacy of the actor rather than the criminal law and adhered to a deterministic model of human behaviour. Positivist criminology provided the impetus for change. Further, the new sciences of psychiatry and psychoanalysis highlighted the importance of childhood experiences in the development of the personality. It was simple logic to spend more money on and provide more resources for the child offender.

But the juvenile court grew out of the fears as well as the aspirations of nineteenth-century social reformers. They sought to advance the welfare of children by removing them from the jurisdiction of the criminal courts and jails and by providing new procedures and institutions based on rehabilitation rather than on punishment. They were also concerned about the social control and moral development of many of the children in the large Victorian cities. The traditional criminal courts had failed to prevent juvenile crime and juvenile crime was highly visible in the cities. This provided an impetus for action: the new procedures humanized the criminal law and its former practice *and* controlled the problematic behaviour of the young.

This reform movement is usually said to have its roots in the general humanitarianism and philanthropy of the nineteenth century, but the concept of humanitarianism covers a wide variety of attitudes and standpoints. Why were various evangelical and philanthropic groups and individuals involved? A simple answer is that they saw themselves as acting on behalf of society and for the benefit of society. But what view of society did they have? From their writings, it appears that they viewed each man or child as having a particular place or station in life and that one of the major aims of the reform movement was the inculcation of certain values and skills. Such aims are characteristic of reform movements in general. Flinn,[17] for example, suggests that social reforms were selected partly for their appeal to humanitarian instinct, partly for their innocuousness to the existing social structure of the country, but also for the purposes of attracting those not in the true religion. Such aims were even more apparent in reforms related to children. Children were too important a resource to be left to their parents; they were an asset to the State and so the State had to intervene in their upbringing. The arguments in favour of the compulsory education of children were that the community would clearly gain, and Flinn[18] suggests that the origin of charity schools and Sunday Schools lay in equipping the poor with the values of humility and submission towards their superiors. Elementary education was linked to the social class of the child. Poor children were instructed 'in those branches of learning suitable to their status' and were taught only to read the Scriptures;[19] anything else 'would produce in them a disrelish for the laborious occupations of life'.[20] Recent work on compulsory education in America suggests similar objectives—those of taking troublesome immigrant children off the streets and confining them in schools where they would be both motivated and taught to take their place at the bottom rung of the industrial ladder.

Similar views were apparent in contemporary writings on the delinquent child. The arguments in favour of reform were founded on Christian principles and on concern for the delinquent child, but also on the threat to society from the dangerous and criminal classes. Thus it was argued that child offenders, just because they were children, should be treated differently from adult offenders. It was unreasonable to expect the same standards of conduct from immature and uneducated children as were expected from adults. Mary Carpenter[21] wrote that children ought never to be considered paupers or delinquents, but boys and girls in need of education. It was also argued that the State should intervene when a child was not being looked after by its parents and that the delinquent, by definition, was not well looked after—there were deficiencies in his upbringing. Throughout the century, Government Committees had isolated such factors as the improper conduct of parents, the lack of education and the lack of suitable employment as causes of delinquent behaviour.[22] The State, therefore, stood as 'parent' to the delinquent child.

Yet another argument was that intervention was in the interests of society—the child offender was a threat to established values. Public attention was turned to the most practical way of defending the community from constant increases in its criminal classes. On this view, the State intervened because of the child's behaviour, not because of his needs—its intention was to control the child's behaviour, to cut off the supply of delinquent children and to point the child in a particular direction—towards Christianity.[23] The role of the reformatory schools was 'to give every child a knowledge and love of Scriptures which may hereafter influence his life'. There, 'turbulent unruly urchins were ... converted into tolerably quiet, orderly schoolboys.'[24] Mary Carpenter wrote of these schools: 'We have thus indicated the way in which young children of the labouring classes may be prepared for their station in life.'[25]

The motives of those urging change, therefore, were quite complex and highly ambivalent—the goal of child welfare was just one of many motivational elements. Dominant concerns were the protection of society from and the social control of children who offend. These aims were presented under the guise of humanitarian concern which, from the standpoint of the sort of society implicitly accepted by the reformers, they surely were. This was a troublesome time indeed for upper middle-class and upper-class persons—social distinctions were disappearing and wealth was becoming more important than birth in determining social status. Their concern with the maintenance of the status quo was quite understandable. The social worker, usually a middle-class woman,[26] taught the poor, especially the delinquent, to respect the values of middle-class life and how to adjust to their image of society.

The First Juvenile Courts

Juvenile courts were courts of summary jurisdiction and, as such, were similar to magistrates' courts in general. To emphasize their separateness, however, the juvenile courts were to sit in different buildings or rooms, or on different days or at different times from the ordinary magistrates' courts. Children were not allowed to mix with adult offenders at any time during their court appearance and proceedings in the juvenile court were private. The new courts had wide jurisdiction over children who truanted, begged, frequented the company of thieves or prostitutes, were beyond the control of their parents as well as children accused of committing criminal offences. Traditionally, society reacted against acts endangering its members but with respect to children this reaction encompassed almost *any* challenge to society's mores. To help mould the child's behaviour into what was seen as appropriate, the courts were given a wide and flexible range of dispositions varying from supervision by a probation officer to commitment to an industrial or reformatory school.

But the juvenile courts were criminal courts. The prevailing idea was that the child was a wrong-doer charged with an offence and the old procedures for dealing with adult offenders were not thought to be inappropriate in most respects in dealing with children. Although there were minor modifications and simplifications in the procedure in order that the child might understand what was happening, the mode of trial was essentially the same as it was for adults. Indeed, the bench acted mainly in their ordinary capacity and acted as juvenile courts only at certain times.[27]

The child welfare movement was an international one. The Second International Penitentiary Conference held in Stockholm in 1878 discussed the question of children in jail and the prevention of juvenile delinquency and both Platt[28] and Stang Dahl[29] have stressed the influence of this meeting on the subsequent development of the child welfare movements in America and Norway respectively. The first juvenile court legislation in the U.S.A. was enacted in Illinois in 1899. This Act set up a separate non-criminal procedure for children who had committed offences or who were neglected. The intention was to treat juvenile offenders 'as a wise and merciful father handles his own child whose errors are not discovered by the authorities'[30] and the aim of the court, instead of determining whether a boy or girl had committed a specific offence, was 'to find out what he is, physically, mentally, morally'.[31] Hearings, accordingly, were informal and criminal procedure was disregarded. This model was followed throughout America.[32]

In contrast, Norway (and Scandinavia as a whole) adopted child welfare boards in the Child Welfare Act 1896. These first boards consisted of the judge of the local court, a clergyman and a physician. Nyquist has suggested that the prior existence of local agencies concerned with the administration of social assistance and the fact that they occupied stronger political and social positions in Scandinavia than elsewhere may have influenced the adoption of such boards rather than juvenile courts.[33] This seems a likely account. What is not valid, on the other hand, is Stang Dahl's claim that Norway played a leading role in the 'invention' of child welfare. This ignores the gradual nature of the reform movement as a whole. Fox, for example, showed that the Illinois Juvenile Court Act of 1899 (like the British Children Act 1908) was, rather than a significant reform, essentially a continuation of the major goals and means of delinquency prevention which had been initiated some seventy years earlier.

Morris and Hawkins referred to these two types of procedures as two alternative paths of development: 'the Chicago path' and 'the Scandinavian path'.[34] But the philosophy underlying the procedures was similar—social welfare—and practice differed little in essentials. Both, for example, paid little regard to the legal rights of the child. Welfare boards and juvenile courts are not alternatives; the philosophy underlying a particular tribunal is more important than its structure. Scandinavian welfare boards and American juvenile courts had, in origin, much in common—more so than American juvenile courts and their British counterparts.

The new juvenile courts in Britain were not without their critics. Some looked fondly to the social welfare orientation of the American juvenile courts. Others drew attention to a basic dilemma in the procedures of the new courts. Sir William Clarke Hall wrote:

The real truth, however, is that no simplification of procedure, no regulations for the 'trial' of children, however perfect in themselves, reach down to the root of the matter. As long as we continue to conceive of the child as a 'criminal' and merely to allow such modification of his criminality as due to youth so long shall we fail to provide the most fitting cure for his misdeeds. What is needed is not the dramatic staging of a trial for a crime, but the provision of the best means for ascertaining and remedying evil tendencies.[35]

Indeed, two contradictory notions of the child offender collided within the framework of these first juvenile courts. On the one hand, the child offender was viewed as a victim of undesirable circumstances who had been denied the benefits of civilized life and it was the courts' task to provide such care and treatment as he required. But he was *also* viewed as a miniature adult who acted with free will and who required control and discipline. As such, both he and society required to be protected by the due process of law and its accompanying procedures and safeguards. The juvenile courts were, as a result, plagued from their inception by conflicting aims and expectations. The principles on which they were based reflect these conflicts.

Herbert Samuel, in introducing the Children Bill in 1908,[36] stated that it was based on three main principles: the child offender should be kept separate from the adult criminal and should receive at the hands of the law a treatment differentiated to suit his special needs; parents should be made to feel more responsibility for the wrongdoing of their children; and the imprisonment of children should be abolished. But closer examination of his words confirms the suggestion that conflict and ambivalence were embedded in the roots of the juvenile court. For example, Mr Samuel went on to say that 'the courts should be agencies for the rescue *as well as* the punishment of children' (emphasis added); and parental responsibility was encouraged because

> [The parent] cannot be allowed to neglect the upbringing of his child and, having committed the grave offence of throwing on society a child criminal, wash his hands of the consequences and escape scot free.

Thus parents could be fined for the wrongful acts of their children. And the abolition of the imprisonment of children was not solely due to humanitarianism. It was said that it would 'destroy the deterrent value if used too soon'. Imprisonment as an adult was the sword held over the young offender's head. This ambivalence towards the child offender led to ambivalence in the structure, procedure and operation of the early juvenile courts.

The Evolution of Social Welfare

In 1925 the Home Office sent out questionnaires to all courts of summary jurisdiction in England to collect information on the conduct of the juvenile courts in their areas. This questionnaire provided information on the practical organization of the juvenile courts, where the courts were held, how often they sat and so on. A diversity of practices existed but one major point emerged: it was the exception rather than the rule for justices to be specially designated to hear juvenile cases. The results of this questionnaire also provided the basic information for the first review of the juvenile courts. This was carried out, in England in 1927, by the Departmental Committee on the Treatment of Young Offenders (The Molony Committee)[37] and, in Scotland in 1928, by the Departmental Committee on Protection and Training (The Morton Committee).[38] Both were critical of certain aspects of the operation of the juvenile courts.

The two Committees examined the validity of applying criminal procedures to child offenders. A number of witnesses had felt that child offenders should not be dealt with within a criminal jurisdiction and referred favourably to the juvenile courts in America. But both Committees argued for the retention of the juvenile court. The arguments in favour of this were that there was

> some danger in adopting any principle which might lead to ignoring the offence on which the action of the juvenile court in dealing with delinquents must be based. It is true that in many instances the offence may be trivial and the circumstances point to neglect rather than delinquency ... but there remain cases where serious offences are committed and neither in the public interest nor for the welfare of the young offender is it right it should be minimised. Two considerations presented themselves strongly to our minds. In the first place it is very important that a young person should have the fullest opportunity of meeting a charge made against him, and it would be difficult for us to suggest a better method than a trial based on the well-tried principles of English law. The young have a strong sense of justice and much harm might be done by any disregard of it ... Secondly, when the offence is really serious and has been proved it is right that its gravity should be brought home

to the offender. We feel considerable doubt whether a change of procedure ... might not weaken the feelings of respect for the law which it is important to awaken in the minds of the young if they are to realise their duties and responsibilities when they grow older.[39]

Images of man and deviant man are clearly linked to social reaction and to methods of social control. In these reports, the delinquent child was viewed as a criminal responsible for his own fate: his law-breaking was conscious and deliberate and, as such, the wickedness of his action was required to be brought home to him by the formality of court-room procedures. The Committees, however, were influenced by a further image: an image of the child as a victim of social or psychological conditions beyond his control. This led to a compromise: the retention of the juvenile court with the addition to it of some of the advantages claimed for the educational or welfare tribunals.

Both Committees recommended a court 'especially adapted for its purpose'.[40] A major criticism of the early juvenile courts had centred on their personnel. The selection of magistrates for the English juvenile courts had been 'largely haphazard' with the exception of London where there was a special procedure. In Scotland the situation was worse because of the structure of the courts. There the Morton Committee felt that magistrates (who were town councillors chosen by the electorate to administer the town government and who accordingly had many other claims on their time) and sheriffs (who were legally trained) were not the appropriate persons to deal with child offenders. Of the magistrates it was said that 'the whole system is clearly not devised to secure the men and women with the best qualifications for the work,' and of the sheriff that 'it is certain that he is not appointed sheriff because of any aptitude he may possess for dealing with juvenile offenders, and he may have no such aptitude'.[41] Both Committees accordingly recommended that the courts should be staffed with people chosen on account of their special qualifications—those with a 'love of young people, sympathy with their interests, and an imaginative insight into their difficulties',[42] and those who showed

concern for the problems of childhood and of adolescence, and an insight into young life and that knowledge of local conditions which will enable them to estimate the influence of the parents, the effect of the environment, and the moral atmosphere of the district in which the offender lives.[43]

Both Committees agreed that the *main function* of the juvenile court should be to consider *the welfare of the children* who came before it and to prescribe appropriate treatment for them.[44] To this end the Committees suggested that the courts should have the fullest possible information as to the young person's history, his home surroundings and circumstances, his career at school and his medical report. They also recommended that the police and schools should collaborate more closely, and that there should be more frequent recourse by magistrates to reports about the child as an aid to determining the appropriate disposition for him. The Molony Committee outlined the basis for these recommendations:

> Once the principle is admitted that the duty of a court is not so much to punish for the offence as to readjust the offender to the community, the need for accurate diagnosis of the circumstances and motives which influence the offence becomes apparent ... (there must be) the fullest inquiries as to the antecedents and surroundings of the offence ... for estimating the personal factors, including especially mental and physical health.[45]

The Committees were aware that such principles might lead to greater intervention in the lives of children and to longer periods of detention. The English Committee wrote: 'The idea of the tariff for the offence or of making the punishment fit the crime dies hard; but it must be uprooted if reformation rather than punishment is to be ... the guiding principle'.[46] What is interesting about both Reports is that these dual images of the delinquent child were placed not side by side but in sequence. In the first instance (the adjudicative stage) the delinquent act was viewed as an act of conscious defiance. Once the act was proved or admitted to, it became possible to view it as a product of personal or external forces and dispositions were to be reached with these forces in mind.

The Committees' recommendations were subsequently accepted and given statutory force in the Children and Young Persons Act 1932 and the Children and Young Persons (Scotland) Act 1932. Parliament subsequently consolidated juvenile court law in the Children and Young Persons Act 1933 and in the Children and Young Persons (Scotland) Act 1937. The new legislation imposed a duty to have regard to the welfare of the child in making the appropriate disposition for him—a major change in the direction of a social welfare approach. But the legislation did not make this the main function of the juvenile court (as recommended by the Committees)—other interests were recognized. It was enough for the magistrate to have regard to the welfare of the child.

Although the English juvenile courts became specially constituted juvenile courts, they remained in practice criminal courts—juvenile court magistrates acted also as magistrates in the adult criminal courts. In Scotland, the clear intention of the legislature was that there should be one juvenile court in each locality but the old system continued except in four areas where special juvenile courts were established. These areas were the counties of Fife, Renfrew and Ayr, and the city of Aberdeen;[47] the provisions of Section 1 of the 1932 Act were never extended beyond these areas. It is difficult now to present explanations for this, but it is unlikely that further developments in the reorganization of the juvenile courts could have taken place during the war years of 1939–45. Subsequently local authorities, on whom the financial burden of providing the new courts lay, may have been reluctant to create special courts unless it could be established that those already in existence were effective in reducing juvenile delinquency, and there was no evidence of such effectiveness. So the juvenile courts in Scotland remained criminal courts; the major part of the work of their personnel, as in the English juvenile courts, continued to be dealing with adult offenders. It is unlikely that the actual operation of the Scottish juvenile courts differed much from the specially constituted English juvenile courts. The courts in both countries were criminal courts and the personnel in both were accustomed to work in the adult courts where considerations of the gravity of the offence and of the protection of the public were relevant. Consequently, juvenile courts did not ignore such considerations despite the statutory obligation to have regard to the welfare of the child. The powers of disposition of the juvenile courts in the two jurisdictions were also similar.

This suggestion that the juvenile courts in Scotland and in England and Wales operated in similar ways is reinforced by the similarity of the difficulties highlighted in England by the Ingleby Committee in 1960[48] and in Scotland by the Kilbrandon Committee in 1964[49] in the operation of the juvenile courts in the two jurisdictions. The dilemma inherent in the procedures of the first juvenile courts had remained: the juvenile courts were based on two quite distinct groups of ideas. The courts were criminal courts and were organized on that basis. But a further principle had been grafted on to that structure—the principle of welfare. These two ideas were not logically compatible:

the one stressed full criminal responsibility and the other stressed help and guidance to suit the needs of the individual child.

Before going on to discuss the changes in juvenile justice policy in the 1960s there are a few further points which must be made about this period. It is impossible to understand the nature and functions of social policy without an analysis of the social, economic and political system in which it operates. Britain, during this period, emerged as a welfare state. The ideas underlying the welfare state are derived from many different sources. Robson provides a useful summary:

> From the French Revolution came notions of liberty, equality and fraternity. From the utilitarian philosophy of Bentham and his disciples came the idea of the greatest happiness of the greatest number. From Bismarck and Beveridge came the concept of social insurance and social security. From the Fabian Socialists came the principle of public ownership of basic industries and essential services. From Tawney came a renewed emphasis on equality.... From the Webbs came proposals for abolishing the causes of poverty and cleaning up the base of society.[50]

Welfare statism was a response to industrialization, urbanization and technological change. Whereas early legislation (e.g. during the Liberal Government of 1906–14) was aimed at the elimination of poverty, at establishing a 'minimum standard of life', gradually welfare legislation was extended to embrace the entire nation (health, education, etc.). Though it was originally conceived in humanitarianism, commentators now draw attention to the latent functions of much of this legislation: raising productivity, fostering economic growth, meeting manpower needs, de-escalating conflict within society and the prevention of anti-social behaviour.[51] An integral part of welfare services is investment in the young, the care and education of children. Social reforms since the 1940s have increasingly been directed towards the welfare of children (and of the family): protection from neglect, exploitation and cruelty. Social values (and social behaviour) are transmitted from generation to generation through the socialization of the young. In Lockwood's words, 'the two major threats to a given social system are infants who have not been socialized and individuals who are motivated to deviance or nonconformity.'[52] Children who offend, therefore, require further socialization; what is of special interest for our discussion is the *form* which control takes within the welfare state. The transition in social controls from punishment to treatment is closely associated with an increased emphasis on public welfare.

The post-war Labour government enacted the Children Act 1948. Whilst the Act did not directly concern the delinquent child it created a child care service and this service was instrumental in the gradual merging, as far as social policy and action were concerned, of the neglected child and child offender into one category: children in need of care. The wording of the 1948 legislation was an attempt to get rid of the remnants of the Poor Law doctrine of 'less eligibility' which had existed until then. Children in care were to have access to the same range of facilities as other children. The Curtis Committee,[53] which preceded the Act, had spoken of the responsibility of Government to see that deprived children 'have all the chances, educational and vocational, of making a good start in life that are open to children in normal homes' and this was echoed in section 12 of the Act. The new children's officers were to secure a normal home life for deprived children; provision was set at an optimal rather than a minimal level.

Young offenders were still primarily regarded as requiring punishment or training rather than 'care'. Attendance centres were expanded during this period and in 1948 detention centres were set up to provide 'short, sharp shocks'. But, although young offenders were not within the Curtis Committee's terms of reference, it indicated that, in its view, there was some overlap between the neglected child and the offender: 'the difference is often merely one of accident'.[54] This thinking influenced the children's officer in his new role.

We also cannot ignore in this discussion what has been retrospectively called 'the Bowlby revolution'. John Bowlby published his major texts in 1946 and 1952.[55] His research purported to show the long- and short-term effects of maternal deprivation on the development of the deviant personality. He wrote that mother love in infancy and childhood was 'as important for mental health as vitamins and protein for physical health,' that separation from the mother during the first eighteen months of the child's life might have a damaging effect on the child's personality and that maternal deprivation stood foremost amongst the causes of delinquency. Indeed, the concept held wide currency and was said to be the cause of a wide variety of conditions. Bowlby's writings had a remarkable influence on social work, especially child care, training.

Gradually, the day-to-day experience of the new children's officers reinforced this premise that there was little difference between the delinquent and the neglected child. Both categories of children were seen as victims of family and environmental circumstances: offences were a response to these. It was increasingly felt that the prevention of neglect would also lead to the prevention of delinquency. But, despite these influences, the basic structure and practice of the juvenile courts remained the same.

The Revolution in Social Welfare: the English Approach

In 1956, the Home Office set up a Committee, chaired by Viscount Ingleby, to inquire into the operation of the juvenile court and to make recommendations for its improvement. The Committee were also invited to consider whether local authorities should be given new powers and duties to prevent or forestall the suffering of children through neglect in their own homes. Perhaps not surprisingly, therefore, the Committee emphasized what had been hinted at in previous reports: the lack of difference in the character and needs of neglected and delinquent children.

It singled out the lack of a satisfactory home as a major cause of juvenile crime as well as of child neglect and, as a result, supported the provision of housing, health, education and other welfare services to families at risk. But the Committee, though given this opportunity of examining the personal social services, felt that recommendations involving radical reorganization went well beyond its terms of reference. This may have been a consequence of the Committee's composition: it was made up primarily of lay justices, lawyers and administrators. There were no social work representatives.

With respect to the juvenile court, the Committee recognized the conflict mentioned earlier between the court's judicial and welfare functions. It stated:

> The court remains a criminal court in the sense that it is a magistrate's court, that it is principally concerned with trying offences, that its procedure is a modified form of ordinary criminal procedure and that, with a few special provisions, it is governed by the law of evidence in criminal cases. Yet the requirement to have regard to the welfare of the child, and the various ways in which the court may deal with an offender, suggests a jurisdiction that is not criminal. It is not easy to see how the two principles can be reconciled: criminal responsibility is focussed on an allegation

about some particular act isolated from the character and the needs of the defendant, whereas welfare depends on a complex of personal, family and social considerations.[56]

The Committee suggested that the weakness of the current system was that it appeared to be trying a case on one particular ground and then to be dealing with the child on some quite different ground. This conflict resulted, in the words of the Committee,

> in a child being charged with a petty theft or other wrongful act for which most people would say that no great penalty should be imposed, and the case apparently ending in a disproportionate sentence. For when the court causes inquiries to be made . . . the court may determine that the welfare of the child requires some very substantial interference which may amount to taking the child away from his home for a prolonged period.[57]

Although the Committee saw this conflict 'as basic to its deliberations', it still argued in favour of the retention of the juvenile court. It agreed with those witnesses who felt that, for the proper protection of those who were the subject of the proceedings, the tribunal should be a court of law, and that the power to interfere with personal liberty should be entrusted only to a court.

> It is not the conception of the judicial decision that is at fault. . . . What is desirable is that the juvenile court . . . should move further away from its origin as a criminal court, along lines which would enable it to deal . . . more readily and effectively with [child offenders] . . .[58]

The Committee developed a novel procedure for getting away from 'the conceptions of criminal jurisdiction'.

It suggested that the age of criminal responsibility should be raised from 8 to 12, but that a child below that age should be deemed in need of care if he acted 'in a manner which would render a person over that age liable to be found guilty of an offence'. Care and protection proceedings were to replace criminal proceedings. The thinking behind the proposal was that by removing the child offender from a jurisdiction based on criminal procedure, one would also remove the expectations that the sentence would be based on tariff principles. The Committee felt that the older child offender should learn to stand on his own two feet and to accept greater responsibility for his actions. Criminal proceedings were, accordingly, to be retained for them and welfare considerations were to be minimized. The Committee held a dual image of the delinquent child, an image determined by the age of the child. Children, it felt, came before the court because those responsible for their upbringing (parents, school, community) had failed to teach them how to behave in an acceptable manner. During childhood, therefore, the responsibility for the child's actions should be shared between him and the parents. The Committee did not go to the extreme of denying the child all personal responsibility for his actions; it was enough that *some* of the responsibility was placed on the parents. As the child grew older, the Committee took the view that his own responsibility increased and that of others grew less.

Of course whether children in the younger age group and their parents would be aware that the proceedings were not 'criminal' is another matter. The decision to initiate proceedings lay with the police; the complaint was to be proved by evidence of the commission of an offence; witnesses could be called to rebut the complaint; rules of evidence were not to be disregarded; and the child and his parents were entitled to legal aid.

Once the complaint was proved, whether as necessitating care and protection or criminal proceedings, the Committee recommended that the court should receive reports from the local authority children's department and probation department, that these reports should include any information which seemed relevant to the treatment of the child and that the offender should be given the treatment he required. The Committee, therefore, at least to some extent supported a social welfare approach towards both categories of children. (One of its recommendations was the setting up of 'diagnostic units' to investigate family problems brought to them by parents and social services and to refer children to appropriate specialists.) But the Committee came out strongly in favour of judicial rather than administrative discretion in the determination of dispositions. It argued that:

> Residence in an approved school involved considerations affecting the liberty of the subject, and we think it important that a decision to commit a child to an approved school should be taken by a judicial body which could not be said to have been influenced by administrative considerations.[59]

Its endorsement of a social welfare approach was modified and the dilemmas so well portrayed in the Report were left unresolved. The reforms suggested by the Committee affected the form and approach, but not substantially the effect, of proceedings involving younger children—they were essentially changes of procedure. The Report drew little criticism. An editorial in *The Times* on the day of the report's publication complained that the Committee had taken an 'unconscionably long time' but generally approved of the Committee's recommendations.[60] Publication did, however, provide a further opportunity for the differing views on the appropriate structure of juvenile court and of social services to be aired. Winifred Cavenagh, in an article which appeared just after the appointment of the Committee, had complained that social action taken under the cover of criminal proceedings was an abuse of justice and of law and had argued that the juvenile courts were in an ambiguous position—their legal structure was bound to clash with what justices appeared to regard as the principal aim of their activities: the promotion of welfare. She was against any modification of the system and suggested a need to 'trim off all those excrescences which do not rightly adhere to a criminal court at all'.[61] Not surprisingly, therefore, she was critical of the Committee's report. She argued that the Committee were trying 'to reconcile incompatible objectives and to sit on two stools at once'.[62] Other critics felt the new 'care and protection' procedure was 'something that would pretend an offence is not an offence' and would 'use . . . a formula to avoid plain speaking'.[63]

For still others the Committee's recommendations did not go far enough. Younghusband, for example, had argued, just after the appointment of the Committee, for the abandonment of offence adjudication and for the substitution of a single care and protection procedure to cover all children—delinquent, neglected and maltreated. She also argued for the creation of a family court and for a family or child welfare service to look after all deprived and delinquent children.[64]

The two main political parties received the Committee's recommendations differently. The reaction of the Conservative party was cool—juvenile crime rates continued to increase and there had recently been disturbances in an approved school. The Labour party felt that the recommendations were not sufficiently far-reaching— they placed insufficient weight on keeping children out of court and there was no structure for the future development of the social services.[65] The Committee's major recommendations—'care and protection' proceedings for children under 12—did not become law. The Children and Young Persons Act 1963 raised the age of criminal responsibility from eight to ten[66] (not to twelve as recommended by the Committee) and Section 1 placed a duty on local authorities to give such advice, guidance and assistance as was necessary to keep young offenders out of court. Henry Brooke, the then Home Secretary, saw the Act as 'the most valuable instrument of all for reducing delinquency and doing it in the best possible way, by saving family life from wreck'.[67] There were no changes made to the structure and procedure of the juvenile courts.

Subsequently, the Labour party in 1964 set up a committee on criminal policy under the chairmanship of Lord Longford. (The Committee included eight future government ministers.) The Report[68] was fairly wide-ranging and a major proposal was the abolition of the juvenile courts. This suggestion was not based on any attempt to resolve the conflicts apparent within the juvenile courts. The Committee's starting point was that 'delinquents are to some extent a product of the society they live in and of the deficiencies in its provision for them,' but that the machinery of the law was reserved for working-class children—children of other classes were dealt with by other means. Their proposals stemmed from the belief that 'no child in early adolescence should have to face criminal proceedings: these children should receive the kind of treatment they need, without any stigma.' Criminal proceedings were felt to be 'indefensible' where the offence was a trivial one and where it was serious this was 'in itself, evidence of the child's need for skilled help and guidance'. The causes of juvenile delinquency and child neglect were traced by the Committee to a primary source: inadequacy or breakdown in the family. 'It is a truism that a happy and secure family life is the foundation of a healthy society and the best safeguard against delinquency and anti-social behaviour.' Delinquency in a child was 'evidence of the lack of care, guidance and opportunities to which every child is entitled'. Accordingly, an alternative framework to the juvenile court was suggested: a 'family service' in which the child, family and social worker would discuss the treatment of the child. Only where agreement could not be reached or where the facts of the case were disputed would the case be referred to a new 'family court'.

There are three central socialist values—equality, freedom and fellowship. Equality, according to Crosland,[69] 'has been the strongest ethical inspiration of virtually every socialist doctrine' as inequality offends against ideas of social justice. Every child, he argued, has a natural right 'not merely to life, liberty and the pursuit of happiness but to that position in the social scale to which his natural talents entitle him'. This egalitarian orientation is vividly apparent in the Report. It was an attempt to construct a system in which the life opportunities of neglected children and of children who offend would be equal to those of law-abiding and non-deprived children.

These proposals subsequently formed the basis of the Labour Government White Paper, *The Child, the Family and the Young Offender*,[70] except that a 'family council' consisting of social workers and other persons selected for their understanding and experience of children replaced the 'family service'. There was considerable opposition to these proposals. Barbara Wootton, a proponent of a social welfare approach generally, criticized the White Paper for 'its complexity, wasteful duplication and probably total incomprehensibility to those who would find themselves trotting backwards and forwards from court to council'.[71] But the main criticisms centred round the inappropriateness of a social welfare approach in dealing with children who offend. Winifred Cavenagh, for example, argued that the family council idea was unsound: it made too little of the cases where the facts were disputed; appearance before the council was just as likely as appearance before the juvenile court to lead to stigma; it created a dangerous precedent to allow detention for observation and assessment without the agreement of the child or of the parents on the basis of administrative rather than judicial action; and it assumed knowledge about the causes and treatment of delinquency which did not exist. There was no evidence, she argued, 'to suggest that we know how to change criminal behaviour by any acceptable means'.[72] Cavenagh was not against the idea of family councils but felt that the arguments for and against such councils should be seen as distinct from the attempt to deal with the offender or his criminality. There *were* differences, it was argued, between the 'deprived' and the 'depraved': the 'depraved' had committed an offence and it was necessary to express society's disapproval of this. A number of lawyers made similar points. Downey complained that the White Paper proposed to abandon justice and established courts in order to follow a 'fashionable' but not well-founded theory of juvenile delinquency.[73] And Fitzgerald argued that the White Paper's aim of protecting children from the stigma of criminality was based on a fundamental misconception—there might well be situations in which stigmatization played a beneficial role.[74]

The major attack against the White Paper came from the probation service and the magistracy, both of whom were concerned with the protection of the legal rights of the child. They felt that there were too many possibilities for abuse in the proposed scheme and that it was undesirable that decisions which might affect the liberty of the young should be reached by social workers. The police were also critical of the proposed machinery.

Some commentators, however, were in favour of the proposals. Kahan saw family councils as a natural development from the recognition that an 'immature human being could not be expected . . . to make mature judgments'.[75] The proposals were, she felt, a corollary of recognizing that social inadequacy was more readily improved by constructive help than by punitive disapproval. Peter Scott argued that the proposals did not go far enough and that failure to include the education authority in the family councils was a 'grave omission'.[76] But he also suggested that the White Paper went too far. He thought it worrying that the impression was given that the nature and causes of delinquency were understood.

In 1968 the Government, in response to the considerable opposition to these proposals, produced a second White Paper, *Children in Trouble*,[77] which was the basis of the Children and Young Persons Act 1969. For this reason it is necessary to spell out the philosophy underlying this White Paper and its proposals.

The second White Paper was an attempt to retain the proposals of the earlier White Paper and, at the same time, to forestall further criticism. The drafters played a skilful game and won. They could not be accused of cheating but there is no doubt that the opposition was tricked or, at least, placated. This was achieved by abandoning the controversial family council concept and retaining the juvenile court. The opposition was thereby deprived of much of its sting. The proposals of the new White Paper have often been described as less radical than its predecessor, but this is not so—what happened was that magistrates and others failed to realize 'how far the traditional functions and operating philosophy of the juvenile court were being eroded by the details of the new framework'.[78] Magistrates, initially at least, considered the second White Paper to be a great improvement on the earlier one.

Basically both White Papers shared an emphasis on treatment or social welfare and on keeping children out of the reach of the criminal law. In *Children in Trouble* it was stated that:

> Juvenile delinquency has no single cause, manifestation or cure. Its origins are many, and the range of behaviour which it covers is equally wide. At some points it merges almost imperceptibly with behaviour which does not contravene the law. A child's behaviour is influenced by genetic, emotional and intellectual factors, his maturity, and his family, school, neighbourhood and wider social setting. It is probably a minority of children who grow up without ever misbehaving in ways which may be contrary to the law. Frequently such behaviour is no more than an incident in the pattern of a child's normal development. But sometimes it is a response to unsatisfactory family or social circumstances, a result of boredom in and out of school, an indication of maladjustment or immaturity, or a symptom of a deviant, damaged or abnormal personality. Early recognition and full assessment are particularly important in these more serious cases.[79]

Consequently, the White Paper suggested that it was necessary

> to develop further our facilities for observation and assessment, and to increase the variety of facilities for continuing treatment. Increased flexibility is needed so as to make it easier to vary the treatment when changed circumstances or further diagnosis suggest the need for a different approach.[80]

Early recognition of delinquency, full assessment of the child's needs and flexibility of treatment were particularly important. A new approach was needed and the White Paper's proposals provided this.

Although the juvenile court was to be retained, the White Paper proposed that all children under the age of 14 would cease to be tried for criminal offences. Further, in an attempt to narrow down the circumstances in which court proceedings would be possible, an offence in itself would cease to be a sufficient reason for a court appearance. 'Care and protection' proceedings would be possible for children between the ages of 10 and 14 who committed offences, but only where it could be established that the child was not receiving such care, protection and guidance as a good parent might reasonably be expected to give. (The same double-barrelled test was to be applied to children exposed to moral danger, beyond parental control, neglected, etc.) Otherwise, such children should be dealt with on an informal and voluntary basis. Children between the ages of 14 and 17, on the other hand, could be subject to criminal proceedings but only after mandatory consultation between police and social workers and after application to a magistrate for a warrant to prosecute. Warrants would be issued only in exceptional circumstances; it was expected that such offenders would also, in the main, be dealt with under 'care and protection' proceedings or informally. The overall aims of the proposals were to reduce the number of cases heard in the juvenile courts and to reduce the number of cases in which the commission of an offence was a sufficient ground for intervention in itself. There was a clear preference for civil rather than criminal proceedings.

Thus far the proposals seem little more than an extension of the approach suggested by the Ingleby Committee in 1960, but *Children in Trouble* envisaged also an enlarged and significant role for local authority social workers. In addition to mandatory social work consultation prior to proceedings and to increased social work involvement with families and children on a voluntary basis, considerable power was also placed in the hands of social workers to vary and implement the disposition orders made by the courts. Commitment to the care of the local authority was to replace approved school and fit person orders; and implementation of the care order would be in the hands of the local authority social service department rather than with magistrates. Attendance centres and detention centres were to be replaced by a new form of treatment—intermediate treatment—and the form that this would take would also lie with the social services; approved schools were to be merged within the community home system and local authorities were to develop a wide range of institutions of different types for all children in need. Magistrates were no longer to be involved in detailed decisions about the kind of treatment appropriate for the child. Social workers, within the limits of the particular order, were to determine this. Thus, although the composition and constitution of the juvenile court was virtually unchanged, its jurisdiction was radically altered.

Revolution in Social Welfare: the Scottish Approach

It would have been possible to extend the Ingleby Committee recommendations to Scotland or to activate fully the provisions of the Children and Young Persons' (Scotland) Act 1937 which permitted the establishment of special juvenile courts there. That this did not happen suggests that the Civil Service in Scotland were dissatisfied with the English Report or desired change in a direction other than that incorporated in it. In 1961, the Secretary of State for Scotland decided to set up the Kilbrandon Committee, chaired by a High Court Judge to 'consider the provisions of the law of Scotland relating to the treatment of juvenile delinquents and juveniles in need of care or protection or beyond parental control and, in particular, the constitution, powers and procedure of courts dealing with such juveniles'.[81]

The Committee began with the assumption that the children appearing before the juvenile court—whatever the reason for the appearance—were all in fact exhibiting the varied symptoms of the same difficulties. It stated that in terms of the child's actual needs, the legal distinction between juvenile offenders and children in need of care or protection was—looking to the underlying realities—very often of little practical significance. Delinquency was described as a 'symptom of personal or environmental difficulties';[82] truancy was said to arise from 'maladjustment whether due to personal or environmental factors'[83] and was in many cases 'a manifestation of emotional disturbance often attributable to factors in the home and family background'.[84] Similarly, being beyond parental control was thought to be 'attributable to factors personal to the child or to the parents themselves'.[85] The root of the problem in all children was felt to be a failure to develop normally. In the words of Lord Kilbrandon: 'the problem is primarily one of arrested or deformed development. There has been a growth failure'.[86] These personality problems could be explained further. The Kilbrandon Committee saw the causes as lying in 'shortcomings in the normal "bringing-up" process—in the home, in the family environment and in the schools'.[87] The Committee stressed that the measures recommended by it were intended not to supersede the natural beneficial influence of the home and the family, but were, wherever practical, to strengthen, support and supplement them. The needs of the child could not be met, it felt, 'by treating the child in isolation, but rather as a member of a family unit in a particular environment'.[88]

The Committee stressed that measures of disposal should be individualized and key notions in the Report's recommendations were 'assessment', 'diagnosis' and 'treatment'. It felt that the appropriate treatment measures in any individual case could be decided only on an 'informed assessment of the individual child's actual needs'.[89] To achieve this the Committee hoped to establish 'a procedure which from the outset seeks to establish the individual child's needs in the light of the fullest possible information as to his circumstances, personal and environmental'.[90] The new system would not work 'without adequate machinery for early identification and diagnosis', without 'adequate facilities for assessment', and it demanded 'a flexibility of approach'. Thus the tribunal should have

> the widest discretion in their application of treatment measures appropriate to the needs of the individual child, who would thereafter remain within its jurisdiction for as long a period as was judged to be necessary, subject to whatever upper-age limit might be fixed by statute. During that period the agency would have the widest discretion to vary or terminate the measures initially applied, and where appropriate to substitute others.[91]

To achieve these ends the Committee recommended the abolition of the juvenile court and its replacement by a welfare tribunal called a juvenile panel, which would be staffed by lay people who either by knowledge or experience were specially qualified to consider children's problems. The panels were to have no power to try issues of fact—they were concerned only with disposition—and the proceedings were to be based on the admission or acceptance of the ground of referral by the child and his parents. A complete separation of judicial and disposition functions was recommended: if the child or the parent denied the ground of referral (for example the commission of the offence) the case was to be referred to the sheriff court (a court presided over by a professional judge) for the offence to be proved. If the child or parent objected to a decision made by the panel on the disposition of the child, they would again be able to appeal to the sheriff court. In both these instances the parents and the child would be entitled to legal aid.

The key figure in the new system was to be the reporter. Police, social workers, education authorities, indeed anyone, including the child's parents, could refer the child to the reporter and it was then his function to decide, on the basis of reports, whether or not the child referred to him seemed to be in need of special measures of education. If he believed that this was so, the child would be referred to the panel. If there was no indication that the child needed compulsory measures of education, the reporter, on his own initiative, could arrange voluntary help from the social work department or the school. Alternatively, he could do nothing at all, he could interview the child, or the child and his parents, or he could write to the child or parents outlining the possible consequences of continued offending. The common element in the measures arranged by the reporter himself was that they lacked the element of compulsion.

The panel was to be a meeting of three panel members who would discuss with the child and his family the reasons why there seemed to be a need for compulsory measures of care. The panel meeting would take place in an informal setting.

The Committee also recommended that the child and his parents should have a right to representation at the panel meeting (but not to legal aid) and that they could be accompanied or represented by, for example, a friend, a teacher, or another member of the family. The powers of disposition to be available to the panel were to discharge the referral or to place the child under the supervision of a social worker—the supervision order could be with or without conditions and could include residence in a residential establishment. The panel would specify the place to which the child should be sent and it would also have continuing jurisdiction, that is, the case would be reviewed on request and would have to be reviewed annually by the panel.

The panels would be served by a new department to be called the 'Social Education Department'. This would amalgamate the functions of the local authority children's department and the probation service, the child guidance service, school welfare and attendance service, school medical service and the approved schools after-care service. The new department would prepare the social background reports on the children, make recommendations for treatment measures, and carry out the treatment orders made by the panels.

The system was to apply to all children up to the age of 16, but a child on supervision would remain within the jurisdiction of the panel until he reached the age of 18. The Committee, however, also recommended that there should continue to be situations in which a child who had committed an offence could be dealt with in the court system. It felt that these situations would arise 'exceptionally' and in 'grave cases'.

Conclusion

These new procedures both in Scotland and in England and Wales were quite explicitly based on a social welfare approach to children who offend. The conceptual framework for such an approach is radically different from that which surrounded the juvenile courts in the late sixties and before. These courts primarily emphasized concepts of crime, responsibility and punishment; they were criminal courts and, as such, their first function was the determination of guilt or innocence. The Kilbrandon Committee neatly summarized the essential differences between this approach and one based on 'assessment-prevention-treatment' in paragraph 54:

(1) *Early preventive measures*: the 'crime-responsibility-punishment' concept militates against preventive action against potential delinquents. Because of the high degree of personal responsibility which it attaches to the criminal, a stigma is attached in the public eye to conviction of a crime, which bears no necessary relationship to the harm done by the action itself or the actual responsibility of the person who did it. Because it is concerned with the deserts of a criminal, the standard of proof is high. In the absence of such proof—even though it is clear that the surrounding circumstances are such as to call urgently for preventive action—no such action can be taken since it would involve treating as criminals persons who have not been convicted by a criminal court.

(2) *Environmental factors:* punishment cannot be extended to any substantial degree beyond the individual offender, since no other person has the degree of guilt for the offence which would be acceptable as a prerequisite for punishment. But treatment can be applied beyond the individual who committed the act, to others, an alteration in whose behaviour might result in a substantial improvement in that individual.

(3) *The needs of the individual:* the 'crime-responsibility-punishment' concept, because the punishment must fit the crime may inhibit the court in ordering the treatment the offender needs. Indeed, it may work in the other direction, for example, in the case of the offender before the court for an offence which, in the eyes of the law, is comparatively minor, but which has causes which require long-term treatment. The court cannot, in such circumstances, impose what would be considered a heavy punishment; indeed, the causes of the crime might well be regarded as mitigating circumstances which would make a lighter than normal punishment appropriate. No such difficulties would arise on the 'preventive' principle since there the prime consideration would be the need for treatment measures.

(4) *Alteration of treatment:* somewhat similar considerations apply in relation to alteration of treatment. Punishment by its nature is 'once for all'. The criminal is entitled to ask that the judge should decide his punishment on the information available at the end of his conviction and, once the judge has weighed out the appropriate punishment, there are no good grounds for its alteration, since the acts which merited it have been done and cannot alter. Subsequent mitigation of

punishment—shortening of treatment because of good response to treatment—may be acceptable, but the court, because its essential function is the taking of final decisions alterable only by a higher court, is not felt to be a suitable instrument for achieving this. This concept, however, is unhelpful from the point of view of treating or training an individual. Even were our knowledge about causes of crime and the formation of offenders much fuller than it is, it is inconceivable that a court could ever have chosen, at the moment of the commencement of its sentence, the exact treatment—to be given perhaps over a period of years—appropriate to the individual person before it.

The philosophy underlying the new systems in both Scotland and England and Wales went far beyond the proposals of previous Reports. Both jurisdictions rejected a criminal justice approach. The essentials of such an approach are: (i) proof of the commission of an offence as the sole justification for intervention—the delinquency itself is the disorder; (ii) a proportion between the nature of the offence and the disposition; and (iii) equality before the law— equal cases demand equal treatment. The proposed new procedures assumed that the child offender was in need of measures of care, that delinquency was a symptom of an underlying disorder. The emphasis was on the shortcomings of the child and his family, whether social or individual. Ideas of justice or legal rights were of secondary importance—the major aim was the identification and diagnosis of the child's needs and the provision of treatment to suit these needs. Treatment measures were to be flexible and wide discretion was to be given to decision-makers both to determine and to vary treatment measures. In both countries there was a preference for administrative and consultative decision-making dominated by professional, primarily social-work, judgments. Protection from the stigma of a criminal status was considered essential and so informal procedures were preferred to formal. That the tribunal in one country was to be a 'juvenile court' and in the other 'a juvenile panel' was unimportant. To reiterate a point made previously in this chapter, the assumptions underlying a tribunal rather than its structure determine its operation.

So far so good. A particular political ideology, the growth of the social service professions and the dominance of a particular view of the aetiology of delinquency converged to create new systems for dealing with children who offend. From now on, the story takes us on different paths. The social welfare principles of *Children in Trouble* reached the statute book in the Children and Young Persons

Act 1969 but that Act has not been fully implemented. The same principles were fully endorsed in Scotland in the Social Work (Scotland) Act 1968. The following chapter discusses how this happened.

II

Social Welfare: its emergence and implementation in Scotland

The juvenile court has provided a fruitful basis for discussions of the creation of laws.[1] Certainly the significance of legislation cannot be appreciated without some attempt to understand its emergence at a particular point in time and the role of key figures in the discussions. The partial implementation of the Children and Young Persons Act 1969 in England raises questions of interest as some three years earlier proposals based on similar aims (though on a different procedure) had failed amidst much opposition. At the same time, the Social Work (Scotland) Act 1968, considered by many writers to be more radical than its English counterpart and sharing many of the essentials of the first English White Paper, experienced little opposition. Indeed, the fierce debates surrounding the English Act make the acceptance of the Kilbrandon Committee's recommendations for the abolition of the juvenile court all the more surprising. It was not that there was no opposition at all—what there was lacked effect. But why did it lack effect? This chapter outlines how the abolition of the juvenile court was achieved in Scotland and how a social welfare approach was adopted in a country of strong Calvinist traditions, traditions which stress individual responsibility and the punishment of wickedness. But first we consider some of the memoranda[2] submitted to the Kilbrandon Committee. These are of interest as they make apparent competing views of delinquency and of appropriate ways of dealing with delinquents. Consideration also enables us to assess whether or not the Committee's recommendations reflect the weight of the evidence submitted to it—what might be called 'the dominant conception' of delinquency and its control. If they do, one would expect little subsequent opposition since interested parties had already had their way.

32

Reason or Rhetoric

Somewhat surprisingly, in view of the recommendations, the majority of the memoranda were in favour of the *retention of the juvenile court*. The Council of the Law Society, for example, considered that no change was necessary, that there was already in operation a workable code. 'But for a few additions and amendments the existing law makes adequate provision for the protection of juveniles and for the successful treatment of juvenile offenders.' The main arguments presented in favour of the retention of the juvenile court were the child's right to a fair hearing and to full protection of the law against any possibility of interference with his liberty, and the preservation of the dignity and impressiveness of the law. It was widely recognized that the courts often lacked uniformity and continuity and that there was little opportunity for selecting people with a special interest in such work. But these criticisms led to suggestions for the reform of the juvenile court rather than for its abolition. Thus the creation of a panel of justices specially qualified for dealing with juveniles was commonly suggested. This would be 'a properly conceived children's court',[3] 'a clinic with powers as well as a court of law'.[4] A few memoranda wished to retain the juvenile court for the purpose of establishing the finding of guilt, and to remit the case thereafter to a 'sentencing tribunal'.[5] The Council of the Sheriff Substitutes Association were alone in arguing that the sheriff court should be retained as the sole juvenile court. This was a surprising proposal as some sheriffs privately acknowledged that they did not enjoy juvenile court work. Most of the memoranda submitted to the Committee were in favour of reform of the juvenile court.

Only three memoranda—those submitted by the Scottish branches of the Howard League, of the British Medical Association and of the Royal Medical Psychological Society—argued in favour of a social welfare approach. This suggests that these memoranda were more influential than the others. In fact the influence of certain submissions is quite obvious; there is a striking similarity between the formulation of the problems and the solutions suggested in the Kilbrandon Report and those presented in these documents.

Thus the analogy between social deviance and illness contained in paragraph 54 of the Kilbrandon Committee Report is explicitly stated in the memorandum of the Scottish Council of the British Medical Association:

While we recognize that by no means all delinquents present medical problems, we feel, nevertheless, that all represent a deviation from the social norm, that is to say they are social deviants. This suggests to us that the approach of the community to the social deviant should be analogous to that of the doctor to the person deviating from the health norm.

The memorandum goes on:

It is important to have available means to investigate fully both the personality and social environment, and to assess adequately the relative importance of all contributing factors . . . to elucidate the symptoms by a thorough examination, to formulate a diagnosis, to prescribe treatment . . . to follow up the case.

This was the crux of the Kilbrandon model. And all three memoranda made the same proposal: the creation of a social welfare board called, variously, the Juvenile Authority or the Juvenile Board—in function no different from the Juvenile Panel.

The major difference between these memoranda and the Kilbrandon recommendations lay in the weight which the memoranda attached to legal rights. They suggested that the board should be advised by a lawyer and should be directly responsible to some legal authority. They also suggested that the board's procedure and decisions should be endorsed by a sheriff. Thus the two idealized conceptions inherent in the juvenile court—social welfare and criminal justice—were retained in the recommended procedures.

The British Psychological Society in its proposals attempted to resolve this ambiguity. It suggested that the functions of the juvenile court should be discharged through two organizations: the juvenile court and a child welfare council. The latter would deal with all children in trouble under the age of 15: the former would deal with the fifteen to eighteen age group, with those under 15 who failed to respond to the welfare approach, and with those who committed serious offences 'where the establishment of guilt is essential'. The memorandum stated that it was necessary and important that justice be done and be seen to be done, and that the appropriate form of re-education be selected for each case.

It is this difficulty of reconciling these two needs, both administratively and in the mind of the general public, which gives rise to our suggestion for providing both a child welfare council and a juvenile court. We view this suggestion as a contribution towards resolving a problem which, if it remains unresolved, is an obstacle to rehabilitation.

These proposals have much in common with two of the Committee's main recommendations: that the *sole* function of the juvenile panel would be the choice of the appropriate method of disposition for the child and that children who committed serious offences would be referred to a court.

Professional ideologies and interests shaped the content of the various memoranda submitted to the Kilbrandon Committee. But why was the Committee more sympathetic to the views contained in certain memoranda? Many of the memoranda submitted pointed in an entirely different direction. Smith and Stockman have written that 'in essence a Report consists of an account of how the world is and how it works, an account of how the world should be, and a series of recommendations as to how this desired state may be achieved.'[6] Government reports, they suggested, embody factual statements and elements of causal models which are intended to be accurate. But what if the case for change rests on unfounded, untested or false assumptions? In our view, and we attempt to show this in Chapter III, the case for a social welfare approach to children who offend has not been established and it certainly was not established by the Kilbrandon Committee.

Criminological theory and research played some part in the formation of the Committee's recommendations, but it was research and theory which were already being questioned. The recommendations seem, rather, to be ideologically based. They are based on a *belief* in a particular approach—not on a real consideration of it. The Scandinavian system of welfare boards was mentioned in the introduction to the Report, but there was no reference to the criticisms being made at that time of American juvenile courts. The President's Commission on Law Enforcement and the Administration of Justice, appointed in July 1965, concluded, after an exhaustive review of the operation of the juvenile courts in America that

the great hopes originally held out for the juvenile court have not been fulfilled. It had not succeeded in rehabilitating delinquent youth, in reducing or even stemming the tide of delinquency, or in bringing justice or compassion to the child offender.[7]

The situation was certainly bleaker there than here. The Commission pointed, amongst other things, to the low calibre of juvenile court judges and to the large, overcrowded and understaffed institutions to which many children were being sent. But the Commission provided a well-argued critique of the philosophy adopted by the Kilbrandon Committee. The Commission report was not published until 1967 but this was the culmination of a growing movement critical of the philosophy operating in the juvenile courts there. Whether the Kilbrandon Committee's omission of some consideration of this critique was by design or through lack of knowledge we cannot assess. Yet the Committee had a strong legal contingent: the Chairman was a High Court judge and its membership included two sheriffs, three magistrates, a professor of law, a chief constable and a clerk to the juvenile court. There was only one psychiatrist, one headmaster, one manager of an approved school and one probation officer. Of course, individual members may have already formed their opinions before considering the various memoranda submitted to them.[8] But, in discussion with some of the members, we were assured that this was not so. In trying to solve this question one is drawn to the conclusion that certain individuals in the Scottish Civil Service played a key role. The influence of the Civil Service is always difficult to measure, but it is clear that there were then civil servants who were very conscious of the conflicts in the existing arrangements. As we said in the previous chapter, it would have been possible to extend the Ingleby recommendations to Scotland or to activate fully the provision of the Children and Young Persons (Scotland) Act 1937 which permitted the establishment of specialist juvenile courts. That this did not happen suggests that the Civil Service may have desired change in a particular direction: indeed, work had already been done on the contrasts between a crime-responsibility-punishment concept and a prevention-assessment-treatment concept—contrasts which, as modified by the Kilbrandon Committee, appeared as paragraph 54, the paragraph which is basic to much of the Committee's approach.

Reactions to the recommendations of the Kilbrandon Committee tended, predictably, to be in line with the submissions already made to the Committee. The Howard League welcomed the Report stating that it would 'bring Scotland into the mainstream of world penal reform'.[9] Most organizations continued to promote their own interests. This is seen most clearly in the discussions of whether social service reorganization should be based in Social Work Departments or in Social Education Departments. Educationalists and school welfare officers were in favour of the establishment of

Social Education Departments, and argued that education and social work had much in common. 'Education has not remained traditional and academic but [its] aims and methods [have] changed with new knowledge and insight'.[10] Child care officers, on the other hand, were in favour of the creation of social work departments.[11] They felt that a family service was ultimately desirable and that the children's department should be given responsibility for the care of delinquent children. Clearly the discussion had a symbolic significance for the various professional groups: the description of 'social education' given in the Report is indistinguishable from what one generally means by 'social work'.[12]

The major critics of the new proposals were sheriffs and probation officers. The Council of the Sheriff Substitutes Association felt that:

> The recommendations that in future the responsibility for deciding the treatment of young offenders should be transferred to panels of lay persons represent a radical departure from the principle that in general the liberty of actions of any age should not be interfered with except by a court of law.[13]

The Council argued that such a departure was justified only if the existing system was 'manifestly ineffective' and if a 'manifestly more effective system can be established'. It was unconvinced that either of these conditions was fulfilled, and so continued to argue in favour of the preservation and extension of the sheriff's juvenile court jurisdiction. The Council stressed that this was based not on reasons of self-interest but on the belief that the Kilbrandon Committee's proposals did not outline a better system. The Sheriff Court, the Council now argued, was better able 'to hold a proper balance between the interests of particular young offenders and the interests of the community as a whole'. The Council did not recognize the conflict which the Kilbrandon Committee saw as the fundamental deficiency in the juvenile court and to which its proposals were directed as a solution. The Council also felt that the Committee had proceeded on an old-fashioned view of how a sheriff was accustomed to separating questions of guilt from treatment; a lay panel was less likely to be able to dismiss from its mind what the offender had done or to deal differently with children involved in the same offence. Further doubts centred on the recruitment of sufficient people of quality as panel members and as reporters, and on the powers, particularly the continuing jurisdiction, of the hearings.

The Council was doubtful that the scale of juvenile delinquency was so serious as 'to justify such inroads into the traditional conception of the rights of parents and the liberties of citizens, however young'.

It also felt that there was a 'real danger of lay panels and their expert advisers, from the best motives, going to unnecessary or undesirable lengths'. The Council's memorandum, in fact, highlights the differences between the assumptions about delinquency outlined in the Kilbrandon Committee Report and assumptions derived from a criminal justice approach. The sheriffs argued in favour of a tariff system, a balance between the nature of the offence and what happened to the child, and for legal protections. Probation officers' objections also centred on the infringement of legal rights—they argued that compulsory measures affecting the liberty of the child and his parents should rest in the hands of a court rather than in a lay panel.

The Police Federation, too, was critical. The Kilbrandon Committee recommended the extension of the police warning system and outlined a change in the traditional police role in handling child offenders. The Committee described the police as 'one of the primary sources of the identification of children in need of special educational measures as well as being part of the sifting or assessment agency'.[14] But the Secretary of the Federation, Dan Wilson, responded as follows:

> The police haven't the time to go dishing out warnings. Police are being paid to be police officers—not social workers. Fear is still one of the great deterrents. Give these juvenile offenders back some of what they give out.[15]

Press reaction was, on the whole, favourable. The Scotsman leader[16] said that the Kilbrandon Committee had applied logically and systematically theories about the treatment of young delinquents 'which have found favour with criminologists' and that the report 'rightly proposes treatment rather than judgement and punishment'. The wide powers which the juvenile panels would have were stressed.

> It does not follow that getting rid of the apparatus of the court will mean that young offenders will get a soft option. A continuous and systematic course of supervision and training may be more irksome than an admonition in the juvenile court.

Overall it was felt that the proposals 'would effect a humane and rational reform in the reclaiming of juvenile offenders'. *The Glasgow Herald*[17] was also enthusiastic about the Report, describing it as 'worth waiting for' and as giving the impression of 'having said the last word on the subject'. The juvenile courts were roundly condemned.

They are the blunt instruments of criminal administration employed for the social and educative development of children . . . the net result is more to bring the law into needless disrespect than to curb delinquency.

The Committee's proposals were described as 'more refined than anything already in practice anywhere in the world'. (It would be intriguing to know the impact of emerging nationalism on these discussions: national pride is often an issue in radical change.) In June 1964 the Government accepted the Committee's recommendations to abolish the juvenile courts and to set up juvenile panels.

After the publication of the Kilbrandon Committee Report, and perhaps before the opposition movement could gather momentum, the White Paper *Social Work and the Community*, was published (in October 1966).[18] The White Paper was the report of a working group and three advisers—Richard Titmuss, Professor of Social Administration at the London School of Economics, Megan Browne from the Department of Social Study at the University of Edinburgh, and Kay Carmichael from the School of Social Study at the University of Glasgow. It is hardly surprising that the White Paper presented the arguments against a Social Education Department and proposed an alternative structure for social services within Scotland—all social workers would come under a single department to be called the Social Work Department. The new department was to be widely based, catering for families as well as children, and, accordingly, a department based on educational services was inappropriate. The case for reorganization was a simple one. Current services had developed piecemeal and in response to the identification at different times of certain groups who needed social help. But troubles seldom came singly—families were often visited by a number of different services or did not know what service to approach. And so the White Paper aimed at providing 'a single door on which everyone might knock to ask for help' and at avoiding 'a multiplicity of services carrying out essentially similar work in the same community or even in the same family'. Where separate departments existed it was also difficult to ensure that efforts were deployed in the most effective and economical way; entrants had to decide at an early age the service in which they intended to work; and the various departments competed for staff. Rationalization of resources would lead to a better and more effective service and, after all—the crux of the White Paper—all social workers used basically the same skills anyway. The probation officer was included within the new department. His main duty—personal social work with the offender and his family in the community—and his skills were seen as basically similar to those of other social workers. The creation of one department would not preclude specialization within it. The advantages were that consultation and co-operation would be easier, and a flexible continuum of care could be offered to clients.[19]

Battles Won and Battles Lost

Subsequent reactions to this statement of Government policy were mixed, but comments continued both to raise points made in the earlier debate on the abolition of the juvenile court and to reflect professional interests. For example, the Association of Residential Child Care Officers welcomed 'the breadth and vision of the proposals being made for an all-inclusive family service', whereas the Association of School Welfare Officers preferred a social work department under the aegis of the education department.

But to some extent the focus of the debate shifted. Both sheriffs and the probation service were diverted from their attempts to retain the juvenile court. They became concerned primarily with the maintenance of a separate probation service for adult offenders. The Association of Sheriffs argued that the White Paper ignored the essential difference between a probation officer's role and that of other social workers: the probation officer intervened where the individual was found guilty of an offence against the criminal law, not because he was a victim of deprivation or experienced some handicap. It argued that 'the duties he performs and the authority he carries are quite different in their nature from those of other social workers'. The National Association of Probation Officers also continued its attack against the children's panels—indeed this attack continued throughout the various stages of the subsequent Bill—but their major assault was aimed at preventing a merger with social workers. Their numerous memoranda were at pains, throughout the discussions, to stress that, in attempting to prevent the merger, probation officers were considering the needs of those whom it was their duty to help and that they were not primarily seeking to protect their own interests or areas of work. Whether or not this accurately reflects their motivations is impossible to assess, but the arguments presented against the merger appear strong, particularly in view of the continuation of a separate Probation and After-Care Service in England. The probation service did not feel that the various services could operate efficiently or easily alongside each other, or that their clients would get the priority they deserved.

Little was heard from educationalists; they mounted no counter-offensive on behalf of the 'social education department'. As John Mack said, its spokesmen had been flattered rather than activated by 'this Kilbrandon borne gift'.[20] Medical Officers of Health wanted the new department reorganized and renamed the 'Health and Social Services Department'. Still others, according to Mack, felt that the proposals did not go far enough—the psychiatric and hospital services were omitted from the reorganization, as were child guidance centres and special schools.

Some organizations were critical of the way in which the new proposals had been reached. The Scottish section of the British Psychological Society wrote that:

> The failure to include representatives of these departments, notably Education and Health, on the panel of professional advisers, who were drawn exclusively from the fields of sociology and social work, must be regarded as a weakness.[21]

Some went much further in their criticisms. A Glasgow psychologist wrote:

> It seems to me that the fundamental criticism of the White Paper is that it purports to be a blue print for the co-ordination of social services, whereas it is in fact no more than a blue print for the social work profession.[22]

He pointed out that no advice was invited from academics or practitioners in the fields of education, medicine and sociology and predicted that the proposals would not gain general support when he asked whether 'the armed forces would be very impressed by a White Paper on the co-ordination of defence drawn up on the advice of three grounded airmen?' But some were impressed. The majority of social workers welcomed the proposals. They had much to gain from their implementation as this was a crucial time in the expansion and professionalization of social work. The Social Work (Scotland) Bill incorporated the proposals both of the Kilbrandon Committee and the White Paper—juvenile panels were to be set up in each area and social work departments were substituted for social education departments.

Why did the critics lose the battle? The probation service in England had prevented a merger with social service departments. Certainly the probation service in Scotland had been criticized by the Morison Committee in 1962. That Committee had concluded that a 'principal cause of the failure of the probation service to develop in Scotland as it should have done is that it has been regarded not as a court service but as a relatively minor local authority service'.[23] Probation Committees, made up mainly of local authority members, had taken little interest in the expansion of the probation service in Scotland and did not serve as a pressure group in the way such committees did in England, in which magistrates were heavily involved. Moreover the English Committees actually employed the officers and, in that sense, they were indeed officers of the court. Other reasons for the merger were that it was less of a change for the probation service in Scotland to come totally within local authority control; the probation service in Scotland was both numerically and politically weak; the proportion of trained officers was small and their duties were narrower than those of the probation service in England. Probation officers in Scotland had less to lose and more to gain by identification with the new social work structure. Even so, it is difficult to see much logic in having different personal social service structures north and south of the border.[24]

Criticism of lay panels had also been sufficiently strong in England to ensure the retention of the juvenile court. As mentioned, opposition to *The Child, Family and Young Offender* had led to the second White Paper *Children in Trouble*. The philosophy and aims of the two White Papers were similar and yet the second White Paper met with general approval. This was partly due to a shift in the balance of power between the opponents and the supporters of the earlier White Paper and partly due to the symbolic retention of the juvenile court. Local authority social workers had recently amalgamated their formerly small professional organizations into the large and potentially powerful British Association of Social Workers. The strong social work orientation in the White Paper obviously met with their approval—implementation of the proposals would provide a useful vehicle in the attempt to 'professionalize' social work. The expected opposition from the National Association of Probation Officers did not emerge—it was temporarily diverted from the White Papers' proposals by internal disagreement concerning the generic concept of social work. (There were two issues: whether or not to join the B.A.S.W. and whether or not to merge with other social services.) There was also some agreement that a new direction was necessary: the juvenile crime rate continued to increase. The stumbling block to the first White Paper had been the different assumptions made by the various interest groups about the main causes of crime and about the best methods of dealing with young offenders. *Children in Trouble* was more successful[25] because it gave the *appearance* of compromise. Similar concerns in Scotland had little impact.

The passage of the Social Work (Scotland) Bill through the legislature was quite smooth in comparison with that of the English Children and Young Persons Bill. Yet the two Bills shared similar aims: to prevent deprived and delinquent children becoming the depraved, inadequate, unstable or criminal citizens of tomorrow, and to build on the resources of the family and of parents by providing, where necessary, effective social work support. The procedures outlined to achieve these aims differed but these differences were such—the abolition of the juvenile court in Scotland and its retention in England—that one would have expected the Scottish Bill to have the more difficult passage. This was not so.

There are a number of possible explanations for this. Bottoms[26] has outlined the difference between the Labour and Conservative parties specifically in their approach towards juvenile offenders (the two White Papers were the creations of a Labour Government) but the basic ethos of the Conservative party—freedom, individualism, self-help—produced a natural opponent to the doctrines being pursued by the Labour party. This divergence of attitudes was reflected in the debates on the English Bill. The Conservatives argued that the Bill was the product of inadequate preparation and consultation,[27] that it was unjust as between different children,[28] that it gave insufficient recognition to the constructive role of the juvenile court and that it interfered with police work with children especially in regard to more serious offences. They also objected to state intervention in a juvenile's life through an executive rather than judicial body. In brief, the Conservatives did not accept the underlying philosophy of the Bill. Sir Peter Rawlinson summed up the views of the opposition when he said: 'The Bill offends against the major principles of fairness, it introduces unnecessary delays and cumbersome procedures, and is the fruit of a philosophy of penology which is unacceptable to the public.'[29]

The Conservative party in Scotland is not numerically strong. The majority of M.P.s representing Scotland were, at that time, members of the Labour party although the Labour party in Parliament as a whole had only a small majority. Also, traditionally, only Scottish M.P.s take part in the debates on Bills which will affect Scotland alone. This meant that English Conservatives played no part in the debates on the Scottish Bill. Furthermore, the Conservative party in Scotland did not present a united front. Certainly, the bulk of the criticism of the Bill came from Conservative M.P.s. Michael Clark Hutchinson, for example, viewed the proposals in Part III of the Bill (the part dealing with the proposed children's hearings)[30] with alarm and apprehension. He was concerned that 'we may be letting loose a lot of amateurs in what should be a judicial process'. He went on:

> In these days of crime and disorder I am not in favour of weakening the judicial process or the procedures of law. I believe in exercising the full panoply of the law and its majesty. I have more faith in the judgement . . . of those on the bench than . . . in inexperienced amateurs who may be motivated by theory or unfounded concepts . . . . There is a great deal of informality about it, with little mention of representation of the child, cautioning or other safeguards. It seems to me that, throughout, the child is to be encouraged to plead guilty or admit his alleged guilt. There is an absence of legal training or of the judicial approach.[31]

Patrick Wolrige-Gordon pointed to the *apparent* removal of the legal aspect from the process. 'This is an inelegant charade. I would not cease to regard these panels as the arm of the law.'[32] He argued that children and their parents should have the right to legal advice and protection. This absence of legal rights was referred to by a number of Conservative M.P.s.[33] But some Conservatives welcomed the introduction of the juvenile panels. Alex Buchanan-Smith, for example, said that he could not agree with his colleagues that a judicial system was the right thing. He felt that the Bill was a great step forward in helping the treatment of the young.[34]

Labour M.P.s, predictably, gave whole-hearted support to the

Bill. William Ross, in introducing it, attempted to allay subsequent criticisms by stressing that the new approach was not soft—'The powers which will be available in future will be just as strong as they are now and much more varied'—and that the Bill had adequate safeguards built into it.[35] The hearings, he said, would work within rules and procedures drawn up in consultation with the Council on Tribunals and the child and his parents would have the right to appeal to the sheriff court (and, on a point of law, to the Court of Session). He also stated that 'no country has made both of these advances [comprehensive social services and new arrangements for children in trouble] and I am proud to introduce a pioneering measure which ... will not only be good for Scotland but which might have something to offer to other countries.' This emphasis on 'pioneerism' may have carried some weight with M.P.s. Some Conservatives had noted that Scotland was moving in a different direction from England. Michael Noble, for example, felt that he did not know enough to favour one form or the other, but hoped that the decision was based 'on important reasons and not just a determination to be different from England'.[36] Bruce Millan, in winding up for the Government on the Second Reading of the Bill, replied that the Scottish Bill was 'ahead of the English'.

The Scottish Bill, in addition to establishing the children's hearings, set out the administrative structure by which local authorities were to provide the new comprehensive service of social support (Part I) and outlined the services which local authorities were to provide (Part II).[38] The new service would cater for the elderly and the handicapped, provide social support for the sick, discharge the local authority's responsibilities for children and provide probation services to the courts and after-care for those leaving penal institutions. These provisions proved to be as controversial, if not more so, as the provisions setting up the children's hearings. Certainly there was far more discussion of these changes in the debates than of those affecting the panels. Attention was diverted from the new system for dealing with children in trouble. Thus there was considerable debate on whether only the counties and cities should handle the social services or also large burghs. Whether or not the timing of the introduction of the new service was right also took up much time. A Royal Commission on Local Government was expected to recommend radical changes in local government structure in the near future and some M.P.s felt that the social services reorganization should be deferred until this took place (possibly in

1975). The proposed merger of the probation service was also debated. The service was praised for having done excellent work in Scotland and it was suggested that nothing would be lost and much would be gained by maintaining a separate probation service. But these points carried little weight—the Government were committed to the merger of the social services in Scotland.

Many of the same points were raised on the Third Reading of the Bill, but there was a general welcome for the move from a court to a hearing. Indeed, although controversies now surround the operation of the children's hearings, the Bill was referred to as 'one of the least controversial of the Scottish Bills which have passed through the house for some time'.[39] The Bill was given royal assent in July 1968.

Postscript

The new system of dealing with children in trouble came into operation in Scotland in April 1971. Although it is clear from the content of the various memoranda submitted to the Kilbrandon Committee and from the reactions to both its report and the Scottish White Paper that views about the appropriate way of dealing with such children differed, there was a greater consensus or, perhaps more accurately, less effective opposition in Scotland than in England and Wales. In England, the Children and Young Persons Act struggled to be born; its life was in part extinguished. The social welfare principles endorsed in it have not yet been put into effect.[40] This was originally because of ideological differences in the two major political parties. The Labour party intended to implement the Act gradually as resources became available. The Conservatives, on the other hand, were committed to raising the age of criminal responsibility no higher than twelve and to the retention of criminal proceedings beyond that age. The Labour Government fell shortly after the passing of the Act and the new Conservative Government did not implement these sections. Subsequent Labour Governments, though still accepting the principles underlying the Act, have taken no steps to implement it fully. In spite of this failure to implement, the current English procedures have been criticized to a greater extent than the procedures introduced by the Social Work (Scotland) Act. We will consider this in Chapter VIII. This chapter has tried to show that a social welfare approach was adopted fairly easily in Scotland though there was no great consensus and some opposition. It is difficult to avoid the conclusion that this approach was adopted because of strong social work influences in the Civil Service at that time. Of course, we can only speculate about this, but it is worth noting that a key figure in the Scottish Office during the Kilbrandon era was subsequently involved in the development of *The Child, Family and Young Offender* in England.

III

Social Welfare: a critique

Critiques of the social welfare approach to children who offend are well developed in discussions on the American juvenile courts[1] but there has been little discussion within the context of the new system of dealing with child offenders in Scotland (or in England and Wales). For this reason we turn in this and subsequent chapters to the deficiencies of such an approach in both theory and practice. In this chapter we develop the critique first generally and then with particular reference to the Scottish system.

To a large extent a critique of social welfare is a critique of positivist criminology. The basic assumptions are, in short, that delinquent behaviour has antecedent causes which explain it: past conditions and situations are emphasized, individual choice is ignored; that these causes can be (and have been) discovered; that their discovery has made possible the treatment and control of such behaviour; that delinquents share pathological conditions which make them fundamentally different from the law-abiding, though similar to others in difficulties; that delinquency gets 'worse' without 'treatment'; that 'treatment' has no harmful side effects; that involuntary 'treatment' is possible and that involuntary 'treatment' is not punishment. In fact, delinquent behaviour is seen in many ways as being similar to medical illness—it represents a kind of social illness. The use of medical analogies in understanding delinquency has a long history. Platt,[2] in his discussion of the first American juvenile courts, described the role model of the judge as a 'doctor-counsellor' who saw his court-room like a clinic. Medical terminology was used frequently in the Kilbrandon Committee report—'diagnosis', 'treatment' and 'symptom'[3]—and the Committee explicitly compared treatment by a juvenile court magistrate to treatment by a doctor.[4] Many of these assumptions, however, are false—they are based on an over-optimistic and at the same time

48

inadequate view of what is known about delinquency—and the analogy with medicine is unsound.

Delinquency, Positivism and Medical Analogies

Critiques of positivism have emerged both from within (from those who hold much the same assumptions but seek to improve the approach) and from without (by those who reject these assumptions and hold quite different perspectives on delinquent behaviour). We encompass both within this chapter.

Differentiation is the basic assumption of positivism. Each school of positivist criminology has pursued its own theory of differentiation between delinquent and law-abiding people: biological, psychological, socio-cultural or whatever. There is no shortage of theories of the aetiology of delinquency. But most research has failed to demonstrate empirically that certain characteristics clearly distinguish the delinquent from the non-delinquent. Walker, in tracing the development of criminological theory has described the various causal landmarks as consisting mainly of 'abandoned assumptions'[5] and Matza has drawn attention to the similarities underlying the behaviour of the delinquent and the non-delinquent.[6]

The Kilbrandon Committee (and the English White Papers), however, endorsed a particular model of causation; it assumed that the causes of delinquency lay primarily within the individual and his family.[7] This led to recommendations of dispositions which centred on individual therapy and family-based casework. The Committee felt that social education could assist parents and children 'towards a fuller insight and understanding of their situation and problems',[8] and it referred to the 'means of solution which lie in their hands'.[9] This confidence appears again in a pamphlet sent to all parents and children who are to appear at a hearing. It states:

> It is the reporter's job to get information about you and your family, maybe about your health and how you are getting on at school. He does this *to find out the cause of any trouble you may be in* so that you may be given *the right kind of help* (emphasis added).[10]

But such confidence is misplaced. The various studies on the effects of family influences have been far from convincing.[11] A recently completed study designed to investigate forty-five hypotheses on causal factors in the development of stealing by adolescent boys found little evidence for the commonly alleged influence of such factors as 'broken homes' and 'parental control over spare time'.[12] There is now a substantial body of literature questioning the deleterious effect on child development of Bowlby's notion of 'maternal deprivation'.[13] And Michael Power found, in a sample of boys appearing before London juvenile courts, that two-thirds came from ordinary families, intact and without serious problems.[14] This is not to say that family relationships or influences are irrelevant in understanding delinquency but rather that we are not able to specify what to look for or what to do about it. In the words of the U.S. President's Commission report: 'Until the science of human behaviour matures far beyond its present confines, an understanding of the kinds of behaviour we call delinquent is not likely to be forthcoming.'[15]

The acceptance of specific explanations hinders, in addition, the development of other 'treatment' (or social reaction) possibilities. By treating delinquency as a problem of individual adjustment rather than, for example, a problem arising out of the social (economic and political) position and condition of adolescents, subsequent social action is both determined and limited. Not only does the choice of the 'cause' affect the choice of 'treatment', it also affects the adequacy of that treatment. Research increasingly shows that 'delinquency is not so much an act of individual deviancy as a pattern of behaviour produced by a multitude of pervasive social influences well beyond the reach of the actions of any judge, probation officer, correctional counsellor or psychiatrist.'[16] To isolate the delinquent from the impact on him of socio-economic change—high unemployment rates (at their highest among the young), technological advances (with the corresponding increase in routine, monotonous jobs) and housing redevelopment (with its accompanying isolation, anonymity and fragmentation of the extended family)—makes no sense.[17] Family orientated and individually orientated casework are likely to have little impact on delinquent behaviour or on delinquency rates.

The medical analogy, in fact, breaks down, for while there still may be doubts in medicine about the causes of certain illnesses and uncertainty about their treatment, there is a far greater body of established knowledge than exists in criminological literature. There, little agreement exists at any precise level about the underlying reasons for delinquent behaviour and there is little evidence that known 'treatments' for delinquent behaviour—for example, probation or institutional placements—have any rehabilitative effect. Failure rates, in the sense of reconviction within a fixed period, are uniform—depending more on the characteristics of the offender than on the nature of the intervention—and high. (Some argue that reconviction rates are an invalid criterion of the success of 'treatment' measures but these rates are reflective of success or failure in other areas of life—for example, industrial life and family obligations.) There is some indication also that intervention may increase delinquency.) Millham and others argue that 'repeated residential treatment is one of the best ways of ensuring that children will continue to experience residential custody in detention centre, borstal and prison.'[18] Other detrimental effects can result from residential 'treatment': poor educational progress, inability to make positive relationships and emotional instability. Yet the new system was based primarily on the same resources as the old; names were changed but probation and residential treatment continue essentially as before.

This must be a matter of concern; for a social welfare approach provides justification for early and extensive intervention in the lives of children and their families: if delinquency reflects a mal-adjustment which can be treated then it is wrong to restrict the availability of treatment or to deprive the child of it. The net of control is cast wider since it is thought that something constructive can be done for delinquent children. But is it likely that 'something constructive' can be done? There is little evidence that rehabilitation, determined by reconviction rates, works;[19] employment prospects may be hindered;[20] the child's self-concept may alter and he may see himself as 'delinquent';[21] and further delinquency may follow.[22] Social welfare systems also provide for wide discretion for referral into the system. For example, S 37 (1) of the Scottish Act states: 'where any person has reasonable cause to believe that a child may be in need of compulsory measures of care he may give to the reporter such information about the child as he may have been able to discover'. The emphasis on the care (and needs) of the child rather than on his punishment (and his offence) encourages referral.

The medical analogy has further deficiencies. Delinquency is not an objective state of malfunctioning. Instances of rule-breaking may be dismissed by decision-makers at one time as being of no significance whereas similar behaviour may be seen at other times as problematic. Where certain symptoms are presented doctors usually agree on the diagnosis—the criteria are in the main objective. This is not always the case—it may, for example, be difficult to establish whether the patient complaining of a pain in his back is 'really' ill or is malingering—but the quality of objectivity is far greater than in the policeman's decision whether or not to caution a delinquent child or the hearing's decision that a child requires compulsory measures of care. Criteria for referral into social welfare systems are often extremely vague. Section 32 (2) of the Scottish Act refers to children who have failed to attend school 'regularly without reasonable excuse', to children falling into 'bad' associations, and to children experiencing 'unnecessary suffering'. And there are no guidelines set out as indicators for compulsory intervention. Can these decisions be objectively determined?

Social characteristics can influence the decision to call an individual an 'offender' or a 'problem' and those who become categorized in this way are so, not merely because of the commission of a delinquent act or of 'shortcomings in the normal "bringing up" process', but also through their interaction with others who witness the delinquent act—police, magistrates, school-teachers, shop-keepers or whoever—and who impose that social description.[23] There is now a significant body of research on unreported delinquency and the process of differential selection reveals anomalies which challenge traditional models of delinquency. How 'something done' comes to be objectified as 'delinquent behaviour' requiring intervention is a critical issue. Cicourel, amongst others, has demonstrated that decisions are made on organizational criteria on ways of thinking, of ordering factors and of interpreting their meaning.[24] Delinquency is not behaviour but the *interpretation* of behaviour by decision-makers, commonly on non-legal criteria. Where there is an absence of objective criteria by which the nature and extent of a 'problem' can be determined, decision-makers can do little more than refer to their own values, beliefs or training.[25] The delinquent is evaluated favourably or unfavourably not because he *does* something, not even because he *is* something, but because *others react to their perceptions of him* as favourable or unfavourable.

Because we do not yet understand the nature or significance of much delinquent behaviour, the various reports presented to decision-makers must contain value judgements and unfounded assumptions. We do not know which factors to refer to, or which situations indicate which form of 'treatment'. Because of this lack of knowledge we tend to collect either information which perpetuates the delinquent stereotype (broken home, working mother and so on) or all possible information in the hope or belief that something might be relevant. As such, these reports are useless as guides to choosing 'treatment', but these 'facts' then justify intervention and the form of intervention. These reports recast or reconstitute the child's identity as a 'delinquent'.

Furthermore, so long as there are differing beliefs about, for example, child rearing, there can be no uniform interpretation of the 'best interests of the child'. Consequently, those who appear before the juvenile court or welfare tribunal are likely to come from particular socio-economic groups because the standards of care expected by the various decision-makers are likely to be based on middle-class standards of behaviour, child-rearing practices and so on. Because of this, particular attention is paid in subsequent chapters to the kinds of factors considered in the children's hearing system in determining the appropriate disposition for a particular child.

The analogy with medicine is clearly inadequate. The process of becoming delinquent differs from that of becoming ill. There is no stigma attached to physical illness (except, perhaps, to sexually transmitted diseases) and compulsory treatment is rare. Outside Erewhon most diseases are involuntary and most crime is voluntary. The analogy is based on an imperfect understanding of social delin- quency, and concepts and ideas have been introduced from the field of medicine without critical discussion of their usefulness. Such concepts are inappropriate in this area—instead of describing the phenomena to which they are applied they tend rather to confuse and obscure the issues.

It might be argued that social work theory and practice have moved away from this naïve and confusing reliance on medical ana- logies (there has certainly been a shift from psychoanalytically dominated to generic training), but this is true only to a limited extent. The White Paper *Social Work and the Community* used much the same language as the Kilbrandon Committee, and the evidence of the British Association of Social Workers to the House of Commons sub-committee on the Children and Young Persons Act 1969 had much the same ring.[26] Their memorandum referred to 'assessment' and 'treatment' of the child's needs. Although age, training, political stance and many other factors influence how social workers see their role, most still tend to see the causes of social need as lying within the characteristics of the client; few point to the material and economic situation of their client as the root cause of his problems. A recent editorial on training in a radical social work magazine concluded: 'Casework is still the major area of social work covered on nearly all training courses; certainly its underlying values are still widely upheld. The orientation of courses, however 'radical', is to define issues as *individual problems*' (emphasis added).[27]

'Personalization' of the causes of the delinquent behaviour means that the 'social reality of crime' (the political and economic realities which govern relationships between man and society) can be ignored. This has been described by William Ryan as 'blaming the victim'. He writes:

> The new ideology attributes defect and inadequacy to the malignant nature of poverty, injustice, slum life, and racial difficulties. The stigma that marks the victim and accounts for his victimization is an acquired stigma, a stigma of social, rather than genetic, origin. But the stigma, the defect, the fatal difference—though derived in the past from environmental forces—is still located *within* the victim, inside his skin. With such an elegant formulation, the humanitarian can have it both ways. He can, all at the same time, concentrate his charitable interest on the defects of the victim, condemn the vague social and environmental stresses that produced the defect (some time ago), and ignore the continuing effect of victimizing social forces (right now). It is a brilliant ideology for justifying a perverse form of social action designed to change, not society, as one might expect, but rather society's victim.[28]

Victim blaming admirably describes the current response to children who offend.[29] Traditional responses and remedies are clung to—all we need is more resources, more social workers—and radical remedies are ignored. The concept of 'adjustment' is commonly used, but it is adjustment to a particular culture or to particular institutions.

The Delinquent and the Deprived

Other assumptions made in a social welfare approach are that offenders are not essentially different from other children who need care, that they have the same problems and that they will respond to the same treatment. This is not a novel idea; such assumptions justified the merger of the industrial and reformatory schools and the wide jurisdiction of the first juvenile courts. But these assumptions are not without their critics. Peter Scott, for example, commenting on the much criticized White Paper *The Child, the Family and the Young Offender*, rejected the suggestion that there was no difference between maladjusted, deprived and delinquent children and argued that there was one major difference: 'the delinquent takes it out on society'.[30] Hood and Sparks suggest differences in attitude between delinquent and deprived children:

> Whatever one may think the predisposing causes of delinquency are, few will deny that delinquency often involves the young person taking a certain attitude towards property and personal relationships, and that these attitudes with their supporting rationalizations may be learned and reinforced through association with other delinquents. Thus, a child may be 'acting out' aggression because of family disturbance, but whether or not his aggression is channelled into housebreaking or whether or not he develops attitudes expressing aggression to school, work and property, may depend partly upon whom he has been associating with. To ignore this seems to deny completely one of the fundamental planks of the sociological view of delinquency ... Persistent delinquents should be recognized as a special group for the purpose of treatment centring round attitude change as, at least, a basis for dealing with their underlying problems.[31]

Some research does indicate that similar factors are associated with the manifestation of both delinquency and deprivation but research also suggests that the degree to which they have factors in common varies. Phillip and McCulloch's data showed statistically significant relationships between various factors but also revealed some important differences.[32] Juvenile delinquency was linked with overcrowding, fewer owner-occupied houses and high infant mortality rates. Child care rates, on the other hand, were associated with separation and trauma in parent/child relationships. Phillip and McCulloch suggest that juvenile delinquency rates were, overall, associated with social disorganization factors whilst child care rates were associated with family disorganization factors. A replication study by McAllister and Mason confirmed this general picture but found that child care rates were associated with low employment and economic status and that delinquency rates were associated with overcrowding, high population density and poor housing.[33] A major deficiency in this kind of research is, of course, its reliance on official rates: factors such as social and family disorganization may have influenced both the behaviour of the child and the behaviour of decision-makers. But it is at least arguable that social policy should be framed to take account of divergences, rather than to conceal them.

This equivalence of care and protection referrals and truants with offenders depends on the view that the offence is irrelevant and that offenders should not be treated as in any way more responsible for their behaviour or conduct than any deprived or neglected child. It ignores choice and denies the delinquent the meaning and purpose of his action. The problems inherent in these assumptions are obvious, but some of the difficulties are avoided by restricting the class of non-offence cases to which offenders are assimilated to non-offence cases involving children who are most like offenders—children from socially disorganized or criminal families and neglected or truanting children: the potential delinquents. Orphaned children are often dealt with under quite different legislation or in different parts of the same legislation.[34]

Other difficulties are avoided when one realizes that it is merely a pretence that the commission of an offence is incidental. If all children in need of compulsory measures of care were in fact alike there would be only one ground of referral: children in need of compulsory measures of care. But usually in social welfare jurisdictions the commission of an offence is a separate and self-sufficient ground for referral into the system[35] and the reason for which most children are referred is that they have committed an offence—but for the offence, few would be referred at all. The commission of the offence must also be proved or admitted.

The Kilbrandon Committee hoped to abolish the notion of delinquency and the kinds of considerations which usually surround it from the deliberations of the children's hearings. The booklet *Children's Hearings: Questions and Answers* sent to all children appearing before the hearing and their parents to help them understand the new system states:

> In coming to their decision, a hearing studies the various reports on the child's health, education and background, enters into careful discussion with the social worker, the parents and the child himself and so tries to build up a good picture of the child, the circumstances in which he lives and the reasons why he behaves as he does.

The booklet goes on:

Because the hearing is concerned with this wider picture and the long term well-being of the child, the measures on which it decides may not seem to be in proportion to any offence or circumstances that may be the immediate cause of his appearance. It sometimes happens that a child who has committed quite a serious offence is not removed from home, because his home background is suitable for him and is not contributing to his difficulties. On the other hand, a child who has committed a very slight offence or no offence at all may have to reside away from home, because he displays problems which his own home cannot help him with.

But is it realistic to expect that the notion of delinquency and the kinds of considerations which usually surround it could be abolished so easily in the minds of the panel members, or the child or his parents? Is it likely that panel members will be able to ignore society's attitude to children who offend or indeed society's attitude to offenders in general? Considerations of individual and general deterrence and the protection of society weigh heavily with the public in their expectations of the penal system. Even quite minor crimes are, in general, viewed as behaviour which requires something done about it. Society's response to offenders is frequently hostile regardless of the nature of the offence or the age of the offender. In fact, adolescence may be an aggravating factor. The adolescent delinquents often become a focus for the frustrations and tensions of the older generation; their acts may be viewed as a collective challenge to cherished values. The official processing of adolescents then takes on an almost symbolic importance—it becomes a means of maintaining the status quo, of providing social education and of defining acceptable boundaries to behaviour. Erikson and others[36] have drawn our attention to the importance of public ceremonies such as court appearances in confirming what is acceptable and unacceptable within society, and Francis Allen has written of the American juvenile court that

in a great many cases it must 'perform' functions essentially similar to those exercised by any court adjudicating cases of persons charged with dangerous and disturbing behaviour. It must reassert the norms and standards of the community when confronted by serious deviant conduct.[37]

The extent to which the offence is relevant in decision-making and whether or not social welfare systems can avoid these expectations in practice will be considered in subsequent chapters.

Social Welfare and Language

Francis Allen wrote some years ago that 'the language of therapy is frequently employed . . . to disguise the true state of affairs' and that it can present an 'obstacle to realistic analysis'.[38] The language of 'help' and 'treatment' is an integral part of social welfare systems in general, and of the children's hearing system in particular. The hearings are under a statutory duty to consider the course of action which is 'in the best interests of the child' and to terminate a child's supervision requirements where it is no longer 'in his interest'.[39] But such decisions take place in an authoritarian setting; the child is referred to the reporter and to the hearing, in the main, against his will. He is compelled to attend and if he does not do so a warrant will be issued for his arrest. Similarly, his parent must attend unless it would be 'unreasonable to require his attendance' or his attendance would be 'unnecessary' to the consideration of the case.[40] Failure on the part of the parent to attend is an offence, punishable by a fine of up to £50. 'Parental co-operation' really means 'parental coercion'.

Also the child is referred into the system primarily for what he *did* (or did not do)—because he committed an offence, truanted or whatever. His behaviour has been seen as troublesome, disruptive or threatening—behaviour which requires the exercise of *coercive* powers. Again to quote Francis Allen:

> It is important . . . to recognize that when, in an authoritative setting, we attempt to do something *for* a child 'because of what he is and needs', we are also doing something *to* him. The semantics of 'socialized justice' are a trap for the unwary. Whatever one's motivations, however elevated one's objectives, if the measures taken result in the compulsory loss of the child's liberty, the involuntary separation of a child from his family, or even the supervision of a child's activities by a probation worker, the impact on the affected individuals is essentially a punitive one. Good intentions and a flexible vocabulary do not alter this reality. . . . We shall escape much confusion here if we are willing to give candid recognition to the fact that the business of the juvenile court inevitably consists, to a considerable degree, in dispensing punishment.[41]

Although the disposition may be presented to the child as 'in his best interests' it is likely that he will see the decision in punitive terms. Research on the former juvenile courts in England indicated that children wanted to 'get off', did not want to be 'sent away', and did not share the treatment-oriented aims of the court.[42] They saw the juvenile court as an agency in which punishment was dealt out and were confused by any disposition which did not conform to the retributive ideal. Recent research on the current juvenile courts in England confirms this. Indeed, the writers suggest that parents may support and children may respect the juvenile court only for as long as it maintains a justice approach.[43]

'Treatment' invariably involves some form of compulsory deprivation. It accordingly falls within the definition of punishment set out by some philosophers, and decision-makers are involved in self-deception if they pretend otherwise. Children see through this hypocrisy. If the child sees the disposition as a means to *his* ends (as opposed to those best for society at large or those judged best for him by society) then the child may be less likely to see the decision in punitive terms, but how likely is this to occur? Hearings are, by their rules, obliged to discover, if possible, what the child wants or to persuade the child that what the hearing wants is, in fact, best for him. But this is a charade. The child knows that if he does not like, for example, this residential establishment he will be placed elsewhere, and he knows that the likelihood is that he will dislike that alternative more.[44]

Against this, it might be argued that 'treatment' is provided only when the child needs it. But what does 'need it' mean? What are our motives in intervention? We explore these issues in subsequent chapters. It is enough for the moment to recall the discussion in the first chapter on the motives of the early social reformers. Their motives were quite complex and highly ambivalent—child welfare was just one of many motivational elements. Other concerns were the protection of society from and the social control of children who offended. These concerns remain relevant. Though often concealed in social welfare legislation, they are nonetheless apparent. By a sleight of hand, the interests of the child and the interests of society are seen to be one and the same. Throughout the Kilbrandon Committee Report and the White Papers we can readily substitute 'the interests of society' for 'the interests of the child' and the meaning would remain unaltered. The assumption that the interests of the individual and of society are in harmony does not suffice. There are instances in which the best interests of the community, if not inconsistent with the welfare of the child, are at least to some degree separate and distinct. Sometimes a conflict in the short-term interests of the child and society is acknowledged and the argument then becomes that it is not in the child's long-term interests to continue to offend without 'treatment'. But there is little evidence for this. We drew attention earlier in this chapter to the deficiencies of current 'treatment' measures. 'Treatment' in effect means 'control' and there is little concern about the impact of 'control' on the child. Current debates on the need for additional secure places for children who offend succinctly demonstrate this point.[45] Such devices of language enable us to do more to the child than where we overtly act in society's interest.

Our real intention in intervening in the life of a child who offends is to create a socially conforming adult rather than a happy and efficient thief. The Kilbrandon Committee, for example, wrote that 'the underlying aim of all such measures must be . . . to strengthen and further these natural influences for the good which will assist the child's development into a mature and useful member of society.'[46] Counselling or casework may have replaced reading the Scriptures, but the aim is the same. The child who commits an offence, is a most efficient method of protecting the interests of doing so again. A social welfare approach, untrammelled by such considerations as equal justice and a tariff of penalties to fit the offence, is a most efficient method of protecting the interests of society. Care, for the purpose of Part III of the Scottish Act, includes 'protection, *control*, guidance and treatment' (emphasis added).[47]

Ambiguity in the New Procedures

So far the social welfare ethos of the new procedures in Scotland has been stressed but other elements are also present. Indeed, the first section of any substance in Part III of the Social Work (Scotland) Act states: 'No child shall be prosecuted for any offence except on the instructions of the Lord Advocate, or at his instance.'[48] The power to prosecute child offenders is preserved—an odd power to preserve within a social welfare framework. The Kilbrandon Committee felt that

> its exercise would arise only exceptionally and on the gravest crimes, in which major issues of public interest must necessarily arise and in which, equally as a safeguard for the interests of the accused, trial under criminal procedure is essential.[49]

The implications of this statement are important. Did the Kilbrandon Committee fail to have the courage of its convictions? If offences are symptomatic of underlying disorders there should be no reason for referring children who commit certain offences to a court. Presumably it was not the Committee's belief that only minor offences were symptomatic of underlying personality or family disorder. What the Committee seem to be suggesting, rather, is that notions of general deterrence and protection of the public are relevant considerations in dealing with some child offenders and may take precedence over the interests of the child. The Committee, accordingly, recommended that cases likely to raise these kinds of considerations should be dealt with separately and differently from other forms of juvenile delinquency. This seems in part an attempt to prevent such considerations from influencing the determination of appropriate dispositions by panel members. But it was also a compromise—a concession to those who felt that such considerations were relevant in dealing with all child offenders. This compromise is most apparent in the section of the Scottish Act which states that the police must report all offences by children to the appropriate reporter *and* to the appropriate procurator fiscal.[50] The child can be dealt with by the reporter only if the prosecutor decides not to prosecute. In practice, as a result of administrative directions, most cases involving children which come to the knowledge of the police are reported only to the reporter, and many cases reported to the fiscal are, in turn, referred by him to the reporter for action.

Nevertheless these provisions represent a substantial breach in the social work ethic of the new system of juvenile justice in Scotland. The retention of these alternative modes of response to the delinquent child embodies within the one system conflicting assumptions about the causation of delinquency, the level of the child's personal responsibility and the objectives of dispositions. It raises issues to which we will return in subsequent chapters about the internal consistency of the values and attitudes underlying current practices. The Scottish legislation is ambivalent about a basic premise in social welfare: the assumption that the delinquent child is a 'victim of circumstances'. The case for trial in the criminal courts depends as much on the view of the delinquent as a conscious lawbreaker as it does on the need to clarify, in public, issues giving rise to concern. Rushforth's survey shows that children dealt with by the courts in Scotland differed very little, if at all, in character from those children appearing before children's hearings.[51]

Legal Rights and Social Welfare

It usually follows from the endorsement of a social welfare approach that legal safeguards are less relevant. Arguments in favour of legal restrictions and controls in the early American juvenile courts were seen as retrogressive steps that would undermine the rehabilitative aims of the court. They were obstacles to treatment. Similar views were presented in this country in the 1960s. Barbara Wootton, discussing lawyers' concern for the principles of British justice, argued:

> Nevertheless, in their application to treatment of the children who now appear before the juvenile courts, I find these arguments less convincing . . . if the welfare, not the punishment of the child is the governing consideration, the safeguards of the criminal trial become irrelevant.[52]

She referred to the compulsory education of children and to the fact that no one has ever suggested that a child ought to have the right to appear before a court before he is compelled to go to school. She continued:

> Why then should judicial process be required before a child can be sent to a different kind of school? . . . Substitute an educational for a penal setting and the need for that procedure will disappear.

The same reasoning was used by Lord Kilbrandon:

> The doctrine is a concomitant of the accusatorial or adversary system of criminal procedure . . . Certainly we hear nothing about 'due process' in the nursery or the schoolroom where it would be totally out of place.[53]

Both writers are guilty of a number of fallacies: they ignore the question of parental rights or choice in education, the difference between making all children go to school and giving some children less freedom than others, and the stigma which may result from such proceedings.

The operation of American juvenile courts has provided some nice examples of the consequences of paying scant regard to legal rights. Chief Judge Weintraub, for example, held in *In the Interests of Carlo* that

> An infant need not be warned that the truth will be used against him, for the very assumption of the juvenile process is that *the truth will be used to help him* . . . With respect to crime, we suppress the truth even if it means the release of one who is plainly guilty . . . I would suggest that it need not follow that the same course should be pursued with respect to juvenile delinquency, since as to it there is still another value to be weighed, to wit, the rehabilitation of the infant. *To deny an infant the attention he needs because the police erred in obtaining evidence of that need may not be the parental thing to do* (emphasis added).[54]

But the situation in the U.S.A. has changed and legal rights are, in theory, gradually being returned to the child. Justice Fortas first questioned the lack of legal rights in *Kent* v. *United States.*[55] He praised the laudable purposes of the juvenile court but asked whether its actual performance measured well enough against its purpose to make tolerable the denial of the constitutional guarantees which applied to adults. Justice Fortas went on: 'The evidence is that he gets neither the protection accorded to adults nor the solicitous care and regenerative treatment postulated for children.' This concern was again expressed by Justice Fortas in the *Gault* case.[56] He said, 'Under our constitution the condition of being a boy does not justify a kangaroo court.' Gerald Gault, a 15-year-old youth charged with making a lewd telephone call, was committed to the Arizona State Industrial School until he reached the age of 21. The offence carried a maximum penalty of a $50 fine or two months' imprisonment for adults. Gerald, while on probation for being in the company of another juvenile who had stolen a wallet, had been taken into custody upon the verbal complaint of a neighbour that he had made an obscene telephone call. The authorities never advised Gerald's parents of his arrest. Upon learning of their son's detention from a neighbour, his mother inquired at the detention home, was advised of the charge and was notified of the hearing to commence the next day. The petition alleging Gerald's delinquency was never served upon his parents, nor did it refer to any factual basis for the intervention of the court. At the initial hearing, in the judge's chambers, the complaining witness was not present; no record of the proceedings was made; and no sworn testimony was offered. There was, however, a testimonial conflict as to whether

Gerald had made the alleged telephone call. The case was adjourned and Gerald spent the next two or three days in custody. At the second hearing, the complaining witness was not present. When Mrs Gault specifically requested the witness' presence, the judge informed her that it was not necessary. The judge himself had never spoken to the complaining witness and the only communication with her was her telephoned complaint to a probation officer. On appeal, the United States Supreme Court held that the due process clause of the 14th Amendment applied to proceedings in the state juvenile courts to adjudicate a juvenile a delinquent. This meant that a juvenile had the right, amongst others, to be represented by counsel.[57]

The reasons underlying the court's decision are worth looking at since the American juvenile courts were founded on a philosophy similar to that of the new systems in Scotland and England. Firstly, the court made it clear that *parens patriae* (the theory that the juvenile court stands *in loco parentis* to a juvenile and is thus primarily interested in his welfare) was an inadequate basis on which to determine the appropriate procedure for an adjudicative hearing—this struck at the informality of the procedures. Secondly, the court dismissed the notion that the 'civil' label attached to juvenile court proceedings justified the denial of rights accorded in criminal proceedings, particularly in view of the possibility of detention within an institution against the juvenile's will. Finally the court rejected the 'quid pro quo' theory which involved the state treating the child instead of punishing him in return for the abandonment of his rights. The court doubted how far the child in fact received individual care and decided that, notwithstanding official policy, the restrictions and deprivations imposed by the juvenile courts were in effect punitive.

This movement towards a more legalistic approach and towards granting basic legal rights to the juvenile is interesting because it was primarily a reaction *against* the procedural concomitants of a social welfare approach. But the debates going on in America were ignored in the British discussions. In effect we were in the process of abandoning criminal procedures for children just when the United States Supreme Court was emphasizing the importance of due process and 'fundamental fairness' in juvenile court proceedings, and was questioning the reality of a social welfare approach.

Are there sufficient safeguards to meet the rights of the child in the Scottish legislation? The more disturbing aspects of the Gault case could not easily arise there. The general law of arrest applies to children as to any other person suspected of having committed an offence and the circumstances in which a child can be detained are limited;[58] but where a child is detained beyond these categories, this would *not* affect the regularity of any subsequent hearing or of the hearing's decision. The child's remedy is an action for damages for wrongful arrest. There is no statutory obligation to notify parents of their child's arrest and detention but in practice the police do notify the child's parents of the arrest. There is a duty to inform the reporter of any child's detention and he may order the release of the child if he considers that the child is not likely to require compulsory measures of care.[59] There are also strict rules concerning the length of any period of detention.[60] *Scottish Social Work Statistics* shows that only 7% of all children referred to the reporter in 1973 spent some time in detention prior to trial and 23% of those were detained for not more than one day.[61]

The child and his parents are also entitled to notification of the time and place of the hearing and to a statement of the grounds for the referral of the child to a hearing. The statement of facts constituting, for example, the alleged offence must be as specific as a complaint under the Summary Jurisdiction (Scotland) Act 1954 which governs complaints generally and, unlike a complaint, must specify the nature of the offence in question. Lack of specification gives the parents or the child the right to dispute the grounds of referral. The reporter must then apply to the sheriff court for establishment of the grounds.

The rules concerning access to information in social work or other reports submitted to the hearing to aid its disposition decisions are less clear. The chairman of the hearing must inform the child and his parents of the *substance* of such reports if it appears to the chairman that this is *material* to the disposal of the case and that its disclosure would not be *detrimental* to the interests of the child.[62] Not only is this requirement vaguely phrased, there is also *no* procedure for challenging or proving any statement in any report. The report may include unsubstantiated and irrelevant information. The parents will not know as they have no right to examine it. The only remedy open to them is to appeal against the *disposition* of the hearing (which, arguably, could be 'appropriate' though based on 'inappropriate' information) or to allege procedural irregularities. But how many children and their parents are likely to recognize these?

The child can be detained or subject to 'care' measures for far longer than an adult convicted of a similar offence—a central tenet in a social welfare approach is that early and extensive intervention is in the child's interests. Doubt has already been raised over whether or not such measures are in the child's interest and the operation of the review powers of the hearings will be considered later. The question to consider briefly here is whether or not the review powers of the hearings provide some protection or safeguard to the child's liberty. Parents can request a review of their child's case at certain statutorily determined intervals (as can social workers and headmasters of residential establishments). The annual statistics suggest that reviews do not provide additional safeguards. In 1973, only 38% of all supervision requirements considered by the hearings were terminated on review; 36% were continued without variation and 26% were continued but varied.[63]

The child's and his parents' major protections lie in the right to deny the ground of referral (if the reporter wishes to continue he must make an application to the sheriff court for establishment of the ground of referral) and to appeal to the sheriff court on questions of law and against the hearing's disposition. But there are some unsatisfactory features in these provisions. A central feature of the new system is the separation of the functions of adjudication and disposition: adjudication is the appropriate role for the courts and disposition is the appropriate role for the panels. But it is only where the child or his parents *actively* dispute the ground of referral (as, for example, in the case of lack of specification in the grounds) that it must be proved in court. And the majority of parents and children are unlikely to know about, for example, the technicalities of specification or the requirements of natural justice. It is also at least possible that pressure is felt by the child and his parents to admit to the ground of referral before the panel in case something 'worse' happens if they do not. If they do not admit the grounds they may, after all, have to appear in court. There are no facilities for legal aid at the hearing when the child is asked whether he accepts the ground of referral (though legal aid is available if the child denies the grounds and the reporter makes an application to the sheriff for the grounds to be established). It can be argued that the hearing is not concerned with legal matters, but this argument is unsound. Whether or not to admit the ground of referral and the possible consequences of any such admission *are* legal questions. Goodwin has provided a number of examples where the child, in his account of the circumstances of the offence, presented facts amounting to a *denial* of the commission of the offence. Yet the hearings proceeded to deal with these cases.[64] Of course 95% of the children appearing before the former juvenile courts admitted the commission of the offence and so it can also be argued that these new procedures do no more than recognize reality. But this is an insufficient answer. The case for an application to the sheriff court where the child does not or cannot admit the grounds of referral is presented by the Kilbrandon Committee as follows:

> If society is prepared on the proof of offences by juveniles to authorise fairly sustained measures of education and training ... it is clearly of paramount importance that the initial basis for action should be established beyond doubt by stringent and testing procedures. This is precisely what criminal procedure aims to do.[65]

The Committee here presents the case *against* proceeding solely on the acceptance of the ground of referral by the child or his parents since hearings also have the power to impose 'sustained measures of education and training'. It is perhaps because of this that applications to the sheriff are more frequent than the expected five per cent. In 1973 11% of all reports to the hearings resulted in an application by the reporter to the sheriff court for the establishment of grounds.[66]

The child or his parents have a right to appeal (and here legal aid is possible—the provisions are comparable to those for legal aid in criminal proceedings) to the sheriff court and to the Court of Session on questions of law (e.g. failure to conform to the rules governing the operation of the hearing or to the principles of natural justice). No-one would question this right to appeal. As Gerald Gordon has written, 'the existence of appeals to the courts on questions of law is uncontroversial and inevitable; it follows from the court's normal function of making sure legal rules are obeyed.'[67] But who is going to notice any such breaches of rules? Legal representation, though possible, is unlikely because of the lack of legal aid at the *initial* hearing and the rules themselves are contained in statutory instruments. The right to appeal may be virtually meaningless: it is certainly rarely exercised. In addition, according to Goodwin, it is a common error in the practice of hearings to forget to tell families clearly of their right to appeal.[68]

The child and his parents also have the right to appeal to the sheriff against the hearing's disposition decision. This right of appeal is more difficult to justify bearing in mind the rationale for the removal of treatment decisions from the sheriff and for the creation of children's hearings. The reasons underlying the new system were that the sheriff was not the appropriate person to determine treatment questions and that decisions in the courts were influenced by inappropriate considerations like the nature of the offence and the punishment of the offender.[69] What is the sheriff's role intended to be? If the result of an appeal is an endorsement of the hearing's view, arguably it could be a waste of time. On the other hand, if the result is to remit to the hearing for consideration of alternative measures then the right of appeal seems wrong in principle. Within the new procedural framework, the 'expert' decision on the treatment measure appropriate to the child's needs has already been made. Resolving this question becomes even more complicated when we consider the factors which the Kilbrandon Committee stated should be taken into account in deciding the appeal: whether or not the decision is in the interests of the child; whether or not the decision amounts to an 'unjustified interference' between parents and their children: and whether or not the decision is an 'unwarranted infringement' of individual liberty.[70] Section 49 (5) of the Social Work (Scotland) Act states the sheriff's function in similar terms. He should intervene where he is satisfied that the decision of the children's hearing is 'not justified in all the circumstances of the case'. But how does the sheriff assess this, other than by reference to some sort of tariff system?

We are then faced with the question whether the real purpose of the right to appeal is to enforce the hearing's decision rather than to safeguard the interests of the child. Certainly, sheriffs have been reluctant to interfere with the decisions of the children's hearings. In *D* v *Sinclair*,[71] Sheriff Mowat took the view that a sheriff should not allow an appeal 'unless there was some flaw in the procedure adopted by the hearing or unless he was satisfied that the hearing had not given proper consideration to some factor in the case'. He felt that decisions of the hearing should be interfered with only exceptionally and not simply because it was felt that another form of treatment might be preferable. Alternatively, the right to appeal may be an attempt to *legitimate* the new system: there is generally a right to appeal from tribunals of first instance. Logically, there should have been some kind of Regional Appellate Hearing, from which an appeal might lie to the Court of Session on points of law. Appeal to the sheriff court may have been preferred in order to encourage public confidence or to allay disquiet about giving wide powers of disposition to a lay tribunal.

The right to appeal may also reflect a fear of the creature created by the Kilbrandon Committee. The panels have wide discretion to determine disposition in 'the best interests of the child'. Other values may, however, take precedence. Indeed, the appeal structure recreates the dilemma sought to be resolved in setting up the hearings: the sheriff must have regard to the interests of the child *and* to considerations of liberty and justice. There is an ambiguity running through the appeal procedures and their application.

Overall, appeal provisions are *secondary* to the main aim of securing appropriate care for the child. According to Grant, 'that there may be laxity in proceedings is indisputable; that the laxity may, on occasion, be serious is probable.'[72] He takes the view if the laxity violates the child's rights then the child or his parents can appeal. But this misses the point. For the most part, parents and children will be *unaware* of these violations. And even where they do appeal the sheriff may, in certain circumstances, hold the appeal to be 'frivolous' and direct that no further appeal shall be possible for twelve months.[73] But what is a 'frivolous' appeal? Parents who want their child to reside at home will appeal against the hearing's decision just because they disagree with it. Is this 'frivolous'? Or is the intention underlying these procedures to provide a disincentive to parents to appeal? In 1973 there were 28 appeals against the disposition decision of the hearing out of 14,961 referrals dealt with by them. Of these, four cases were discharged, four were remitted to the hearing for reconsideration of the disposition and in 20 cases the disposition was confirmed.[74]

Conclusion

We have suggested in this chapter that the recommendations of the Kilbrandon Committee were based on inadequate premises. This may mean that social policy and action which have their origin in the Report are similarly inadequate. The question then arises as to whether or not the operation of the children's hearings meets or exemplifies these criticisms. We explore this in the following chapters.

Social Welfare in Practice

Introduction

In the previous chapter we made a number of criticisms of the philosophy underlying the children's hearing legislation in Scotland. These criticisms were, in summary, the lack of objective criteria for assessing the needs of the child; the conflict between the needs of the child and the needs of society; and the possibility of greater intervention in the lives of children and their families. Moreover, the new system involved a radical shift in values and challenged traditional ideas on justice and the law. Reporters decide, on the basis of a child's need for compulsory measures of care, whether or not to refer a child to a children's hearing. Formerly, the fiscals prosecuted children appearing in the juvenile court. In a few areas operating a special juvenile court there were specialist juvenile fiscals who dealt only with juvenile cases, but, in the majority of areas, the fiscals appointed to prosecute in the juvenile courts were those appointed to the ordinary adult courts—they dealt with all cases referred to them by the police; juveniles formed only a part of their routine work. Reporters deal solely with juveniles. But there are further important differences between the two roles: the nature of the decisions made by them, the nature of the discretion exercised by them and the criteria of decision-making used by them. The procurator fiscal's main duty, whether dealing with adults or with juveniles, was to decide whether or not the nature of the offence was, in itself, of such public importance as to justify prosecution. Reporters, on the other hand, for the most part are concerned with the measures to be applied 'in the child's best interests'.[1] The basis of the referral to the children's hearing is the need for compulsory measures of care and this marks a substantial change, in theory, in the type of questions to be asked and in the kinds of factors to be taken into account.

The former juvenile courts were courts of criminal law; and juvenile court procedure, though modified in certain respects, did not represent any fundamental alteration from the principles of criminal procedure. Sheriffs and magistrates focused on the specific act alleged to have been committed by the child and on the degree of the child's personal responsibility. Although the range of powers available to the hearings was not to be much different from those available to the courts, the Kilbrandon Committee stated that 'the *manner* in which they could competently be exercised would be very different'[2] (emphasis added). Measures applied by the children's hearings were to be determined 'on the criterion of the child's actual needs'.[3]

Similar kinds of changes were envisaged in the role of the police. The Kilbrandon Committee saw the police as 'one of the primary sources of identification of children in need of special educational measures: as well as being part of the sifting or assessment agency'.[4] The Report of the Working Party on 'Police Procedures under the Social Work Scotland Act' concluded that the spirit in which the police handled suspected child offenders ought to reflect the fact that the object was not to secure conviction and sentence but to establish and take those measures, *if any*, needed in the 'best interests of the child'.[5]

The children's hearing system required changes in procedure, in the conduct of those dealing with children and in the criteria of decision-making. The question arises whether or not these changes have been achieved. Have changes in the philosophy underlying the system led to changes in the pattern of referral of children to the reporter or to the hearings, to changes in the characteristics of the children referred to the reporter or to the children's hearings, or to changes in the pattern and use of measures of disposal? In this and subsequent chapters we attempt to answer these questions. In this chapter we consider the operation of the new system at a national level and in Chapters V, VI and VII we examine more closely the operation of the system in two areas of Scotland, a large city and a mainly rural county.

The General Picture

In 1973 a total number of 35,932 children who had committed offences were dealt with in the Scottish juvenile justice system: 3,192 (9%) were dealt with in the courts; 22,176 (62%) by the re-porters (a proportion of these went on to the children's hearings);

9,824 (27%) by police warnings; and 740 (2%) by police juvenile liaison schemes.[6] A further 3,648 were referred to the reporter as truants, children beyond the control of their parents, children in moral danger or children suffering from neglect.[7]

The great majority of grounds for referral to the reporter relate to offences. The police and procurators fiscal were responsible for 90% of all reports to the reporter; educational sources for 5% and social work departments for 2% (60 of the remaining reports were made by relatives).[8] The majority of crimes alleged in the offence referrals were crimes against property—the most common offences were theft (27%) and house-breaking (24%). The next most common offence was breach of the peace (23%).[9] Most children referred to the reporter were in the 12–15 age-group, with more than half in the 14–15 age-group.

When the reporter receives information which suggests that a child may have to be brought before a children's hearing, he makes whatever initial investigation he thinks necessary. His basic task is to decide whether or not the child may be in need of compulsory measures of care. If he thinks these are necessary, he must refer the child to a children's hearing; if he does not, he then decides what other action on his part, if any, is necessary. The following diagrams outline what happened to the children referred to the reporters in 1973.[10]

DIAGRAM I: *Action by the reporter (total referrals), 1973.*

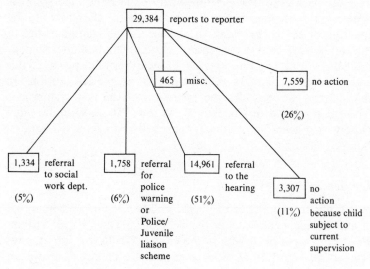

DIAGRAM II: *Action by the reporter (offence referrals), 1973*

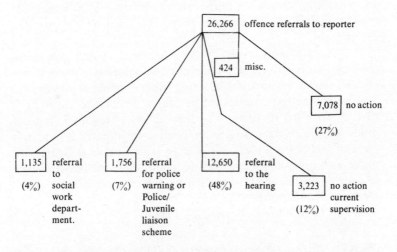

It is clear from these tables that the decision not to refer to a hearing does not necessarily mean that nothing happens to the child. 'No action' frequently does not mean 'no action', but rather 'no compulsory action'. The phrase 'no action' can include an interview (similar to a police warning) in which the reporter usually warns the child of the consequences of his action, a letter with similar aims, voluntary social work help or psychiatric care, restitution, working in children's homes, cleaning walls sprayed with paint, compensation and other forms of community service.

Reports alleging offences were much less likely to be referred to a hearing than non-offence reports; 83% of reports alleging truancy, for example, were referred to a hearing compared with 48% of those alleging offences.[11] Overall, fewer children appear before the children's hearings than appeared before the juvenile court. In 1969, 25,047 children were dealt with by the juvenile courts[12] — as opposed to 12,650 who appeared before a hearing in 1973 (a further 2,577 appeared before the sheriff court[13]) — an overall reduction of 39%. The reporters, unlike procurators fiscal, sift out a large number of children who do not appear to require compulsory measures of care. In England, this sort of decision—whether or not to refer to the juvenile court—is made by police officers in the juvenile bureaux where these exist, otherwise by divisional officers. In comparison with Scotland there has been no reduction in the number of children appearing before the juvenile courts in

England. Although 40% of those known to the police in England and Wales in 1973 were cautioned, the number of children proceeded against in the juvenile courts increased by 4% over the 1969 figures.[14]

The hearing can proceed to consider the case only where the child and his parents accept the grounds of referral. In the majority of cases (80%), grounds are accepted either in whole or part and the hearing proceeds. If the hearing decides, after consideration of the case referred to it, that no further action is required, it must discharge the referral. Where the hearing decides that a child is in need of compulsory measures of care, it may make a supervision order with or without conditions (conditions can include residence in a specific residential establishment—for example, one of the former approved schools). The following diagrams outline initial disposals by the children's hearings in 1973.[15]

DIAGRAM III: *Initial disposal of total referrals to the hearings, 1973*

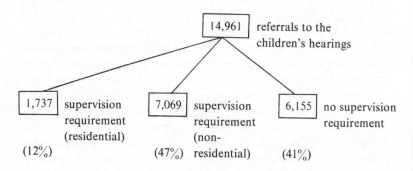

DIAGRAM IV: *Initial disposal of offence referrals to the hearings, 1973*

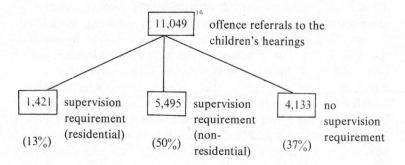

It is difficult to make comparisons between the use of measures of disposal in the new system and in the former juvenile courts in Scotland as the range of measures is different.[17] But there has been a considerable increase in the use of probation-type measures. In 1970, 3,529 (13%) of the children dealt with by the court were placed on probation;[18] in contrast, 5,495 (50%) of offence referrals dealt with by the hearings were placed on supervision in 1973— an increase of 56%. This compares with a decrease of 14% in the use of supervision in England and Wales over the same period.[19]

An intriguing but unanswerable question is what is happening now to the type of child who was previously fined. Is he being dealt with by the reporter as a 'no action' disposal, or being placed on supervision by the hearing? The fine was probably regarded by the juvenile courts as a nominal measure—children were usually fined only a small amount. Its use seems to have been largely symbolic, a way of reinforcing acceptable patterns of behaviour. If this was so, such cases are likely to be dealt with now by a 'no action' disposal. But Duncan and Arnott[20] found in their research that the children fined in one area were quite similar to the children placed on probation in another area where probation was freely and widely used. They attributed the frequent use of the fine in the city to a policy preference rather than to any differences in the characteristics of the two samples. If this was a general occurrence, then a policy change—particularly a change to a policy which emphasizes the need for early intervention—is likely to lead to increased use of supervision. The Kilbrandon Committee envisaged that their recommendations would result in 'a substantially greater use of community measures of casework with children on the lines of the present probation'[21] and this, as we have just shown, has happened.

Commitment to a residential establishment is also being used more frequently now than before. The rate of referral to a residential establishment has risen dramatically since 1967. In all there are 1,600 'List D'[22] places in Scotland and this is thought to be inadequate—many schools are full; 10 out of the 26 schools closed their waiting lists in 1974 and children spend an average of three months in the assessment centres awaiting[23] placement in a school. In 1970 there were 1,208 children subject to an approved school or a fit person order.[24] In all, 5% of the children dealt with by the court were dealt with in this way. In 1973, 1,421 children referred to the hearings as offence referrals were removed from their homes by the hearings (that is, 13% of all disposals in offence referrals), and in addition, 259 were removed from home by the court (that is 10% of the disposals made by the court)[25]—in all, a total of 1,680 children, an increase of 23% on the figure for 1970. This compares with a decrease of 8% in the number of children in residential establishments in England and Wales over the same period. There, the number of children in approved schools *fell* continuously throughout 'he first twelve months following the implementation of the Children and Young Persons Act 1969 to a figure about 15% lower at the end of that period than at the beginning. In March 1973 there were 5,636 boys in the former approved schools compared with 6,122 in December 1970.[26]

The rate of discharge in the children's hearings has remained much the same as in the juvenile courts. Formerly, about 30% of all cases dealt with by the juvenile courts were discharged or admonished. The Kilbrandon Committee expected discharges in the new system to occur infrequently—children were to be referred to hearings only where there was a prima facie case that compulsory measures were necessary. But the Committee was envisaging an ideal world. Often, full information (e.g. a social background report) is not available to the reporter until after the child has been referred to a hearing. This may change with increasing social work resources, but, until then, a high rate of discharge is likely to continue in the new system. As in the old, it reflects, in the main, that compulsory measures of care or control are not necessary. Discharge is also used fairly frequently in the English juvenile courts, although discharges there are mainly conditional rather than absolute.[27]

Children in the Courts

In 1973, 3,192 children were proceeded against in courts (an increase of one third over the 1972 figures).[28] The Kilbrandon Committee envisaged that prosecution would only arise 'exceptionally and on the gravest crimes'.[29] Yet most of these prosecutions were summary. Has something gone wrong with the system?

The expectation at the time of the implementation of the Act was that the consent of the Lord Advocate would be required for every prosecution of a child. During the committee stage of the Social Work (Scotland) Bill, the Lord Advocate was reported as saying that 'the purpose of the clause is to see that every case involving a child is brought to the notice of the Crown Office before any proceedings are taken'.[30] It is unlikely that more than a handful of the 3,192 prosecuted were directly referred to the Crown Office. The majority would have been dealt with in terms of a general directive issued to fiscals and the police by the Crown Office in August 1970 which stated that children who committed certain offences must be referred by the police to the procurator fiscal. The list of offences included cases which would formerly have been dealt with in the High Court—murder, culpable homicide, serious assault and like offences. It also included offences which might involve disqualification from driving, forfeiture of an article (for example, a weapon), and offences in which an adult is involved with the child (for the purposes of the Act an adult is anyone over the age of 16). Children, therefore, could be referred to the courts for technical or procedural reasons. The hearings have no power to order forfeiture or to disqualify because they were not to have any powers which were purely penal.[31] In the words of Gerald Gordon, it was 'thought better to break the spirit of the Act by prosecuting children in such cases than to spoil the image of the hearing by giving it the necessary powers'.[32] Many of the children prosecuted are, indeed, sacrificial lambs on the altar of social welfare ethics. Few come under the category of the 'gravest crimes': 1,103 children were charged with breach of the peace and 1,020 with theft (including theft by house-breaking).[33] The courts' dispositions convey a similar picture: 242 were placed on probation, 857 were fined, 845 were admonished or discharged; only 259 were placed in some sort of detention (List 'D' school, detention centre, borstal, etc.) and 359 were remitted to a hearing for disposal.[34]

The Secretary of State for Scotland has since made a statement in the House of Commons (in July 1974) outlining a change in the instructions issued by the Lord Advocate. The Lord Advocate has directed procurators fiscal not to commence proceedings against children under 13 years of age without reference to the Crown Office for his authority, or against children alleged to have committed offences while acting along with an adult unless there are circumstances which make joint prosecution essential. This change was a response to the publicity and resulting controversy surrounding the trial in the sheriff court of a 9-year-old girl charged with stabbing a playmate. These directions have led to some reduction in the number of children appearing before the sheriff court.[35] Of course, the fiscals have considerable discretion whether or not to

refer children initially referred to them by police to the courts
or to the reporters.[36]

In practice, it may make little difference to the child whether he
appears at a court or a hearing. Courts have a statutory duty 'to
have regard to the welfare of the child' and have social background reports to aid their disposition decisions. Indeed, at certain
points, prosecution may be *more favourable* to the child than proceedings before a hearing.[37] A child appearing before a court, for
example, is eligible for legal aid. It all depends on whether hearings
do in fact determine their decisions *solely* on the needs of the child.

The Case Study

The discussion in the following chapters is based on a study of the
new system of dealing with 'children in trouble' in two areas of
Scotland, a large city and a mainly rural county. The aim of the
study was to describe the operation of Part III of the Social Work
(Scotland) Act as it affected a particular group of children. This
involved tracing the development of the process from the stage
of initial referral to the police or to the reporters through to the
final disposal by the hearing. One cannot, of course, talk of *the*
system of dealing with child offenders in Scotland. There are a
number of systems operating within the same statutory framework
and, as a result, practices differ. Each area is influenced by the
differing organizational structure of its police force, social work
department and reporter's office, and by the differing professional
and operational ideologies of senior police officers, social workers,
reporters and panels. Consequently another aim of the project was
also a continuation and extension of a project on the juvenile
courts in the same two areas.[38] This meant that we had some com-
parative information from which we attempted to measure change.

The initial sample comprised all children referred to the reporters
in these areas during the period January to March 1972: 473 in the
city and 170 in the county. A second sample, similarly defined, was
drawn from the same period in 1973: 651 in the city and 302 in the
county. The two samples were first looked at separately to assess
whether or not changes (e.g. in the characteristics of the children
referred or in disposition patterns) had occurred over the year.
Few changes occurred, and the discussion in the following chapters
is based on a consideration of the two samples combined: a total
of 1,596 children. Individual case histories are used to highlight

points under discussion. In addition, we discuss those cases retained during the same period by the police for police warning. We had access to all files held by the reporters, police and fiscals for the children within our sample and collected information on the presenting behaviour (for example, the child's delinquency) and on the child's social and family characteristics as described in the various reports presented to the reporters and hearings.

Though we describe to some extent the children dealt with under the new system—their characteristics, delinquencies and so on— more emphasis is placed on the processes by which various kinds of decisions and selections were made because of the impact of different organizational structures on these decisions and because we wished to assess whether the changes predicted did in fact occur. The social background of the children referred to the children's hearings reflects the by now familiar picture of deprivation: a high unemployment rate among fathers, large families, financial difficulties, disturbed peer and family relationships, extreme physical need, and so on. It is possible that there is an association between these kinds of factors and the child's behaviour.[39] But such a picture also reflects the way in which children are defined as being in need of compulsory measures of care or control. What distinguished children who were dealt with by 'informal' methods from those who appeared before the hearing? and what distinguished those children dealt with by the hearing in different ways? We suggested in Chapter III that decisions and dispositions within the system would depend not merely on the characteristics of the children involved, but also on the ways in which these characteristics were perceived by the various agents in the system. Law-breaking, or any other kind of problematic behaviour, may not in itself mark a child as in need of compulsory measures of care. That behaviour is always subject to interpretation and the position which the child achieves within the system depends on this. Decision-makers interpret actions and events and relate these to other factors concerning the child—for example, his past record or his family situation. They must determine whether or not this particular event indicates that the child before them is 'really' troublesome, or whether it means that the child is 'really' a good child who has been, for example, led astray. The final designation of the child is conferred on him by agents of the system; it is not something which he achieves only by his own efforts. The Scottish system of juvenile justice, like all social welfare jurisdictions,

specifically intended such interpretation to take place. The underlying philosophy, its concern with needs rather than with deeds,
clearly directs agents to consider the actions of the child in the
widest possible context.

V

Police Warnings: a study in
value conflict

Most of the children dealt with in the children's hearing system are offenders—82% of all referrals to the reporters in 1973 were from the police (a further 8% were referred by procurators fiscal).[1] As a result, the police remain key decision-makers in the new system—the nature of their decisions limits or delimits the decisions of others. The decisions open to the police are: to warn the child on their own initiative; to warn the child and place it under the supervision of the juvenile liaison officer (if such a scheme is operated in the area); to refer the child to the procurator fiscal for the consideration of prosecution in the courts; or to refer the child to the reporter. The routine is much the same in most areas. An offence by a child is reported, preliminary investigation is carried out and the officer submits a report on the case to his superior officer. But the system of subsequent reporting may vary according to the internal structure of the department— for example, whether or not the police warn on their own initiative, or whether or not a police juvenile liaison scheme exists. In those areas operating a juvenile liaison scheme all police reports about juveniles are dealt with by the divisional police liaison officer. In other forces reports are received by whichever officer is on duty at the time and referred by him to his superior officer. Warnings are given with the consent of and in the presence of the child's parents and only where the child admits the commission of the offence.

The majority of police forces in Scotland administer police warnings—in 1973, 27%, of all child offenders were dealt with in this way.[2] But there are clear regional variations. In the two survey areas the pattern of police decision making was as follows:

DIAGRAM V: *Police decision-making in the city, 1973*

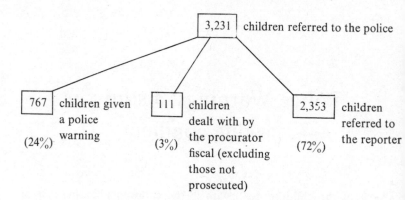

DIAGRAM VI: *Police decision-making in the country, 1973*

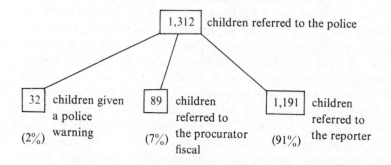

In the city it was usual practice for the police to warn children of their own initiative, whereas in the county area it was rare to do so. There are a number of possible explanations for this: different organizational structures in the individual police forces, different role-orientations in key figures in the police or different crime 'problems' in the two areas.

The city was divided, for administrative purposes, into six divisions and, for general police purposes, into four territorial divisions each commanded by a Chief Superintendent. Most areas were policed by the unit beat system although the city centre was policed by more traditional means. The city was one of the few areas in Scotland which did not set up a community relations branch in 1971. Rather, the policy there was to consider all constables as community relations officers in that such work was considered part of the normal duties of all police officers.[3] The county was divided into three divisions and the major urban areas were policed by the unit beat system. There was no specific community involvement branch,[4] but there was some informal involvement at a local level. There was no police juvenile liaison scheme in operation. Although both areas had an actual strength below that authorized, neither area was experiencing severe staff shortages in 1973.[5]

The total number of crimes and offences reported to the police in the city in 1973 was 52,224 and in the county 24,468.[6] This represents a rate per 1,000 of the population of 116.4 in the city and 73.2 in the county.[7] The crime pattern in the two areas was slightly different. In both areas the majority of offences reported were minor offences (Class VII) but the proportion was larger in the county than in the city: 67% in the county and 55% in the city. There were also proportionately fewer crimes of property without violence in the county: 15% compared with 25% in the city; but the proportion of property crimes with violence and violent crimes was much the same in the two areas.[8]

The Chief Constable's reports in the city do not examine separately the contribution of juveniles to city crime figures and so comparisons cannot be made between the juvenile crime rates in the two areas. But the crimes committed by the city and county samples in our study period showed that the city sample did commit significantly more offences of violence than the county sample, and that the county sample committed significantly more offences of malicious mischief. (This reflects a continuing trend as the research carried out in these two areas in 1967 found much the same.) But it did not seem that differences in the 'crime rate' in the two areas were such as would explain the difference in warning practices. The crimes committed in the two areas were, on the whole, predominantly petty—social nuisances rather than social dangers. Most of the assaults were minor playground assaults involving no weapons and requiring no medical attention for the victim. Slightly fewer than one third of the property offences committed involved sums of more than £25; the majority of cases of malicious mischief involved damage of less than £100.[9] Organizational differences were also not sufficient to explain the differences in warning practices—neither force operated a juvenile liaison scheme and the work done by community relations departments in other areas was done in both the city and the county as part of ordinary police work. What did account for the difference in warning rates was policy differences in the two areas, as determined by the Chief Constables.

The practice of police warnings was well developed in the city before the implementation of the 1968 Act. For example, 293 children were given police warnings in 1968 and 237 in 1969.[10] The county, on the other hand, had operated two systems of warnings—one given on the initiative of the police themselves and the other given after cases were returned to the police by the procurator fiscal for police warning. The majority of warnings fell into the latter category. In 1969, 53 warnings were given by the police in the county on their own initiative: 231 were given on the instruction of the procurator fiscal.[11] Under the new system the old pattern has continued although cases are now returned by the reporter to the police for subsequent police warning instead of by the fiscal. The police in the county warned 32 children in 1973, but a further 192 were returned to the police by the reporter for a police warning.[12]

By combining these two categories of police warnings in the county we can construct a new police warning rate. This then means that 17% of those referred to the police in the county in 1973 were subsequently warned by them. This was closer to the city and national picture. Did this mean that there was a 'typical' police warning case? If this was so, had the various directives on changes in the police role under the new system had an impact on policy and practice, and, consequently, on the characteristics of the 'typical' case?

Warnings—Sifting the Sheep from the Goats

Police procedure in relation to warnings was operated before the Act in accordance with the recommendations of the Scottish Advisory Council Report of 1945. This report stated that warnings were not intended 'to settle the appropriate course of treatment for the young person or to invoke punishment, but to warn him firmly as to the folly of antisocial behaviour and as to its consequences'.[13] Police warnings were reserved, except in exceptional circumstances, for first offenders who committed minor offences. The great majority of cases given a police warning under the juvenile court system were minor offences (Class VII), offences which the procurator fiscal would probably have regarded as too trivial to bring before the court. Police warnings continue to be reserved for such cases.

Those given police warnings in the city were, on average, younger and had committed fewer previous offences than the children referred to the reporters by the police. The offences involved primarily petty thefts from chain stores in the city centre, were usually committed in groups after school on weekday afternoons or on Saturday mornings, and most of the property taken was recovered. Most of the children also came from what were described as supportive homes, lived with both parents and came from social classes 1, 2 and 3. The proportion of females was higher than among the children referred to the reporter, but this was due to the nature of the offences committed by females (minor acts of shoplifting) rather than to discrimination in favour of female offenders as male shoplifters were also usually warned. In fact, those warned by the police in 1972 and 1973 were markedly similar to those warned in the same city in 1967. Research then found that 'the city warning cases follow a very distinct pattern. The juvenile concerned is usually a first offender coming to police attention for a theft offence, very often shoplifting, where the property involved is of low value and is fully recovered'.[14]

The picture in the county was similar. Children given warnings on the instructions of the reporter were broadly similar to those given warnings by the police in the city on their own initiative, that is to say, they were mainly first offenders or had committed minor offences. But there were slight differences in the type of offences committed by the two groups. In the city the majority of the offences were petty property offences or shoplifting; in the county a large number of children who had committed offences involving malicious mischief were returned to the police by the reporter for a police warning, as were a number of children who had committed minor assaults and breach of the peace.

Overall, the allocation of police warnings continued in both areas to be determined by the type of offence committed by the child and by whether or not the child had a previous record. What is remarkable about this is the *lack of change* despite the implementation of a major piece of legislation which incorporated clear changes in the role of the police. Our research confirms the findings of John Mack[15] in other areas of Scotland: the new legislation had little impact on police policy in changing the criteria for the allocation of police warnings.

Although the number of police warnings increased throughout the country—from 5,422 in 1969 to 9,550 in 1973—this represents only a slight increase proportionately: from 22% of those reported to the police in 1969 to 27% in 1973.[16] It is likely that these, too, are cases which conform to the 1945 recommendations. Mack argued that this does not indicate a widening of the police warning mesh. Rather, he suggested, it was 'more of the same'. But more of the same *is* a widening of the net. The increase in recorded juvenile crime in Scotland in 1973 was mainly attributable to an increase in the number of children given police warnings. In 1969, 27,220 children were proceeded against in the juvenile courts;[17] In 1973, 25,368 children were proceeded against in the sheriff court or were referred to the reporter.[18] It is only when we add to this the number of children given police warnings—by definition minor offenders—that an increase in recorded crime results: 32,642 in 1969[19] and 35,932 in 1973.[20] Since one of the aims of the legislation was to deal with children informally as far as possible and to keep children out of the formal control system, such an increase must be scrutinized carefully.

In the United States the general aim of youth bureaux was also the diversion of children from the juvenile justice system. But it appears that where these have been set up the police now send children to youth bureaux when formerly they would have taken them home and persuaded their family to deal with them, and that schools and other organizations refer troublesome children to the bureaux almost as a matter of course.[21] This happened in this country, too, in the former police juvenile liaison schemes—schemes in which a police warning was followed by a period of supervision by specially selected and trained police officers. The West Ham scheme dealt with children who in the absence of such a scheme would probably not have been taken before the juvenile court.[22] It is also possible that children who would previously have been dealt with informally are now, in England, being referred to juvenile bureaux precisely because such agencies exist, and are subsequently formally cautioned. A recent report points to two features which provide some support for this suggestion.[23] First, taking the police forces of England and Wales as a whole, Ditchfield found a close connection between the growth of juvenile cautioning since 1968 and increases in the known offender rate for juveniles. Those areas with the greatest number of cautions, also recorded the largest increases in the number of known offenders. Second, some areas with increased cautioning rates also showed large increases in the ratio of juveniles to adults in the offender population, often much larger than could reasonably have been accounted for by changes in the age structure of the population. For example, juvenile cautions increased in the Metropolitan Police District from 207 in 1965 to 12,125 in 1973. This increased cautioning was accompanied by a significant increase in the proportion of juveniles to adults in the offender population: in 1966 there were 25 juveniles for every 100 adults in the offender population compared with 37 in 1973. In urban police forces which made no special arrangements for dealing with juvenile offenders, on the other hand, little change in the ratio of juveniles to adults in the offender population was found—the ratio of juveniles to adults in the offender population in Birmingham was 52 in 1966 and remained so in 1973. As Ditchfield stresses, it would be misleading to draw too firm conclusions from these figures, but it at least raises the question whether changes in police practices resulting from the 1969 Act led to some juveniles being officially cautioned who would previously have been dealt with informally.

'No Action' Decisions—Redefining the Goats

It was thought that police warnings would relieve the new system in Scotland at an early stage of a considerable number of cases, but those cases currently warned by the police are of a 'sub-hearing' type—minor offenders with little or no record. This again reflects little change in police practice: Mack and Ritchie[24] described police warnings issued before 1971 as catering for children 'at the sub-court level', cases which the procurators fiscal would not have considered serious enough to warrant a court appearance. Indeed, as diagram II showed on page 73 many of the cases actually referred to the reporters by the police were not subsequently referred by them to the children's hearing for consideration of compulsory measures of care. The number of 'no action' decisions in cases referred to the reporter by the police is considerably higher than in, for example, educational referrals. In 1973, 52% of offence referrals were given a 'no action' disposal by the reporter compared with 17% of educational referals.[25]

The reason for this difference in 'no action' rates is that educational referrals usually take place after a number of measures have been attempted. For example, in the city the child or his parents is usually sent a card from the school asking why the child has not attended and then the family is visited by a schools attendance officer. If these steps do not bring about improvement in attendance, the child and parents are then referred to the Day School Management Committee which is a committee of the town council. This Committee in turn refers the child to the reporter where it feels further measures are necessary.[26] Casual truancy is dealt with internally by the schools or not at all, and further action is taken only where the truancy is prolonged, where there is some indication of emotional disturbance in the child, or where the child is seen as 'troublesome' by the school. There has already been a period of unsuccessful pressurizing and bargaining. The request to the reporter, therefore, is phrased in terms indicating compulsory action *is* necessary. It is specifically a request to use the hearing's authority to induce conformity (that is, school attendance) or to remove the child from the school community. The school is seeking to use the coercive powers of the hearing in handling its problem cases.

The police similarly refer to the reporter those children whom they find troublesome in the area. The police are subject to pressures from the community to 'do something about' juvenile delinquency. The police refer a child to the reporter for 'something to be done' to that child; those cases retained for warning by them are those about which, because of the nature of the offence, they do not perceive any pressure from the public to 'do something'. Police officers tend to feel that when reporters take 'no action' this discredits them in the eyes of the delinquent and also within the community. Consequently, the police are highly critical of the reporters' 'no action' rate in offence referrals. The majority opinion of the Association of Chief Police Officers was that

> in some cases at least, the best interests of the child are not served by taking 'no action'. Indeed the reverse might be the case as the most criminally minded will be likely to regard 'no action' as an inducement to commit more crime and therefore continue on a criminal career.[27]

These views were echoed by John Mack who assumed that reporters would take 'no action' decisions in only a few cases. He wrote:

> It is desirable that the youngster who has offended and has admitted the offence should be made aware of the error of his ways without delay

and without postponement; if this is not done and if he gets off as he thinks scot free on an admitted offence, he might well be expected to go on to commit other offences.[28]

This may be so, but the Kilbrandon Committee explicitly stated that referrals to the children's hearing should be made for one reason only, namely 'that prima facie the child is in need of special measures of education and training'.[29] The Scottish Act refers to the need for 'compulsory measures of care'.[30] The views of the police on reporters' 'no action' decisions highlight a major point of conflict within the new system.

The Role of the Police—an Issue of Value Conflict

The new system required changes in the police handling of juvenile offenders and this has put the police into a conflict. Traditionally, it is the role of the police to detect offenders (juvenile and adults alike) and to refer them to the procurator fiscal for prosecution in the courts. (In some jurisdictions, for example in England, the police refer offenders directly to the courts for prosecution.) The Kilbrandon Committee expected the police to become 'one of the primary sources of identification of children in need of special educational measures'.[31] This is not a task for which the police have been given any special training, and it is a task which is at odds with demands made on the police by the public to 'do something about' juvenile delinquency. This can create a conflict in the various roles to be performed by an individual officer, and can lead to conflict with his colleagues. Officers will experience pressures, implicit in their desire to maintain good relations with their colleagues and explicit in the demands of the public for certain kinds of action. This means that the police are unlikely to become integral parts of a social welfare approach to children in trouble—welfare values have a low or marginal position in the values of their profession. The fact that in our sample the police took little notice of the child's personal or social characteristics in deciding whether or not to refer the child to the reporter and were reluctant to differentiate in their treatment of co-offenders suggests that to do otherwise would have offended values held by them: for example, justice, equality before the law and deterrence. The reporters' role is at variance with these values. In the words of the Kilbrandon Committee

The issue confronting the reporter to the panel will be whether the child requires treatment of the kind such as to justify formal referral to the panel, as distinct from informal measures. In other words, the issue is essentially how best to treat the needs of the child, and whether this aim would be better furthered, *or could be attained only*, by a formal referral to the panel (emphasis added).[32]

In these circumstances it is inevitable that there is tension between the police and reporters.[33]

The fact that the courts still have jurisdiction over *some* child offenders serves to reaffirm many of the views of the police and to indicate that real or radical change is unnecessary. The opinion of the Association of Chief Police Officers was summarized in a recent memorandum as follows:[34]

> a: no benefits have accrued in regard to the treatment of offenders and children's panels are less effective than the former juvenile courts in securing treatment which will serve the best interests of child offenders;
>
> b: there is a hard core of juvenile offenders who have little or no respect for children's hearings;
>
> c: there are too few places in residential establishments, particularly for unruly offenders for whom there is a marked lack of accommodation;
>
> d: the former probation service commanded more respect from offenders than the current social work departments;
>
> e: the operation of children's panels has reduced respect for the police by many juvenile offenders;
>
> f: children's panels as presently constituted do not have sufficient powers to deal with the problems brought before them;
>
> g: a higher proportion of cases are marked 'no action' than was the case in the former juvenile courts.

This memorandum also showed that pupils in 'List D' schools and other residential establishments committed more offences during the first three months of 1974 than in a similar period in 1973 and that during the first six months of 1973, 1,450 children previously dealt with by the hearings committed further offences.

The police clearly blame the children's hearing system for this apparent increase in offending. According to Dan Wilson, Secretary of the Scottish Police Federation, there is 'a great deal of disquiet among police officers of all ranks' about the operation of the children's hearings. He goes on:

The Federation was not asked specifically to comment on the hearings before the Social Work Act became law. Now we are getting all the anomalies and the police are helpless. All they can do is carry out their instructions and keep reporting these people.[35]

The comments reveal a clear lack of faith in the new system. If strains and tensions amongst those operating the system become severe, it is unlikely that the shared objective—the prevention or control of delinquent behaviour—can be reached.

The Kilbrandon Committee also saw the need for what can be called 'symbolic' sanctions. The Committee stated:

Much juvenile delinquency, particularly among younger children, consists of acts of petty mischief which do not require elaborate or sustained treatment measures; and that, *in so far as they do need to be dealt with by public action*, they can very appropriately be met by means of warning (emphasis added).[36]

The continued use of police warnings symbolizes society's insistence that the law should not be broken and that children should not break the law with impunity—it is an example of the wish 'to do something' although the child is considered not to need measures of compulsory care. Police warnings are an anomaly in a welfare-oriented system. It might be argued that it is not 'in the child's interest' to allow him to break the law without incurring a sanction but there is little support for this. Indeed, research suggests the converse.[37] The retention of police warnings suggests that society is unable to respond to child offenders solely within a welfare framework.

This raises the wider question of the role of the police in a social welfare jurisdiction. An important thesis of the Kilbrandon Committee (and one which the police appear to accept) was that a trivial offence can indicate that the child is in need of care.[38] Should the police, therefore, bring even the most trivial offender to the notice of a social work department or a reporter? The Standing Conference of the Organisation of Social Workers favoured this, stating that it was undesirable that the decision of how to handle offenders should be left to the discretion of the police whose background, they considered, did not equip them to make such decisions. The opposite view (presented by the Howard League for Penal Reform and the Royal Medico-Psychological Association) favoured the retention of warnings on the initiative of the police because the majority of delinquent acts committed by children did not, in the words of the Working Party on Police Procedures, 'represent the first stages of the slide into delinquency but merely childish irresponsibility, and the number is so great that the resources of the social work department would be wasted trying to investigate them'.[39] But this begs the question. The Working Party did not say, for example, in what way police resources are equipped to distinguish the 'irresponsible' from the 'disturbed' or 'truly' delinquent. The Kilbrandon Committee itself was confused on this point. Having stated that minor offences may be symptomatic of underlying emotional disturbance, the Report goes on: 'The risk of such situations arising in relation to the type of cases in which police warnings are at present given seems to us to be extremely remote'.[40] How do we know this? The Committee seems to assume that the seriousness of the offence is an indication of the seriousness of the 'need', but there is no evidence to support this.[41]

Currently, the level of social information known to the police is slight and in some areas, for example, in the survey city, the procedure followed before a police warning was given to a child was that the police notified the appropriate social work department that they were considering warning the child so that a record check could be made to see whether or not the child was known to the department. Such a procedure has a number of consequences—it provides the social work department with an excuse to intervene in that family (by asking the police to refer the case to the reporter); it increases the chances of the child coming into the formal control system where his family is already known to the social work department for some reason; and it means that the child not known to the social work department is likely to avoid referral to the formal control system. As a result, the delinquent stereotype—delinquents come from 'problem' families—is maintained.[42]

The police are not keeping out of the system children who could be kept out. The reporter in the county area, where few police warnings were given, had a very high 'no action' rate in offence referrals (74% of offenders referred to the reporter in our 1973 samples were given a 'no action' disposal) and even the reporter in the city area, where there had already been a police sift, decided that a considerable number of offence cases did not require compulsory measures of care (51% of offenders in our 1973 sample were given a 'no action' disposal).

The conflict of correctional values with welfare values may well be a universal and inevitable feature of any system which deals with children who offend. The police cannot be expected to submerge correctional values to welfare values in their handling of such children. If we wish to create a system in which welfare values dominate, the role of the police requires reconsideration. We return to this in Chapter VIII.

The Reporter's Role: a study in diversion

Defining Diversion

Diversion was not, until recently, a word much used in Great Britain and yet, as we outlined in Chapter I, the ideas underlying the concept are not new and have influenced social policy in relation to children who offend.

Why the increased emphasis on diversion? The juvenile court itself was originally planned to divert children from the more formal court procedures applied to adults and many of the arguments now presented in favour of diversion from the juvenile court derive from a feeling that the juvenile court has failed—failed to provide the sort of care envisaged by the proponents of the early courts, and failed either to stem increasing rates of juvenile crime, or to reduce recidivism. Now Edwin Lemert has argued that if there is a defensible philosophy for the juvenile court, it is one of judicious nonintervention—in other words a policy of diversion.[1]

Advocates of diversion point to many possible advantages—some of which contradict each other. First, diversion is seen to provide an earlier opportunity of working with defendants than would otherwise be possible and this, in turn, provides hope that such work will be more successful. Diversion in this approach is a *gateway* to resources—the juvenile court only failed because treatment measures were applied too late in the child's career. Conversely, it is argued (because we have too little information about appropriate and successful ways of dealing with children who offend) that diversion can *protect* children from the consequences of these same treatment measures. The other major arguments in favour of diversion (the theoretical basis of which lies in labelling theory[2] and differential association theory[3]) are variants of this view. Diversion can avoid the stigma often associated with a court appearance and, cer-

94

tainly, there is some evidence that such stigmatization can intensify a deviant self-image and can lead to further acts of deviance, that intervention may exacerbate delinquent behaviour.[4] Diversion, it is also argued, can avoid contamination; it can prevent naïve offenders from associating with more experienced offenders. It is commonly felt by proponents of these views that too many minor offenders appear in our juvenile courts, that many of the acts committed by children referred to juvenile courts indicate family, educational or welfare difficulties, or just difficulties in growing up. The juvenile justice system, it is felt, is too heavy-handed for such offenders; its processes should be a last and limited resort. Finally, of course, there is the argument of cost, that diversion saves scarce resources.

But it is also claimed that there are disadvantages in the notion of diversion. The major ones, in summary, are: the loss of the possible deterrent value of a court appearance and a diminution of the symbolic importance of the court process; the possible pressure on children and parents to admit guilt in order to avoid an appearance before the juvenile court; the possibility that diversion may involve greater interference with the offender's liberty than if he was dealt with by the juvenile court; the decision to divert may involve discriminatory practices; the possibility that diversion may extend rather than limit the network of social control; the possibility that diversion may involve greater interference with the liberty of those offenders still dealt with by the juvenile justice system; the possibility that insufficient weight may be given to the rights of the victim; and the question whether or not further offences occurring after the decision to divert should lead to formal processing of the child. The Scottish system developed a unique form of 'minimising penetration'[5] into the juvenile justice system. A case study of the role of the reporter provides a framework in which to discuss many of these issues and throws some light on a vital question in any discussion of diversion: who should divert?

The Basis of the Reporter's Role

As we have seen, about one quarter of the children referred to the police in Scotland each year are warned by them. The police refer those whom they are unwilling to caution to the reporter—the key figure in the new system. It is his function to decide, on the basis of reports, whether the child referred to him by the police, by social work department, or, indeed by anyone including the child's parents, is in need of 'compulsory measures of care'.[6] Only when he believes that this is so, does the reporter refer the child to a hearing. The reporter should ask first whether action is justified and, if so, whether it is necessary.

Built into the Scottish system, then, is a *double* screening device. The reporters stand as independent and visible sifts between the police (and other referring agents) and the children's hearings. Their independence is such that, although employed by the local authority, their contracts of employment cannot be terminated by the local authority. Nor are reporters subject to any controlling authority. Traditionally, of course, in the Scottish legal system an independent assessor exists between the police and the adult courts, namely the procurators fiscal.

Reporters were created as a professional group only in 1970— what kind of people are they? The Kilbrandon Committee felt that the role called for 'a degree of practical knowledge and understanding of children's problems', and that a reporter 'should preferably be an officer combining a legal qualification with a period of administrative experience relating to the child welfare and educational services'.[7] Such creatures are rare to find and, in fact, the majority of the reporters appointed in 1970 were lawyers or social workers; indeed many of the reporters who were legally qualified were part-time and continued in their practices.[8] Other groups were also represented—for example, former police officers and clergymen. In the county at the time of our research the reporter was a former probation officer and his deputy was formerly a solicitor in private practice. In the city the reporter was a lawyer with considerable juvenile court experience and his deputy was a social worker. The appointment of representatives of both the legal and social work professions was a common pattern throughout Scotland in those areas where more than one reporter was appointed. But why should the 'ideal' reporter have 'legal qualifications'? This seems at odds with a social welfare approach—an approach dominated by social work values. It may have been an attempt to introduce legal or justiciary considerations into the social welfare approach. If so, this surely recreates the conflict which was to be resolved in the new system, the conflict between criminal justice and social welfare criteria. But, if it was such an attempt, it was a somewhat half-hearted one. The reporter is meant to be satisfied that the information stated in the grounds of referral contains sufficient evidence to enable him, if need be, to establish the grounds in the sheriff court.

But there is nothing to prevent a reporter taking the risk that the child will accept the grounds of referral—he can always subsequently abandon the application to the sheriff if he thinks that he is unable to prove the case. Such practices are encouraged by social welfare principles and do occur in the Scottish system. Also, although the reporter alone is responsible for the decision to refer the child to the hearing, there is no machinery for appeal against it, there are no criteria set out anywhere which might be considered relevant in determining whether or not compulsory measures of care are necessary, the decision is made in private and the reporter need not give reasons for his decision.

The reporter is a hybrid creature—neither lawyer nor social worker. But he is likely to be influenced by his prior role orientation, training and professional ideologies. Reporters who were formerly lawyers are likely to develop different policies and practices from reporters who were formerly social workers. Certainly, the national figure for rates of referral to the children's hearings by reporters conceal considerable regional variations: the rate of referral to the children's hearing in 1973 varied from 32% in the city of Aberdeen to 81% in Stirling.[9] Such variations have a number of possible explanations: they may result from different crime patterns in the areas; from different police policies and practices; or from differences in the policies and practices of the reporters themselves. The different referral rates in the two study areas provided an opportunity to explore these hypotheses.

Diversion in Practice

The administration of juvenile justice can be viewed as a delinquency processing 'system'. Individuals are passed from one stage to another with selection processes occurring at each stage. The nature of this processing may affect and be determined by a number of factors, not least the needs of the 'system' itself.

The county reporters had a considerably lower rate of referral to the hearings than the city reporters: 32% compared with 56%. The distribution of disposals during the 1973 study period shows that regional practices and resources differed and had an impact on the eventual disposition of the child. There was, for example, no system of reporters' interview or 'warning' in the county; nor did the city reporters return children to the police for warning; the use of voluntary social work reflects differences in available resources in the two areas.

DIAGRAM VII: *'No action' disposals by the city reporters 1973 (3 months)*

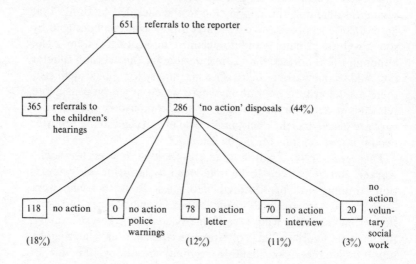

DIAGRAM VIII: *'No action' disposals by the county reporters 1973 (3 months)*

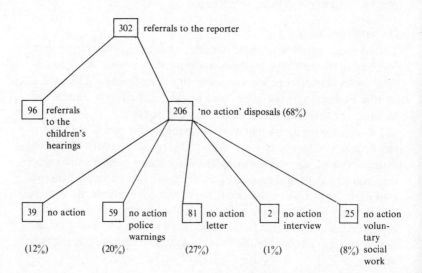

The overall 'no action' rate disguises marked differences in the 'no action' rate for different grounds. In January to March 1973 the county reporters gave 'no action' disposals to only 18% of the educational referrals compared with 74% of offence referrals. The corresponding percentages in the city for the same period were 5% and 51%. This reflects the point made in the previous chapter about the nature of referrals to the reporter by different referral agents.

We outlined in the previous chapter some differences in the juvenile crime pattern in the two areas—namely a higher proportion of crimes of violence in the city than in the county and a higher proportion of malicious mischief in the county—but this was not sufficient to explain the differences in the rate of referral to the children's hearings. The nature of the offence had no influence on the reporter's decision to refer to a children's hearing in the county; and children who committed property offences or malicious mischief were *more likely* to be referred to a hearing in the city than those who committed breach of the peace or assault. The major difference between the two areas was that in the county there was a higher proportion than in the city of property offences in which the property was not recovered. In general, however, the crimes committed by children referred to the reporters in the county and in the city were similar (on such criteria as value of property stolen, extent of damage to property, injury to the victim, etc.). And the children in one area were not more persistent offenders than in the other—just less than half of those referred to the reporter by the police in both areas had court records. The higher rate of 'no action' by the county reporters could not be explained by reference to the different types of crimes committed in the two areas.

We also noted in the previous chapter that police warnings in the two areas operated differently. The practice of police warnings in the county was not well developed, whereas the police in the city warned a large number of children on their own initiative. It was possible that this difference in police practice explained the different 'no action' rates, since the more trivial cases would have been sifted out by the police in the city before they reached the reporter. In the county, on the other hand, the first major sift was carried out by the reporters. In an attempt to test this, we added together the police warnings and the reporter's 'no action' decisions in the city and created a new, overall, 'no action' rate. When the new 'no action' rate for offence referrals was compared with that of the county the difference in the 'no action' rates disappeared for the

1972 sample, but remained (and was statistically significant) for the 1973 sample. The new 'no action' rate for 1973 in the city was 64% compared with 74% in the county. Organizational differences at the police level in the two areas were not sufficient to explain the differences in the 'no action' rate.

In the previous project on the juvenile courts in these two areas there were similar, and quite marked, differences between the fiscals' rate of referral to the juvenile courts: 95% in the city and 60% in the county.[10] Three possible explanations were considered: (1) the cases referred to the city fiscals involved more serious offences or more persistent offenders; (2) the two systems operated differently because of their different structures (the city had two levels of juvenile courts: the burgh court for more trivial cases and the sheriff court for the more serious; the county had only one juvenile court—a special juvenile court. It was thought that less serious offences might have been dealt with in the county at the pre-court level); (3) the attitudes and policies of the fiscals in the two areas differed. The first explanation was rejected. The researchers found —just as we have found—that those cases reaching the fiscals in the two areas were fairly similar; the number of offences committed, the value of property stolen and the amount recovered showed little variation. There were a larger number of first offenders among the cases referred to the county fiscal than amongst those referred to the city fiscal, but this did not explain the difference in the two areas in the proportion sent to the court. The researchers adopted as an explanation a combination of the second and third explanation— that the system itself and the personalities and attitudes of the fiscals operating it created and accounted for the differences. In the current context, the framework of the system is the same for both areas. This draws us to the view that differences in the training, personalities and attitudes of the reporters accounted, in part, for the differences in the 'no action' rates in our survey.

Styles of decision-making also differed in the two areas and were such that they seemed to affect referral rates. In the city the reporter's staff operated as one unit and all the staff met once or twice weekly to consider the appropriate action for each referral. Decisions were group decisions. The reporter there felt that there were considerable advantages in making decisions in this way—in particular it meant that in reaching a decision he had the benefit of the opinions of people of previously different backgrounds. In the county, the problem of distance led to a pattern of children's hearings being held in different centres at varying intervals and so the county was split geographically between the reporter and his deputy. Referrals were allocated accordingly, with each reporter making his own decisions. When people from different professional backgrounds make decisions together it is likely that they reach *compromise* decisions—where there is some doubt or disagreement the decision is likely to be to refer the child to a hearing. This would occur less frequently where reporters were working independently of each other and may again, in part, explain the lower rate of referral to the hearings in the county.

A further explanation for the different referral rates is, quite simply, the availability of social work resources—in many cases the city reporters did not have social work reports prior to making their decision whether or not to refer to the hearing due to shortage of staff in the city Social Work Department. Again, where the reporters were in some doubt about whether the child required compulsory measures of care it is likely that the child was referred to a hearing. There was no single explanation for the different referral rates—professional ideologies of the individual reporters, styles of decision-making, availability of resources all influenced the eventual outcome.

Criteria for Diversion

The reporter's decision whether or not to refer a particular child to a hearing for consideration for compulsory measures of care is clearly the key decision in the new system. What kind of information do reporters have to make this decision? What kinds of factors shape their decisions?

The system is intended to be 'a procedure which from the outset seeks to establish the individual child's needs in the light of the fullest possible information as to his circumstances, personal and environmental'.[11] The reporter, therefore, gathers and pieces together information about the child's actions, school behaviour, social characteristics and family background so that a clear picture of the child emerges. The significance of the original ground of referral—for example theft—is understood by considering the action in its wider social context. The decision taken depends on the type of picture which emerges.

The reporter begins with the report of the referring agency which is, in the majority of cases, a report from the police giving details of the offence or offences which are the reason for the referral. But it is clear from the high proportion of children who are not referred to a children's hearing that the original ground for referral, particularly in offence referrals, is not necessarily seen in itself as indicating a need for compulsory measures of care. The reporter must attempt to distinguish between the 'normal' delinquent and the 'problematic' delinquent, between the 'normal' runaway and the 'problematic' runaway. He is, in essence, making a prediction. He is attempting to assess whether or not the behaviour will continue or will grow more serious if compulsory measures of care are not applied. He is not concerned with what has happened, but with what 'caused' the behaviour. He is assessing what kind of person the child is or, in Emerson's words, he is making an assessment of the child's 'moral character'.[12] The reporter looks for indicators which confirm or deny the preliminary diagnosis of a 'problem' which the referral represents. There are, of course, a number of possible indicators of compulsory measures of care. In one instance, information about the child's previous offence history may serve this function; in another, it may be information about his family background. There may be one such indicator or, as is more likely, several; and there may, at the same time, be indications in the opposite direction, that compulsory measures of care are not necessary. Decisions then depend on some assessment of the relative importance of various factors. This explains why all cases manifesting similar behaviour patterns are not necessarily treated in the same way—some delinquents emerge from the encounter with the reporter firmly identified as 'troublesome', while others are regarded as not 'really' troublesome despite having committed an offence or having run away from home.

In attempting to answer such questions as whether the behaviour was part of a pattern which was likely to continue, or whether it was related to other kinds of problematic behaviour, the reporters, in our survey, looked first at the incident itself. If the act was an isolated occurrence—if, for example, the child had committed no other offences or had no previous history of running away from home—some form of 'no action' disposal was likely. Where the child had no court record or had not previously been referred to the reporter it was also likely that he would be dealt with by a 'no action' disposal. On the other hand, repeated behaviour tended to confirm the 'problem' diagnosis and referral to a hearing then became likely.

'Michael's' case illustrates this. 'Michael' was charged with two offences of theft by house-breaking—he had stolen money from some pre-payment gas meters. He had previously been given a 'no action' disposal by the reporter for a similar type of offence and at that time the social worker had suggested that his co-accused were not his usual friends and that 'Michael' had been led astray by them. On this second occasion, however, 'Michael' was referred to a children's hearing *without* a request for additional social work information—the repeated pattern of behaviour was seen as confirming the 'problem' diagnosis.

But the process is not an automatic one. 'Luke' had previously been on probation and was currently on supervision. When he became involved in a further offence of theft it seemed likely that he would be referred to a children's hearing with a view to a possible placement in a residential establishment, but he was dealt with by a 'no action' letter. 'Luke' was described by the social worker concerned as quiet and withdrawn, and as unsuitable for a residential establishment. The reporter balanced these factors against the others.

The incident itself, of course, could be of such seriousness that it determines the form of the decision. The value of the property stolen and total number of offences committed at the time of a particular referral appeared to influence the reporter's decision to refer the child to a hearing. The value of the property stolen was a greater discriminator in the county, but, generally speaking, where the value of the property stolen was more than £25 the child was very likely to be referred to a children's hearing. (In the county the child was very likely to be given a 'no action' disposal where the property value was less than £5. In the city, however, about half such cases were referred to a hearing.) Similarly, the more offences a child committed the more likely he was to be referred to a children's hearing. The likelihood of a child who had committed one offence being referred to a children's hearing was low.

In the county the nature of the offence committed by the child had no influence on the reporter's decision to refer to the children's hearings, but this was not so in the city. There, children who committed malicious mischief were more likely to be referred to a hearing than those committing breach of the peace or assault. This indicates the minor nature of most such assaults and breaches of the peace.

Factors traditionally thought to influence decision-making—age and sex—did not appear to influence reporters' decisions. The reporters in the county (unlike the city reporters) seemed to discriminate in favour of females, but the sample of female offenders there was very small. This difference was not due to the trivial nature of most of the offences committed by females in the county, for their offences were not more trivial than those committed by female offenders in the city.

Reporters also had access to social background information. Some social information was included in the police reports, but the level was usually slight. There might be a comment of a general nature on the child and his family—for example, the structure of the family, the number of children in the family, whether or not the father (or mother) was employed and the physical appearance of the home—but in the majority of cases the comment was non-committal: 'The parents say he attends school regularly and is well behaved at home,' or 'he is not a member of any youth club or organization.'

Reporters sometimes have reports from the child's school and from the local social work department. As the schools have become more involved in the new system, the number of reports sent to the reporters has increased, and the number of reports from the social work department has also increased in recent years. Resources in the city were less well developed at the time of our research, however, than in the county and so social work information in the city tended at this stage to be that already on the files in the social work department—the child came, by definition, from a family already seen as a 'problem'. Where the child was not already known to the social work department, the reporters had no additional social background information. In the county the practice of requesting a visit to individual families and of receiving a report before the reporter made his initial decision was quite common.

In the various reports written for the reporter there was a mass of 'soft' data which was impossible to quantify. The framework of factors which could be referred to in such reports was vast; and it was diffuse. Information was not systematically collected or presented, and it was impossible to assess whether or not a particular piece of information which was missing was missing because it was not known, because it was considered irrelevant to the particular child's difficulties, or because the social worker forgot to include it. In order to make some use of the information available to us in the various reports we coded the report as a whole as either a) indicating problems or difficulties within the family or in the child's behaviour or attitudes or b) indicating favourable aspects within the family or in the child's behaviour or attitudes. Examples of the former are:

> undisciplined behaviour ... control rather than treatment required ... problems reflect disturbed family patterns ... cannot be managed by mother ... father had frequent police contact and served prison sentences for breach of the peace and assaults ... anti-authority ... heavy drinker ... mother ineffectual.
> boy with poor self-image ... repression of feelings leads to outburst of aggression ... father disciplinarian of the old school ... had to give up work because of health ... mother depressive ... quick and uncontrollable temper ... unconscious rejection of boy since early age.
> boy ... physical development in excess of years and uses this to detriment of others ... no remorse or concern ... pursues own path regardless of consequences ... father basically a good father but well known to authorities for anti-social behaviour.

and of the latter:

> boy self-assured and responds easily ... offence isolated incident ... family stable ... affectionate, supportive.
> boy open and friendly ... communicates freely on both descriptive and emotional levels ... drawn into offence by older boys ... family extremely co-operative ... in agreement on upbringing and discipline.
> boy well-balanced youth ... good relationships ... ashamed of misdemeanour ... family aware of problems of young people ... good home ... no indication of the need for supervision.

Our codings were inevitably impressionistic, but, in this context, this is justifiable. The writer of a report selects from a pool of available information that which is to be contained in the report itself—the report is geared towards achieving certain ends. The writers of these reports were usually attempting to persuade the reporters to accept their recommendations for a particular form of action—they were attempting to convey in their report a particular impression. The same impression was probably conveyed to us. Our analysis was limited to the extent that it was based only on the records held by the reporters and made available to us. The reporters' range of information might have been greater than this—from our period of data collection based in the reporters' offices we know that reporters were in contact by telephone with both social work departments and schools. But, from our discussion with the reporters in the two areas, any additional information was 'more of the same', it was confirmatory of the impression already conveyed by the reports.

In 1973, 37% (in the city) and 32% (in the county) of the children referred by the police to the reporter had 'problems' according to the police report. The majority of cases, however, in both areas were 'non-problematic' in police eyes and this, to a large extent, accounted for the high proportion of offenders given 'no action' dispositions by the reporters. The extent of 'problem' indication, in fact, varied distinctly according to the grounds of referral and corresponded closely with the reporters' subsequent decisions to refer particular children to the children's hearings. Favourable reports quite clearly increased the likelihood of the child being given a 'no action' disposal. On the other hand, it was highly likely that a child would be referred to a children's hearing where there was an indication of 'problems' in the police, social work or school reports.

It was possible to isolate further a few socio-demographic factors —factors which did consistently appear in the reports. These were social class, family structure, family size and the employment record of the father. Family structure was the only factor which was reflected in the decision-making in both areas. Children from 'broken homes' or 'single parent families' were more likely to be referred to a children's hearing and less likely to be given a 'no action' disposal than children living in the normal two-parent family. None of the other factors mentioned seemed to be associated with the process of decision-making in the county. But in the city, all of these additional factors, except social class, seemed to be associated with the reporters' initial decisions. Where the child's father was unemployed he was more likely to be referred to a children's hearing than a child whose father was in employment and as the size of the child's family increased so, too, did the child's chances of referral to a children's hearing.

Reporters could decide on one of several actions within the so-called 'no action' category and it is possible to point to factors which seem to be associated with these different 'no action' disposals. The chances of a 'no action/voluntary social work' decision rather than a decision to take no action at all were high where the various reports indicated 'problems'. For example, in the city 71% of those given such a disposal had problems mentioned in their initial social work reports, 72% in their school reports and 70% in their police reports. On the other hand, the mention of 'favourable' aspects in the various reports was likely to lead to a straight 'no action' disposal. In the county those returned by the reporter to the police for a police warning were also a quite distinct group—the majority of these children had no court record, no previous referrals to the reporters, had committed, in the main, only one offence and had a high level of 'favourable' aspects in their initial social work and school reports. They were, in fact, broadly similar to the group given police warnings in the city—the main difference was one of administrative procedure.

Some factors seemed more closely associated with the various reporters' decisions than others. By ranking the values of the contingency co-efficients we can get some idea of the factors which seemed to have a closer association than others. The most important factors, in order of significance, were, in the city, the total number of offences committed, police comment, initial social work comment, and school comment. In the county, the most significant factors were initial social work comment, the total number of offences committed, police comment and school comment, again in order of significance. Frequently decisions in the city had to be made without a social work report and this probably explains why the presenting behaviour itself is reflected in the city reporters' decision-making to a greater extent than in the county reporters'. The county reporters more often had social work reports, and the comments in these reports were more closely associated with the decision than the presenting behaviour.

It was also likely that some factors had no influence independantly of the influence of another—the total number of offences committed by the child or the comments made in the initial social work report might, for example, have dominated the decision-making process, the significance of other factors being determined by these two. Further analysis confirmed that some factors had no independent influence. The existence of a previous court record did not have a significant influence on the city reporters' decisions where the number of offences currently committed was one, or four or more. But, where the child had committed two or three offences, the existence or otherwise of a court record was relevant in *confirming or denying* the original diagnosis of 'troublesomeness'. At the extreme ends of the spectrum—the commission of one offence or four or more offences—the reporters' actions were influenced to a large extent by the number of offences committed;

but, in considering what action was appropriate for children who committed two or three offences, the city reporters seemed reluctant to act on the basis of the behaviour alone. They looked elsewhere for clues—for confirmation or denial of the original diagnosis.

The existence of previous referrals to the reporter and the value of the property stolen also made no contribution in the city independently of the number of offences committed. Indications of 'favourable' or 'negative' aspects in the police, social work and school reports, however, were associated with decision-making independently of the number of offences committed by the child. Amongst those committing one offence and referred to a hearing 69% exhibited 'problems' according to the police reports, 85% according to the school report, and 77% according to the social work report.

A quite different picture emerged in the county. The existence of a previous record seemed associated with the reporters' decision-making independently of the number of offences committed by the child, as did previous referrals to the reporter. For example, whereas just over half of those who committed four offences and who had no previous court record were referred to a children's hearing, more than 90% of those who committed four offences and who did have a court record were referred to a hearing. Again, a third of those who committed two or three offences and who had no previous referrals to the reporter were referred to a hearing compared with two thirds of those who committed a similar number of offences and who had previously been referred to the reporter. The presence of 'favourable' and 'problem' aspects also seemed to influence decision-making in the county over and above the number of offences committed.

What appeared to be happening in both areas was that other factors were being used to confirm or deny the initial impression conveyed by the presenting behaviour—a predictable finding. Decisions were rarely made on the basis of one factor alone—a number of elements were present in any one case—and the reporter made a decision by balancing one against the other. The absence of a previous record could be balanced against previous knowledge of the family or against the number of offences committed. This process is best demonstrated by referring to some case histories.

'Norman', for example, was involved in a number of relatively serious offences, but had no previous record, a good school report and a favourable family background. In the light of all these factors the reporter made a 'no action' decision. Similarly 'Bill', who had three referrals for three offences of theft by house-breaking, was given a police warning for two of the referrals and the third was dealt with by a 'no action' letter. In one of the offences the property involved had exceeded £30 in value but 'Bill' had no previous convictions and there were a number of other positive indicators. The police report indicated that his father was co-operative, had made his son confess, and it stated that it was 'apparent that he had the best interests of the boy at heart'. 'Bill's' school report indicated good progress and stated that he was a 'well-integrated member of the class' and was 'well-behaved'. The initial social work inquiry indicated that the father 'had taken considerable care in helping his son to solve his problems'. The parents were described as 'insightful and competent'. The boy's behaviour was described as 'improving due to the father's good handling'. In these two cases positive social characteristics counterbalanced the seriousness of the offences committed by the boys.

Sometimes, however, the offence was seen as sufficiently serious in itself to require formal action. 'Tom', for example, was referred to the reporter for theft by house-breaking in which more than £100 worth of cigarettes and alcohol had been stolen. He had no previous record and his reply to the charge was 'I'm sorry I did it. It won't happen again.' The police report indicated that the parents were separated, the school report was non-committal and there was no initial social work inquiry. In light of the limited background information available the seriousness of the offence seems to have been the main factor in the decision to refer 'Tom' to a children's hearing.

But there are also instances where the offence is trivial and intervention is recommended because of family circumstances. 'Jane' was referred to the reporter because of four charges of malicious mischief—she had sprayed paint from an aerosol can over a car, a telephone kiosk, and other property. She had no previous findings of guilt, admitted the charges, paid the car owner for the damage caused, and said she would pay for the other damage. The school report indicated that although she was not working to capacity she was doing five subjects to 'O' level and described her as 'shy and irresponsible ... but no real trouble'. However, the initial social work inquiry indicated that the parents were separated because the father was having an affair with another woman. The mother was described as a very tense woman with 'bottled-up feelings' and was currently undergoing psychiatric out-patient care. 'Jane' was said to feel great hostility towards her mother, and the social worker suggested that this covered an even greater hostility towards her father. The social worker's recommendation was that 'Jane' should be referred to a children's hearing with a view to a supervision requirement being made because 'the mother and child are wrapped up in their own problems, are unable to communicate with each other and need social work help'.

'David' was also referred to a children's hearing although he had committed only one offence of theft by house-breaking (the value of the property involved was less than £25) and had no previous record. The police, school and social work reports, however, all indicated a situation where a widow had no control over her son, who was becoming increasingly violent and aggressive. In both of these cases the reporters looked beyond the offence to the child's family and social circumstances.

Frequently children involved in the same 'incident' were dealt with differently. In one case involving two girls aged 14 who had run away from home, one was referred to the hearing and the other was given a 'no action' disposal. Although the parents of the former were concerned, the girl was unhappy at school because of academic pressures and was afraid to tell her parents of this. The social worker felt that support would be helpful as the girl found 'communication with her parents difficult'. The parents of the other girl themselves arranged for the girl's referral to psychiatric and child guidance services and so the reporter felt that 'no action' was appropriate.

The Implications of such Criteria

But what does all this mean? In both areas 'offence' criteria and the indication of 'problems' were associated with decision-making and, to the extent that 'offence' criteria by themselves did not determine the decisions taken, the philosophy of the Kilbrandon Committee and the Social Work (Scotland) Act was being put into practice. Decision-makers looked beyond the behaviour. This marks a substantial change from the process of decision-making among fiscals in the former juvenile court. In Duncan and Arnott's study, the city fiscals referred 95% of the cases referred to them to the juvenile court and their decisions were primarily on legal criteria—whether or not there was sufficient evidence to prove the case—and this was the predominant pattern throughout the juvenile courts in Scotland.

The difference between the new system and those jurisdictions which operated special juvenile courts is not, however, so marked. The county fiscals in the Duncan and Arnott survey referred to the juvenile courts only 60% of the cases referred to them by the police (20% were returned to the police for a police warning and proceedings were dropped in the other 20%), and though the criteria of decision-making included legal reasons these were not the sole basis for the decisions. Many of the cases not referred to the court were very trivial—riding a bicycle on the pavement, stealing bread from a doorstep and so on. But there were some cases which were more serious and which were committed by boys with previous records. Two boys, for example, who stole lead from the roof of a factory and who both had previous convictions were returned to the police for police warnings. Different members of a group of boys involved in the same offence were also on occasion dealt with differently by the county fiscals, so it was not simply the nature of the offence which determined the form of action taken. Decisions in the special juvenile courts were also determined by balancing various considerations. This reinforces a point made much earlier in this book: the type of tribunal (juvenile court or welfare tribunal) is largely unimportant. What is crucial is the philosophy underlying that tribunal and the ideology of its practitioners.

But to the extent that 'offence' criteria were relevant to the reporter's initial decision, the Kilbrandon Committee's and the legislature's intentions were not met. The city reporter, in a report prepared for the local authority probation and after-care committee, admitted that the nature and gravity of the offence formed a serious part of his consideration although this was not the sole criterion. In both areas there was some evidence that a 'tariff' system was in operation, that the existence of a previous court record and previous referrals to the reporter made referral to the children's hearing likely. This was less so in the city when the number of offences committed was taken into account, but the relationship remained strong in the county area. Such children could, of course, present a greater number of problems than other children; but often reporters did not have much social background information when they made their decisions. Where reporters did have such information, there is a further difficulty in accepting this suggestion. Whereas 'offence' criteria are objectively identifiable the 'comments'

made by the various writers of the reports are not—they are con-
structed. It is possible, therefore, that the 'making up' of a report
is *premised* on 'offence' criteria. Those who construct the reports
do so subsequent to the commission of the offence and they are
knowledgeable of it. It is plausible to argue then that the construc-
tion of these reports, by any of the agencies concerned, might
'mirror' the perceived seriousness of the offence. In other words, the
perceived seriousness of the offence might be reflected in a report
which proclaims the seriousness of the offence in terms of 'needs'
rather than 'deeds'. This would mean that the spirit of Kilbrandon
has merely been glossed on to a basically unchanged system and that
'offence' criteria continue to dominate. Some evidence for the
validity of this point is found in the commonly held belief that the
seriousness of the 'deed' is a pointer to the seriousness of the 'need',
that there is a direct link between the two. There is no evidence
to substantiate this link—the important point is, however, that
this lack of evidence does not prevent action being suggested, and
taken, as if such evidence did exist. 'Offence' criteria then become
a shorthand way of determining the extent of the 'need'.

We found some support for this in comparing 'need' scores and
'deed' scores for a sample of our cases. We isolated and gave scores
to certain offence characteristics (total number of offences, previous
court record, etc.) and certain need characteristics (social work
comments, school comments, etc.). The maximum score on either
scale was 12. We found considerable correspondence between the
two scores; this suggests that writers of reports were influenced
by knowledge of 'offence' information. But the process was by
no means clear-cut—there were instances where the 'offence' score
was low and the 'need' score was high. On the other hand, it was
rare to find a high 'offence' score and a low 'need' score. We would
not wish to put much weight on this evidence—but it at least raises
the question whether 'need' criteria are in fact determined by
'offence' criteria.

This case study of decision-making by reporters revealed that
conflicting ideologies and pressures are built into the system. Although reporters might view their primary task as the promotion of
social welfare and 'helping' juveniles in need, they do not, in dealing
with such children, ignore ideas of law enforcement and community
protection, nor do they ignore the community's expectations of
appropriate behaviour for children. There is a fairly explicit acceptance of the importance of not letting juveniles 'get away' with too

many offences. In our sample there were no instances in which a 'no action' disposal was given more than twice, and there were only 10 cases out of 473 in the city in 1972 in which a 'no action' disposal was given even twice. In reaching their decisions, reporters balance various, sometimes conflicting, criteria. Decision-making by reporters is a seemingly pragmatic amalgam of social welfare, social control and, with respect to offenders, tolerance. On closer investigation, however, assessments and dispositions turn out to be primarily focused on notions of control. We return to this point in the next chapter.

To the extent that it was an easy matter for us to make accurate predictions in relation to decision-making, decision-making has become routinized. Processing the child through the system follows fairly precise rules of thumb. Some of these 'rules' are discriminatory; we will also discuss this in the next chapter.

To end on a note of hope: the existence of reporters has enabled the Scottish system to divert a considerable number of children from the formal control system. To the extent that they are prepared to give a large number of 'no action' disposals, reporters are resisting pressures to act primarily as law enforcement agents. A recurrent theme in the reports on those cases given a 'no action' disposal was that the presenting behaviour was not symptomatic of any real 'problem', either for the child or for society. It was often described as 'an isolated incident' or 'out of character', and families were seen as concerned and supportive. Often the child and the family had already accepted control or treatment through voluntary arrangements with the psychiatric or social work services. Children referred to the hearing, on the other hand, tended to have long histories of problem behaviour (offending, truanting, etc.) or personal, family and environmental difficulties. Diversion or non-intervention, though currently widely supported, is not without its difficulties; these become apparent in the operation of the children's hearings themselves.

The Children's Hearings: a study in ambiguity

Panel Members—Expectations and Accomplishments

The sole concern of panel members was described by the Kilbrandon Committee as the consideration and application of training measures appropriate to the needs of the individual child. The Committee accordingly felt that panel members should be 'persons who either by knowledge or experience were considered to be specially qualified to consider children's problems'.[1] This is similar to the language of the 1933 Children and Young Persons Act which referred to a 'panel of justices specially qualified for dealing with juvenile cases' and the 1969 Children and Young Persons Act made no changes to these requirements. But a crucial difference between English juvenile court magistrates and panel members is that the latter are selected by means of a complicated process of interviews and group discussions. English juvenile court magistrates, on the other hand, are elected, in the main, from their own number by fellow magistrates after serving a minimum number of years on the bench in the adult court.[2] They are not appointed initially as persons 'specially qualified to consider children's problems', and they may have considerable experience of the sentencing practices in adult criminal courts in which, arguably, different considerations apply.[3] Panel members have no such experience of the adult courts (and play no part in the adjudication stage).

The responsibility for the recruitment and selection of panel members lies with the Secretary of State for Scotland, but this responsibility is discharged locally through Children's Panel Advisory Committees which were set up in each local authority area. In fact, when the new system was set up more than 3,000 people applied for panel membership—a number far in excess of needs—and 66% of all applicants were unsuccessful. A major problem in the selection process was the reconciliation of two different sets of criteria, both of which had been set out in various documents preceding the legislation. These criteria were: panel members should be representative of the community and panel members should be specially qualified. It was stressed that 'the need for the involvement of the community generally is at the heart of the children's panel process'[4] and, further, that 'the aim (of the children's panel system) will be that decisions on how to deal with a particular child should be taken by members who have personal knowledge of the community to which the child belongs'.[5] Panel members, accordingly, 'should be drawn from a wide range of occupations, neighbourhoods, age-groups and income-groups'.[6] The same document, however, continued: 'Panel members should have knowledge and experience in dealing with children and families ... they require the right personal qualities ... and a genuine interest in the needs of the child in trouble'.[7] How were these two sets of criteria reconciled?

The qualities looked for in prospective panel members were described by Mapstone as 'not only the social confidence and intellectual discipline which may result from further education or long participation in public affairs, but also the controlled involvement, a combination of concern and detachment, commitment and independence, characteristically developed in training for the professions'.[8] Other qualities required were a high standard of literacy and the ability to communicate verbally. Such qualities were unlikely to be found frequently amongst those living in the areas from which most children appearing before the hearings were likely to come. Consequently, the eventual outcome was a 'professional' lay panel rather than a panel representative of the community. The original panels were overwhelmingly middle-class —in the country as a whole, only 14% of those selected were from social classes three, four and five.[9] In the survey county, although professional groups formed only 3% of the county's population, they formed 17% of the initial applicants for panel membership and nearly 25% of those selected. In the city more than half of the original panel came from social classes one and two—none from classes four and five.[10] Subsequent research attempted to allay possible criticism by showing that panel members, as a group, were upwardly mobile and that many had, in fact, grown up in social classes three, four and five. The assumption made was that panel members could accordingly represent and understand the communities from which most children referred to the hearings came. But their very upward mobility distinguished them from the majority of families in these areas. Their values and norms were likely to be quite different.

Yet another factor suggests that panel members were not likely to be representative members of such communities. The process of selection was, according to Mapstone, geared towards those with 'the essential qualities and attitudes of a good social worker'.[11] There was a tendency not to select applicants who took a 'tough line' on discipline, punishment, the protection of society and so on. The selection process moulded the panel in a particular way—the members were chosen for their receptivity to social welfare ideology and language. In their attitudes towards delinquency, social problems and so on one would expect to find considerable uniformity.

Those qualities sought among prospective panel members are quite different from those said to be required for membership of the magistracy, and accordingly of the juvenile bench, in England. In describing the functions of juvenile court magistrates, Cavenagh[12] wrote that these were to define compulsory powers in relation to care, or to regulate the imposition of sanctions—she stressed that the decision was judicial rather than clinical, and that the question was whether the proposed grant of powers or the suggested sanction was justified by the gravity of the situation as revealed by the evidence in the reports. She emphasized that this was not necessarily the same as the question of what was in the best interests of the child.

Another major difference lies in the subsequent training of panel members and magistrates. The extent and type of training given in Scotland was left to the four areas (north, west, east and south-east) and, as a result, training varied considerably. It could involve an intensive programme of visits to institutions, discussions, lectures and case study sessions—or it could amount to a few weekend training sessions. But even at its very lowest level, such training amounted to more than what is standard practice in relation to training in England.

Consideration of the type of training given to panel members leads to a point of some importance. Not only were hearing members *selected* primarily on the advice of social workers, but they were also *trained* by them.[13] This raises interesting questions about the function of the lay panel. It is *not* primarily to determine training or treatment for, in the report of the working party[14] set up by Social Work Service Group to discuss the operation of the new system, there was little mention of the skills and functions of panel members in this respect. Rather, it referred to the need for the establishment of multi-disciplinary teams 'which will draw together the professional expertise of the workers concerned with each child whose difficulties are under consideration'. It also stated that 'assessment teams should accept responsibility for evaluating the success or otherwise of their recommendations and for satisfying themselves as far as they can that the child is progressing satisfactorily and that his present treatment is still appropriate to his needs'. Are the children's panels mere tools in the professionalization of social work? Social workers, after all, are the major presenters of information to the panel and the choice of disposition can probably be determined by the presentation of information in a particular way. Panel members, in fact, followed the recommendations of social workers in 88% of all cases dealt with by them in the research areas in 1973. In contrast to this, Phillip Priestley[15] found in an English city that although magistrates accepted and implemented over 90% of the recommendations made by social workers for supervision orders they rejected one in three of the recommendations made for care orders. English magistrates seem to retain considerable independence in reaching their decisions; panel members, on the other hand, readily accept, possibly because of their training in the values and ethics of social work, the recommendations of social workers.[16]

Panel members did disagree in some—admittedly few—instances with the recommendations made. Is their task to supervise the professionals? or even to balance the rights and liberty of the child and his parents against the disposition proposed by the social worker? Analysis of the cases in which the hearing disagreed provides negative answers to these questions. Disagreements usually occurred where the circumstances had changed between the making of the recommendation and the hearing—*real* disagreement was rare. Paterson[17] has suggested that the function of the lay panel was to *legitimize* the actions of the professional. 'It gives credence in the eyes of the community for a new structure which could deprive individuals of some of their rights and liberty without the structure of the courts'. Although the professionals make their recommendations to the panel, Paterson argued that 'the decision lies in the hands of the community's appointed representative'. But this, as we have just pointed out, is assuredly not where the decision lies. The panel is a professionally orientated group; even if it was at the outset representative of the community it served, training made it less so. But, arguably, panel members, as representatives of the community, are likely to give at least some consideration to such factors as the nature of the offence, the protection of society and deterrence. Subsequent training could only *modify* the influence of such considerations in determining the appropriate disposition. If this is so, and we believe that it is, the ambiguity between criminal justice and social welfare values inherent in the juvenile court was recreated in the structure and function of children's hearings.

The Case Study

The diagram on page 74 gave the national figures for dispositions by the children's hearing in 1973 but these figures conceal considerable regional variation. The annual figures for the two survey areas were:[18]

DIAGRAM IX: *Initial dispositions by the hearing in the county, 1973*

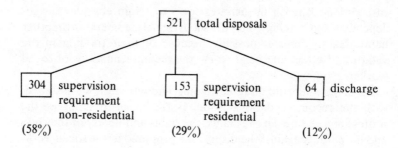

DIAGRAM X: *Initial dispositions by the hearing in the city, 1973*

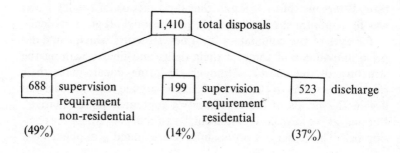

There were marked differences between the two areas: a high discharge rate in the city and a high rate of residential placement in the county. The distribution of disposals during the research period was broadly similar.[19] These disposals can serve, therefore, as a case study of the reasons underlying patterns of dispositions and of decision-making in the children's hearing system. The rigidity of dispositions made in the former juvenile court system was much criticized by the Kilbrandon Committee. It stated that there was

> no general provision whereby an order, once made, may be reviewed, even where it may be clear, at any stage to the supervising agency concerned, that the measures adopted are not achieving the result hoped for. Further formal action can in these circumstances only be taken in the event of even more serious circumstances arising, which justify the bringing of entirely fresh proceedings in consequence either of a further offence or of a situation justifying 'care or protection' proceedings. Existing procedure, focused as it is on certain defined acts and situations, and resulting in training measures subject to . . . preconceived and . . . arbitrary limitations of time, is inimical to any idea of continuing educational process.[20]

To serve the needs of the child better the hearings were given wide discretion both to determine the original dispositions and to review them—the call was for 'flexibility of approach'. It was intended that criteria of decision-making would change: the over-riding criterion was the needs of the individual child.

As we pointed out in the previous chapter, the county reporters referred significantly fewer offence cases to the children's hearings than the reporters in the city, and frequently had social work reports available before deciding whether or not to refer the child to a hearing. One might expect, therefore, that the children referred to the hearings in the two areas would differ somewhat, that, for example, the county sample would include more persistent and serious offenders, or that there would be a higher incidence of 'problems' indicated in those cases. This proved to be so.

There was not much difference in the extent to which the two samples had previously been involved in the children's hearing system—about half of the children in each sample. On the other hand, the city sample had a significantly larger proportion with previous referrals to a court: one half compared with one third in the county sample. But the county sample did contain a higher proportion of children who had committed four or more offences—about one half compared with a quarter of the city sample. Indeed just over 40% of the city sample had committed only one offence. It was possible that these children had been referred to a hearing because their offences were more serious than those committed in the county, but this was not so—the city sample had a higher proportion of offenders who had committed property offences of a value less than £5.

There was no difference in the two samples with regard to family structure, whether or not the father was employed, social class or family size (though more than half of the children in both samples came from families with more than five children). But there was some difference in the indication of 'problems' highlighted in initial social work reports. (Reports were not, however, available on all children within the samples.) Although the indication of 'problems' in the reports was uniformly high, almost all of the county samples were described as problems compared with 85% of the city sample.

The fact that the county children's hearing sample differed from the city sample—it seemed to include more serious offenders and more 'problem' referrals than the city—may have explained the lower rate of discharge and the higher rate of sending the children to residential establishments there. But there are other possible explanations. The various dispositions being used by the panels may have been used in different ways for similar types of children or different factors may have influenced the decisions reached in the two areas. The extent to which supervision was used in the two areas differed slightly: 58% in the county, 49% in the city in 1973. This was probably because 'something happened' to most children dealt with by the children's hearings in the county; the reporter there had already sifted out many of the children who did not need compulsory measures of care. But the children placed on supervision in the two areas were remarkably alike. There was, for example, little difference in what we have called 'offence' criteria or in the indications of 'problems'; similarly, although the county had a higher rate of referral to residential establishments than the city, there were no significant differences between the residential samples in the two areas. Both reflected a high degree of 'problems'. For example, more than 95% in both areas were described as coming from 'problem' families and there was no difference in the two areas in the value of property stolen or in the number of offences committed by these children. A large number in fact had committed fairly minor offences. 60% of those sent to residential establishments by the city hearings and almost half of those in the county had committed offences of a value of less than £25. And more than two thirds in both areas had been charged with and admitted only one offence on the occasion on which the order was made. Commitment to residential establishments was being used in the children's hearing system in much the *same* way as it had been in the juvenile court system. It was used then after other methods had been tried and after the child had committed a number of previous offences.[21] The same was true of the children's hearing samples. Whereas half of those placed on supervision had not previously been referred to the reporter the majority of children sent to residential establishments had previously been dealt with within the system. This points to the continued operation of a tariff system. The kinds of resources available to the hearings in the two areas did not explain the differences in the use of measures: 'List D' schools are operated nationally and the county had greater social service resources than the city. The higher rate of removal from home in the county may, however, be a reflection of panel members' attitudes and working philosophies—the two panels may have held differing views of the role of residential establishments. Also Bruce and Spencer[22] have shown that panels do vary considerably in the emphasis given to the interests of the child and the interests of society. Panel members in the two areas may have varied in this respect but this is not likely as the two panels were trained in a similar way and shared, overall, similar characteristics. Because it seems that the higher rate of commitment to residential establishments in the county was attributable to the higher indication of 'problems' in this sample than in the city sample at the outset we discuss critically later in this chapter the meaning of 'problems'.

But first it is necessary to look more closely at decision-making by the hearings. The children's hearing has two main decisions to make—whether or not compulsory measures of care are necessary and, if they are, what form of treatment is appropriate to each child.

1. The primary decision

Although there was this marked difference in the rate of discharge in the two areas there was little difference in the kinds of cases which were discharged. The higher discharge rate in the city (37% as opposed to 12% in the county) reflected the lack of initial social work information available to the city reporters. Because of this, minor cases of a 'non-problematic' nature were referred to hearings there. If social work information had been available, it is likely that many of these children would not have been referred to a children's hearing.

The reasons attributed by panel members to cases which they discharged centred on the ability of the family to discipline the child. They included such statements as 'the parents are capable of disciplining the child', 'the mother is caring', 'good parental intent', 'the parents can control the child's behaviour'. On occasions, reference was made to the child himself or to his behaviour: 'out of character', 'marginal involvement', 'led into the offence', 'isolated incident', 'normal boy with normal problems'. Such phrases reflect a denial of the original diagnosis of troublesomeness—either with reference to the characteristics of the family or to the child himself. The offences committed by those discharged were by no means all trivial. In one case the reporter referred to the hearing a boy who admitted unlawful intercourse with a girl under 12, breach of the peace and possession of an offensive weapon. The referral was discharged. The hearing described the family as a caring one and capable of keeping the boy out of trouble. In another case involving seven thefts from cars the hearing felt that there was sufficient support in the home. The boy had had a short term of voluntary supervision but further external supervision was considered unnecessary.

A number of cases were also discharged where a social worker was already involved in the family—for example, a brother or sister was already on supervision. In such cases the social worker was requested to keep an 'informal' eye on the child discharged. There was also some evidence of the use of a hearing to create a salutary effect—for example, 'the hearing has had the desired effect on the family; they are determined to do better', and 'the boy is chastened by his experience at the hearing'. In a number of instances the case was discharged where help had already been sought by the parents, for example, psychiatric or social work help. This is in line with the spirit of the Kilbrandon Committee. It stated that the hearing should 'enlist the co-operation of the parents and as a result adopt the appropriate measures informally and by agreement without resort to an order of the panel'.[23] A discharged referral, therefore, sometimes meant that although help or control was necessary, compulsion was not. In one case, involving a boy said to be out of parental control, the hearing discharged the referral as the father, who had been troubled by the son's behaviour (taking money from home) and who had discussed the boy with his doctor, arranged for the boy to attend a child guidance clinic. The family were concerned and stable, though known to the Social Work Department for many years because of financial problems, and the social worker had recommended that the case be discharged. In another instance the hearing specifically stated that the help required was educational and not social and that the school and child guidance clinic together should help the child with his difficulties. There were also instances of informal restitution being made and, in one instance involving two girls who had sprayed paint on walls, the girls were invited to work in a children's home on a voluntary basis as a means of recompense.

Another recurrent theme was that the child was about to get a job. Thus in two cases which were discharged, the early entry of both boys into the Royal Navy seemed to influence the hearing's decision. Neither of the boys had a previous record and while there were four offences, none of them was particularly serious. The family situation was not very favourable, but early entry into the Royal Navy was seen as removing the boys from this and as providing support to the boys. Generally, obtaining a job presented to the panel members a picture of the child reaching adulthood and accepting responsibilities, and again served to deny the earlier diagnosis of troublesomeness.

What was happening in these cases was that the significance of the ground of referral was minimized in the light of social factors which indicated that there was no need for the use of compulsory measures. There were, however, a few cases in which discharge of the referral indicated that the children's hearing felt no longer able to cope with the child. In one instance in the city, where a boy of 16 was described as not responding to supervision and where charges were pending against him in the sheriff court, the referral was discharged so that in future he might be dealt with in the sheriff court. The hearing decided that he was 'as well considered as an adult and answerable to the adult court for his behaviour', and that 'none of our disposals meet the current situation'. In another case a boy was referred to the reporter on a charge of breach of the peace and disorderly conduct. He had a long history of previous offences and had been in three approved schools. The family situation was described as very unsettled and he was presented as an aggressive individual. The children's hearing decided that it was pointless to keep him within the children's hearing system; being over 16 he could now be dealt with in the adult system. In such cases 'total denunciation', to borrow Emerson's phrase,[24] had taken place—these children were regarded as hopeless by all concerned, including their social workers and 'fault' was attributed to the child himself.

2. The secondary decision

The broad distinction between all the cases dealt with by supervision within the community and those dealt with by supervision with a residential requirement was that a greater number of unfavourable aspects were, predictably, found in the residential cases. But the factors which seemed to influence such decisions were more difficult to determine. As in decision-making by the reporters, a complicated process of balancing various considerations seemed also to take place in decision-making in the children's hearings. In the city, a great number of factors seemed to be associated with the decisions to place the child in a residential establishment: 'lack of remorse', 'previous court record', 'previous referral to the reporter', 'total number of offences committed', 'family problems' and 'relationship problems'. In the county only two factors appeared to be significantly associated with this decision: 'family problems' and 'previous referrals to the reporter'. This, of course, did not mean that other factors were not considered and did not influence the outcome. This process of balancing by which one aspect of behaviour, for example an offence, was interpreted in the light of other aspects of behaviour, for example school performance, is best illustrated by reference to some case histories.

'Stuart', though he had committed twelve offences, including nine of theft by house-breaking, and had three previous court appearances, was placed on supervision by the hearing. The social worker reported that he had responded well to probation and had a good relationship with his social worker. His parents were seen as people who were trying hard to 'provide a decent home' for their large family and no other member of the family had been in trouble. The boy was enjoying work in a technical college. This was regarded as similar to satisfactory behaviour in school or obtaining a job; they all indicated that the child was settling into a more acceptable behaviour pattern and identifying with the values of the community. The non-residential supervision requirement was a response to this favourable assessment.

'James', who had committed sixteen offences (fourteen thefts by house-breaking and two charges of malicious mischief) was also placed on supervision. He had a limited previous record of police warning and discharge. The social worker stated that 'James' 'appreciated the seriousness of the situation' and was making restitution to the people involved. His actions 'were not the actions of a hardened delinquent'. 'James' was at the time of the hearing a trainee with the National Coal Board and the family situation was described as favourable. The parents were described in the social worker's report as 'sensible and insightful', and as 'anxious, concerned and shocked' by their son's behaviour. The social worker felt that the boy would comply with a supervision requirement, but suggested that the children's hearing might feel that some other means of disposal was appropriate in view of the number of offences. The children's hearing mentioned in their reasons for the decision that a placement in a residential school had been considered because of the 'serious nature of the offences', but nevertheless placed the boy on supervision. These comments emphasize that the hearing felt that this was a case in which the number and nature of the offences were a pointer to the boy being 'in difficulties', but the nature of the disposition indicates that the existence of favourable factors counteracted these negative factors.

But the balancing worked both ways. 'John' had been involved in fifteen offences (all property) and had previously been on probation and in an approved school. He was sent to a 'List D' school, despite recent signs of improvement. On his release from the approved school he had been placed in a special school on the advice of a psychologist. He had responded well there and when he had appeared at a previous children's hearing he was discharged because of his improved behaviour. The school report for the current hearing indicated that he was now well behaved and always ready to help. His parents, however, were described as having little control over their children, and the boy's brother was also in trouble. While there were undoubtedly a number of unfavourable factors in this case, the marked improvement in the child's behaviour in the special school, which had been recognized at the previous hearing, suggested that the child was responding to treatment there. The new set of offences, however, combined with his previous record, counterbalanced these signs of improvement.

A similar situation arose in 'Andrew's' case. He had committed twenty-six offences, had one previous court appearance and was, on that occasion, sent to an approved school. The family was described as warm, affectionate and caring, but also as ineffectual and disorganized. The father had changed jobs frequently, with spells of unemployment, and the family had a history of moving house. 'Andrew' had been placed on licence when he left the approved school and had established a good relationship with his social worker. The family also responded well to social work help. The circumstances of the family and 'Andrew's' response to supervision seemed to indicate a case for further social work intervention, especially as the boy had never had a proper period of supervision before. The hearing, however, sent the boy to a 'List D' school.

Some children, on the other hand, were removed from home even although their offence history was very limited. For example, 'Charlie' was sent to a 'List D' school although he had committed only one offence of theft by house-breaking and had no previous court record, or referral to the reporter. Other aspects of the boy's behaviour indicated 'problems'. He was described as verbally and physically aggressive, as emotionally disturbed, and had had psychiatric care. He was involved in vandalism, truancy and theft at school, and this behaviour was seen to be related to the home background. His father, although dead for six years, had been a frightening figure—a man with drinking problems. 'Charlie' was seen as anxious and frightened by male authority figures and his mother, described as very anxious and depressed, had no control over him and seemed terrified of him. Voluntary supervision from the Social Work Department had not been successful. In the light of all these circumstances the social worker recommended, and the hearing agreed to, placement in a 'List D' school.

The need to 'do something' about continued offending—to contain the problematic behaviour—was apparent in many decisions. 'Chris' had, in the company of a friend, taken money from playing-field dressing-rooms. He was currently on supervision for earlier property offences. The school report said that 'Chris' was now just coping with school work and that he no longer truanted so much. His father was described in the social work report as a heavy drinker and gambler and his mother, who had a history of mental illness, admitted that she could not control her children. 'Chris' was enuretic and aggressive, and the social worker felt that his problems stemmed from his parents' own emotional problems. Psychiatric reports indicated that 'Chris's' problems stemmed from the home and that he should have treatment at a psychiatric unit, preferably as an in-patient. The hearing decided to continue the supervision order with a requirement of psychiatric treatment and recommended that he be admitted to the psychiatric unit at the earliest possible date. 'Chris' subsequently committed further offences; theft from a factory, a van and a canteen, and throwing stones at a train. The hearing was told that it had not been possible to place 'Chris' in the psychiatric unit and that there was no chance of an early vacancy. The hearing sent him to a 'List D' school—a decision which seems more a response to 'Chris's' continued offending in the community than to his 'needs'. Similarly, 'Alice', a girl of fourteen who persistently truanted and ran away from home, was sent to a 'List D' School by a hearing after her fifth referral to it in a year, although the hearing explicitly stated that she was unlikely to benefit from that placement.

Control or Care?

The children's hearing system was an attempt to implement 'treatment' as an organizational goal. 'Treatment' was the *official* goal priority. The new system, however, was dealing with children already defined as 'troublesome' by some agency or other. Control of the behaviour of these children therefore became a concern—the *'operational'* goal priority. The hearing made a further assessment of whether or not a particular child was 'troublesome'. Resources were not limitless; not everyone could be sent to a 'List D' school, placed on supervision and so on. Some method of developing a list of priorities had to be sought. The panel had to ask themselves: 'Are compulsory measures of care *really* necessary?' They had to look for 'tip-offs' that something was *really* wrong, that the child was *really* troublesome.

Both Emerson[25] and Matza[26] have argued that, in the end, juvenile courts focus on the behaviour of the child, usually the offence committed, in deciding appropriate dispositions. According to Matza, the offence and its seriousness were re-instituted as guides to dispositions in the American juvenile courts because of the vagueness and ambiguity of the principles of individualized justice. 'The principles of individualized justice turned out . . . to be a nameless guide for action.' He went on:

> It depends first on the total risk of danger in the juvenile's current offence and prior offence record . . . qualified by an assessment of . . . the willingness and the ability of the parents to sponsor the child.[27]

Emerson suggested that the act retained its significance as a short-hand means of inferring what the child was really like.

On the surface, offence criteria were not highly associated with the hearings' various disposition decisions in our survey. This could be due to two factors: firstly, most of the offences dealt with by the hearings were relatively minor—serious offences are by law referred to the procurator fiscal and are likely to be prosecuted in the sheriff court; and secondly, the children's hearings do not receive a police report—they receive only a very brief statement of the circumstances of the offence, sometimes as little as the phrase 'theft by house-breaking'.

As a result, the hearings concentrated on the family. The model presented by the Kilbrandon Committee was that the cause of delinquency lay within the family and it was to the family that the hearing looked for help in assessing what sort of person the child was, whether he was likely to offend again, and so on. A 'good' home led to a reassessment of the 'trouble' as 'normal'; a 'bad' home confirmed the diagnosis of 'problematic' behaviour. Those cases discharged by the hearing can best be described as exhibiting 'normal' delinquency, the sort of thing most children do. Where such children reappeared within the system, the reappearance *per se* cast doubt on the original diagnosis of 'normal' delinquency.

But is there any agreement about the designations of 'good', 'adequate', or 'poor' home? Cicourel[28] suggested that judgments by social workers and courts of the quality of the delinquent and the delinquent's family were biased against lower-class families, that middle-class families provided the model for what a 'good' home should be. Emerson[29] disagreed with this and argued that juvenile court judges distinguished between the family life of the 'reputable' and the 'disreputable' poor. But this too reflects a bias; 'disreputable' is likely to mean 'different from the life style' of the decision-maker or, at least, a life style that the decision-maker disapproves of. Our experience of the operation of decision-making in the children's hearing system confirms the views we expressed in Chapter III —there is an absence of objective criteria by which the nature and extent of a 'problem' can be determined. Because of this, decision-makers referred to their own values and beliefs (and these were predominantly middle-class).[30] The decisions made by them depended on the degree to which the individual was seen as conforming to what was considered acceptable behaviour.

Reference was frequently made to the child's attitude to the offence, whether or not he had a job, whether he was involved in organized youth activities and so on. These factors can be seen as being part of an assessment of 'needs' in that a child who fails to attend school or who is troublesome when he is there, or who finds it difficult to fill his leisure time, may need some form of help. However, it cannot really be argued that these represent objective criteria which enable one to judge that someone suffers from some malformation of personality. They are all concerned with the question whether or not the child is generally involved in behaviour acceptable to, and approved by, most adults in society. Criteria of 'needs' were in fact criteria of 'social conformity'. Children from broken homes, for example, were more likely to be committed to residential establishments than children living with both parents. This might mean that the 'needs' of such children and their families were greater (certainly, this is commonly assumed), but it might also indicate a wish to control or intervene with the lives of certain types of families—such families were assumed to be less able to cope with the behaviour of their children.

The following two case histories give some indication of what seems to be meant by the concept of 'need'. 'Fred', a boy of 14, was discharged on his first referral to the hearing. The offence was fighting at school and, according to the school, 'Fred' was continually involved in fights, did not like school and did not try hard with his schoolwork. The social work report stated that some supervision might be helpful, but that it would be better to have it on a voluntary basis as 'Fred' wanted to join the army when he left school. The hearing decided that his parents could adequately deal with the home situation and that compulsory supervision was not necessary. The parents were told that if they wished any help the social work department would provide it. 'Fred' subsequently did fifty pounds' worth of damage to a teacher's car and committed a breach of the peace and assault. The school at this stage said that he was an extremely bad influence. The Child Guidance Clinic's report stated that he was determined to be a non-conformist in school and it suggested a psychiatric assessment. Both this report and the social work report recommended a residential placement. The hearing decided that it would be 'in the child's best interest' to be removed from home to the controlled environment of a 'List D' school, because of the serious nature of the offences and of the very real risk of serious trouble if he remained in the community. The hearing felt that 'Fred's' behaviour might be the result of deep-seated emotional problems, but stated that *his need for containment was more important than his need for psychological assessment.*

The facts in 'George's' case demonstrate the same point. 'George' was a boy of 10 who had previously been discharged by the hearing and who was also sent to a 'List D' school without any prior supervision. The offences committed by him were theft of cycles and entering a house with other children. He had previously committed three offences. The home circumstances were described as 'difficult': 'George' lived with his father and grandmother neither of whom, though concerned, was able to control or care for the family. He was described as suffering from material neglect, as being of low intelligence and as having no awareness of social norms. The social worker involved recommended a residential placement so that the boy might learn social values and self-discipline, and the hearing agreed to this. Should learning 'social values' and 'self-discipline' be referred to as the 'needs' of the child? A more accurate description is the 'needs' or 'interests' of society. If it is argued that these are in the interests of both society and the boy, surely it is possible to learn them in a non-residential setting. The fact that the boy was detained in an institution suggests that other aspects of society's interest are more important than the boy's 'needs'.

Reference to criteria of 'need' was often used to justify different dispositions for children involved in the same incident. 'Jane' and 'Jill' had, together, defaced a wall in a common passage by painting names on it in black paint. 'Jane' was removed from her home by the hearing; 'Jill' was discharged. 'Jane' had no previous court or hearing appearances, but the school report described her as uncooperative and disruptive. Considerable tension was said to exist between 'Jane' and her mother and the mother was described as resentful towards the father who often worked in the evenings. The social worker felt that the girl's general dissatisfaction and discontent was a result of family relationships and recommended supervision, stating that the girl needed outside help to enable her to cope with life and that supervision might reveal some insight into the causes of her behaviour. A letter by the reporter to the psychiatrist who examined 'Jane' revealed that when she was originally referred to the children's hearing there was not thought to be any indication of the need for compulsory measures of care; the objective was to get 'Jane' involved in more worthwhile pursuits than painting walls. The hearing, however, was a very tense occasion and revealed what were seen as 'problems' in the family. The hearing's decision was to remove the girl from home and to place her in an institution 'where she would get emotional support which would allow her to develop normally'. 'Jill' also had no previous court or hearing appearances. Her home was described by the social worker as stable, but the social worker also said that discipline was strict and that 'Jill's' parents were not providing her with sufficient help and understanding. The social worker recommended supervision, but the panel initially continued the hearing to allow the girl the opportunity to work in a children's home, and then discharged the referral.

So-called 'need' criteria seemed to dominate considerations at this stage, but there was also a natural progression from some kind of 'no action' or discharge disposition to supervision to residential placement. Twenty-six children in the city and fourteen in the county were committed to a 'List D' school at the first decision made about them during the first three months of 1972. Of these only one in the city and two in the county did not have some previous experience of either the court or children's hearing system and half of each group had been previously, or were currently, on supervision. The same picture emerged in the 1973 samples. Thirteen out of twenty-three sent to 'List D' schools by the city hearings and six out of ten sent to 'List D' schools by the county hearings had been previously, or were currently, on supervision. Only one of the twenty-three and two of the ten had no experience of the court or hearing system. This adds weight to our suggestion earlier in the chapter that a tariff system emerged in the children's hearing system.

Is it a tariff system based on the number of offences committed and on the number of previous referrals into the system as in the former juvenile courts? Or can there be a tariff of 'needs'? Martin Davies,[31] in discussing social work reports prepared for adult offenders, coined the phrase 'reverse tariff'. By this he meant that the social worker or sentencer determined where on the continuum of social need the offender stood and what, consequently, was the appropriate recommendation or sentence.

> If the need is minimal, then the residual tariff element is used to deter-mine whether the offence warrants a fine or can be dealt with by dis-charge; if problems exist (within a very wide range of circumstances) then a probation order is made . . . ; where personal or social problems are more severe or perhaps where probation had already failed . . . a range of alternatives may be employed . . . training in a borstal or deten-tion centre . . . or imprisonment.

The same sort of process seemed to occur in the children's hearing system. The child with 'few problems' was likely to be given a 'no action' disposal or was discharged; the child described as having some 'problems' was likely to be placed on supervision; and the child described as having 'severe problems' was likely to be removed from home. At the same time, the first or trivial offender was likely to be discharged and the persistent or serious offender was likely to be removed from home. The 'middle-range' offender with some record was likely to be placed on supervision. The child committed to an institution was often seen as a 'problem to the community' and someone for whom supervision is 'no longer realistic'; but at the same time, reasons for commitment to an institution were often phrased in 'need' terms: for example, 'she needs a physically secure environment to help her form relationships with peers and adults', or 'the home offers no security or support. He needs a structured setting to function well and develop self-control and self-respect'; or placement in a 'List D school might be more beneficial now than later'. Has a tariff based on 'needs' been grafted on to a tariff based on 'deeds'? This is a complex issue. The high rate of commitment to residential establishments is probably best understood by reference to this merging of tariffs. The child who has committed many offences in the past, or currently, or who has committed a serious offence is likely to be dealt with in this way. But so, too, is the child with a light record who commits a minor offence but who is described as 'problematic'. The net of intervention pulls in both groups. But because 'needs' are in fact related to social conformity, a tariff of 'needs' becomes a further device for control. If the child's offence behaviour is not such as requires control, *other* aspects of his or his family's behaviour may indicate that control is necessary (he comes from a broken home, single parent family, etc.) 'Needs' and 'deeds' both relate to *control.*

It can be argued that 'needs' and 'deeds' are not separate entities— that the seriousness of the 'deed' reflects the seriousness of the 'need'. We discussed this in the previous chapter and concluded that there was no evidence for this assumed link and that there was at least some evidence to suggest that writers of reports may be influenced by *knowledge* that the child has committed a particular offence, has committed offences in the past and so on. Seriousness of the 'needs' of the child may be determined by knowledge of the seriousness of the 'deeds' of the child and recommendations premised on 'needs' may really be based on 'deeds'.

The operation of subsequent reviews of initial decisions by the children's hearings provides further support for the view that this assumed association between 'needs' and 'deeds' is a device which enables us, with good conscience, to control the child's behaviour. Twenty-one (4%) of the children in our 1972 city sample came into the system on five or more occasions within twelve months. It would be difficult to argue that the child's 'needs' changed quite so markedly within that relatively short period of time; or that 'treatment' was tried for a sufficiently long period to justify change on 'treatment' grounds.

Dispositions Reviewed—a Chance to Think Again?

Unless a child was given a 'no action' disposal by the reporter or was discharged by the hearing, the decision reached about each child must, by statute, be reviewed within a twelve-month period. Early reviews can be requested by the child and his parents, by the social worker involved in the case, by the headmaster of the residential establishment in which the child was detained, or by the hearing itself. Continuance of the 'problematic' behaviour or improvements in the child's situation can lead to a request for a review of the original disposition or to a further referral to the hearing. How was a reassessment of the situation made? What kinds of factors were considered? Was the situation reassessed positively as well as negatively? How flexible was the new system? How frequently were decisions changed?

Two hundred and eighty-seven children from the original 1972 city sample and eighty-nine from the county sample had their cases reviewed at least once within the following twelve months. A case study of these subsequent decisions confirms our suggestion that a tariff system developed in the new system as in the former juvenile court and that the child's behaviour (e.g. the nature of the offence committed by him) was the main consideration in determining the appropriate disposition. The following case histories demonstrate these points.

'Pete', a boy of 11, had committed a number of offences including playing street football, stealing newspapers and house-breaking. When he entered our sample he was already on supervision for property offences and assault. The social work report indicated that the father had left the family many years before and had no contact since with the family. 'Pete's' mother had since re-married.

The stepfather was currently ill but the mother, though experiencing hardship, was managing to cope. The report suggested that the family as a whole needed the support of a social worker. A psychiatric report referred to 'Pete's' 'personal inadequacy', but said that he did not need to go to a 'List D' school; rather he needed someone to take an interest in him and it was doubtful whether he could get this in a 'List D' school where he would be open to the influence of other delinquents. The social worker recommended supervision at home and the hearing agreed to this. 'Pete' subsequently committed a series of house-breakings and attempted house-breakings. The social worker again referred to 'Pete' as being under the influence of older boys, but the hearing decided to send him to a 'List D' school as he was unable to keep out of trouble in spite of supervision from his social worker. A short time previously referral to a 'List D' school had been considered inappropriate on the basis of the boy's *needs*; his subsequent *offending* led to commitment to a 'List D' school.

The circumstances in 'Angus's' case were similar. He had committed six property offences, three of which involved considerable sums of money. The police report stated that 'Angus' was mentally retarded and that his parents had no control over him or his brother. He had already been in a residential home for disturbed children and it was noted that he required special education and medication. The advice from the psychiatrist was that if there *had* to be a residential placement it should be in a local 'List D' school to enable the family to stay in contact, but that if his brother was away from home then 'Angus' should stay at home on supervision. The hearing decided that although he had been involved in a series of thefts, 'Angus' should be placed on supervision at home. A psychiatrist agreed to see him on a weekly basis. A short time later, 'Angus' committed another series of housebreakings, involving property worth about £100; most of it was recovered. The hearing sent 'Angus' to a 'List D' school—again a disposition recently felt to be inappropriate. Continued offending led to a reconsideration of the previous decision, to a negative reassessment of the situation.

A supportive family background can, however, counterbalance a continued pattern of offending. 'Ian', aged 14, and currently on supervision, stole 4 bottles of whisky from a shop after breaking the shop window. According to the school report, he was mixing with other delinquent boys and was becoming truculent. The hearing decided to continue the supervision. 'Ian' was subsequently charged with breach of the peace and disorderly behaviour, was convicted in the sheriff court and the sheriff remitted the case to the hearing for disposition. The social work report stated that both parents were very co-operative, were in agreement about the upbringing and disciplining of their children, and were upset at the boy's offences and behaviour. The hearing decided that supervision should continue because he seemed to be responding and there had been no trouble for some time. 'Ian' again got involved in a gang fight and was referred to the hearing on the grounds of breach of the peace and assault. Again supervision was continued—the reason given was the support provided by the boy's family. 'Ian' committed a further breach of the peace and again supervision was continued. Throughout, the family background counterbalanced the continued offending and gang involvement, the family continued to be seen as able to control 'Ian's' behaviour.

'Will's' father had taken him to a police station to confess that he had broken into a store-room along with some other boys and had then broken into a joiner's work-shop and stolen tools. The social work department gave very little information about 'Will' or his family, except to say that the parents were upset over his behaviour. The social worker was already involved in the family through supervising 'Will's' sister and he felt that the parents were responsible people and had tried to make the boy see the possible results of his action. The hearing decided, in view of the repeated offences and to prevent further delinquency, that the boy should be placed on supervision with a condition of membership of the sea cadets. 'Will' then broke into a warehouse, a school and a shop. The social worker said that 'Will' was not responding to supervision and that he should be sent to a 'List D' school. The hearing agreed, stating that 'a reasonably long stay in a 'List D' school would be to his advantage'; he had not reacted satisfactorily to supervision and the thefts made a nonsense of continuing the supervision. Continued offending led to a negative assessment of 'Will'. While at the school, he committed various further offences, but after some months in the school he requested a review. The school felt that he had made a genuine effort towards his rehabilitation and 'Will' himself was confident that he should return home. The school was not so sure, but thought he should be given the chance and said that it would take him back if need be. 'Will', having left the school, committed yet further offences. The hearing decided that because of the gravity of the recent offences it had no alternative but to return him to the school: the subsequent offending confirmed the school's uncertainty about the degree of change in 'Will'. But a few months later, 'Will' again requested a review. The school this time said that recent months had been trouble-free and that weekend leaves had passed without incident. Material conditions at home were better and 'Will' himself had written to his former school asking whether or not there was a place available for him. The hearing decided that because of all these satisfactory responses, he could return home. His initiative in asking for a review and in making arrangements with his former school were indications of a definite change for the better. This time, the boy was reassessed positively.

These case histories suggest that at least one aim of the new system has not been fulfilled. The fact that the offence is relevant to decision-making—and it was naive to have expected otherwise— means that the system has not in practice resolved the conflict which plagued the juvenile courts and which the Kilbrandon Committee set out to resolve in establishing the children's hearings. It is not even clear that the hearings have reduced the conflict. Decision-makers specifically refer to the offence and to its accompanying considerations and they still have to reconcile the various expectations held of the system—their own, those of referral agents, the public, the child and his parents.

Conclusion

Although more children were referred to the reporter than to the former juvenile courts, fewer were in turn referred by him to the children's hearings. The reporter acted as a major sifting mechanism. But, once children reached the hearings, the level of intervention was greater than in the juvenile courts—more children were removed from their parents' homes in 1973 than in 1969 and more were placed under the supervision of a social worker.

This greater level of intervention highlights a deficiency in Edwin Lemert's model of 'judicious non-intervention'. He suggested that referral to a court or hearing should be a measure of last resort—a sign that all else had been tried and failed. He seems to assume that these agencies will know better how to deal with those appearing before them, but there is no reason to suppose that this is so. For, if all else has been tried, what can courts or hearings do other than punish or attempt to deter these children. In other words, children are controlled and punished in the guise of 'care' or 'treatment'; and because action is disguised as 'treatment' the number of children subject to such measures increases.

Such children also continue to be stigmatized perhaps to an even greater extent than in other kinds of systems because they are, by definition, the *most* troublesome, the *most* disruptive and so on. As Emerson writes: 'The principle of judicious non-intervention would seem not to change the juvenile court's handling of such hard-core, discredited delinquents most in need of salvaging'.[32] Lemert's response to this criticism is that *any* system of social control is stigmatizing;[33] but the point is that the approach categorized by him as 'ideal' may lead to *increased* stigmatization. He also argues that even if these children are being 'warehoused', it does not matter too much because they will pass out of the jurisdiction of the court or hearing at 18 (or at whatever age is determined by statute). But children come *into* such systems when quite young—at the age of 8, in Scotland, if they have committed an offence, and at a younger age where referred on other grounds. Few adults are given 'sentences' of ten years.

This higher level of intervention could reflect changes in the kinds of children referred to the reporters or appearing before the children's hearings from those who previously came into the juvenile court system. But it is by no means clear that any such changes have occurred.[34] This raises the question whether children now being sent to, for example, residential establishments might have been dealt with otherwise in the former juvenile court system. It is, at least, possible that this is so.[35] We must make explicit that 'needs' frequently mean 'social conformity' and that 'care' frequently involves measures which we know to be damaging or, at least, ineffective in preventing subsequent delinquent behaviour. 'Care', in reality, means 'control'.

Children who Offend:
an irresolvable dilemma?

Current Criticisms

The children's hearing system is not without its critics. It has been variously described as a 'costly experiment',[1] a 'baneful influence'[2] and an 'abysmal failure'.[3] The hearings have been blamed for failing to prevent an increase in juvenile crime. It is said that 'vandalism flourishes'[4] and that 'offences have increased dramatically'.[5] But as we pointed out on page 86 it is only when the number of children given police warnings is added to those referred to the reporter or proceeded against in the sheriff court that an increase in recorded crime results: 32,642 in 1969[6] compared with 35,932 in 1973.[7] This increase in recorded crime is mainly attributable to an increase in the number of offenders who were, by definition, minor offenders—offenders who constituted no grave threat to society. It is, of course, difficult to determine what any increase in recorded crime means. Because of the 'dark figure' of crime, that is crime which is unrecorded and unreported, it is impossible to say to what extent there has been a real increase in juvenile crime. Both public attitudes towards reporting the child offender to the police and police attitudes towards the referral of the child to the reporter may have changed as a result of the legislation. But it is impossible to assess the direction of this change. The public may have become more tolerant of the child offender and the police less tolerant—or vice versa. We just do not know. What is clear is that changes in public attitudes can profoundly affect crime rates.[8] Similarly, studies of the exercise of discretion indicate that decision-makers can also make an independent contribution to increasing rates of crime. Wilson,[9] for example, showed how the growth of specialized juvenile units and police professionalization were associated with higher rates of juvenile delinquency.

Nevertheless, it is the way in which we perceive a situation which determines our views and attitudes towards it and it is commonly felt in Scotland now that crime has dramatically increased and that the reason for this lies in the hearing's lack of effective powers. The hearing has no power to fine, to order the finding of caution by the parents, or to order restitution by the child or his parents, and so it is argued that the new system, instead of having a wider range of dispositions, is more restricted and limited in scope. Possibly the most controversial issue has been whether or not to re-introduce the fine. The Kilbrandon Committee came out strongly against this. It stated:

> Most of these fines were, we assume, in fact paid by the parents, the alternative (where imposed on the child) in event of default being the child's detention in a remand home. We cannot regard either of these results as being satisfactory either as an effective measure of training for the child or as being likely to secure genuine parental co-operation.[10]

But it is now argued that at least in the former juvenile courts:

> the citizen who had suffered at the hands of criminal children did have the satisfaction of knowing that the children would be taken before some sort of court with the ability to fine culprits . . . the children's hearings cannot hurt the malefactors where it hurts most, on the hide and in the pocket.[11]

Such claims have met with the contrary arguments that fining does not necessarily change the attitudes of the offender or his parents, and that no-one has established that the fine is in fact a deterrent. Future policy is not yet determined.[12]

Further, it is argued that the hearings are in reality powerless—that there are insufficient residential places, that many 'List D' schools are full, and that supervision is meaningless because social work departments are overworked and under-staffed. This has led to calls to give the hearings power to impose a 'short, sharp piece of punishment'[13] and it has been suggested that it is perhaps time to trust the children's hearings 'to identify the merely naughty child and impose minor penalties'.[14] There is also some feeling that the hearings have neglected the interests of the community in favour of the interests of the child: The juvenile court may have had its shortcomings and failures, but it was armed with powers which enabled disposals to have regard to society as well as to the interests of the child.'[15] Yet another argument is that the new system is creating new generations of delinquents. 'The degeneration of the young is being actively encouraged by those who are determined not to face the elementary fact that the Social Work (Scotland) Act has been a failure.'[16] The language used by some critics is reminiscent of the 'war against crime'. It is claimed that there is a need for 'weapons . . . some sort of armoury, otherwise the law of the jungle will prevail'.[17]

Do these feelings have a sound basis in reality? It is true that resources are lacking. There are few psychiatric units for young people, few small family group units and few schools for maladjusted children. In April 1971 the case loads of most social workers were between 80 and 100. Edinburgh was 20% short of its establishment staff and in Glasgow less than half the social workers were trained. In 1972 the average proportion of fully qualified field staff was almost 50%, but the output of social work students from universities and colleges that year nearly doubled the 1970 figure. This means that many social workers are young and inexperienced, and although there has been a steady development of services— public expenditure amounted to 40 million in 1972/73—there are still heavy pressures in most areas.

But it is wrong to suggest that the children's panels have less stringent powers than the juvenile courts. A child can be detained by a children's hearing for far longer than he could have been by the former juvenile court system. The hearings have jurisdiction over a child until he reaches the age of 18 unless the case is terminated at an earlier date. The hearings also have the power to place the child on supervision in a residential establishment without the commission of a further offence throughout this period.

Also, there are no comparable figures for subsequent offences committed by children dealt with in the juvenile courts in the period before the implementation of the Act and so we cannot say with certainty whether the picture is worse or not. Certainly, well before 1971, children were being sent home because of the shortage of residential places and committed further offences while at home. Children have always absconded from institutions and committed offences while absconding; children on probation also committed further offences while subject to that order. It is an over-simplification to lay the blame for these 'failures' at the door of a single piece of legislation, and it is false to pretend that all was well before the implementation of the Act. Most of these criticisms stem from an unwillingness to accept the underlying philosophy of the Act. The important point is, however, that the situation is *perceived* as worse now than before and is responded to in that way.

We discussed in Chapter V the tension which exists between the police and reporters. Nigel Bruce has shown that tension also exists between social workers and teachers. He refers to 'misunderstanding' and 'mistrust' between the two and provides abundant evidence of negative attitudes between teachers and social workers by quoting various spokesmen. For example, 'differences of approach generate a lot of heat in the area' or 'social workers are often immature and inexperienced young adults'. At the root of this, Bruce suggested, was a lack of understanding of (or sympathy with) the new approach, He wrote:

> The lack of co-operation from many schools today arises because teachers feel that they are extraneous to the system rather than an integral part of it ... Articles and letters appear in educational journals which indicate unawareness of the novelty of the system; unawareness, for instance, that hearings are obliged by statute to make decisions in the interest of the child—the interests of the community and the school find no mention in the act; unawareness too that the examination of evidence and adjudication of guilt is not part of the role of the hearing and is legally beyond their power; unawareness again that punishment is not the prime concern of the hearings, but that they are endeavouring to provide something more positive for the family.[18]

There have been few points of contact between the courts and the hearings, but the courts have, on occasion, been critical of the hearings—for example, some of the recommendations made by the hearings to the High Court on the appropriate disposition for a child have been attacked. In one case the hearing recommended a deferred sentence for a 16-year old boy who had committed an assault. The court sentenced him to three years' detention. In another case involving perjury by a boy of 16, the hearing recommended a fine. Lord Wheatley, in sentencing him to two years' detention, said that the hearings had disregarded the problem of perjury which bedevils the administration of justice. In this particular context the hearing was, one assumes, concentrating on the effect of the measure on the child; the court, on the other hand, was probably more concerned with deterrence and with maintaining a balance between the crime and the disposition. The 'yardsticks' of the courts and hearings differed.

We raised the possibility of such a conflict of ideologies in our discussion in Chapter III of the court's role in appeals to it by parents against the hearings' decisions. This was made apparent in a recent decision in the Sheriff Court. A children's hearing had been convened by the reporter on the ground that three children of the family were suffering from the lack of parental care. At the hearing, the mother denied the grounds of referral and so the case was referred to the Sheriff Court for the establishment of the grounds. The Sheriff found that the grounds were not established as to the two younger children, but established as to the oldest girl. This girl was, accordingly, referred back to the hearing for disposition. The panel members decided to remove the girl from home and place her in a children's home. The mother appealed to the Sheriff against this decision. During the appeal it was conceded by the reporter that the decision concerning disposition was based on information before the hearing which was not part of the original grounds for referral. This is normal practice in all cases dealt with by the hearings and in accordance with both social welfare ideology and the Kilbrandon Committee's recommendations. The reporter argued that once the grounds of referral were accepted at the hearing or were established in the Sheriff Court, the hearing was not bound by the information contained in the grounds of referral and that the hearing had absolute power to take any steps considered by it to be in the child's best interest. The Sheriff held that the hearing could consider only that information which served as grounds of referral. She held that:

> Any other interpretation is not only a misinterpretation of the law, but a breach of natural justice which must allow to any person fair notice of the crime or fault of negligence, call it what you will, with which they are charged ... I find it unthinkable that a person who has denied the original grounds of referral against her ... should be judged as unfit to carry out any part of her parental role (for that is really what the condition of the child's residence in an institution amounts to) on grounds which have not been stated as grounds of referral, and which she has had no opportunity of denying or having examined in court.[19]

So far the effect of the case has been minimal and reference continues to be made to factors outside the ground of referral in the determination of disposition measures. But the implication of this decision is that, in for example an offence referral, the hearing should look no further than the nature and significance of the particular offence outlined in the referral. This is clearly at odds with the philosophy and spirit of the Kilbrandon Committee Report and of the Social Work (Scotland) Act, though in accordance with principles of criminal justice. This decision is a further example of different yardsticks being applied in the courts and in the hearings. The following case history makes the same point. The social work department in the city requested a review of the supervision order of 'Don', a boy aged 15, as he was continuing to truant from school. The school said that 'his behaviour and general attitude had not improved' and they feared deterioration if the supervision order was removed. The children's hearing continued the supervision. The social work department made a further request for a review of the supervision one month later. 'Don' had failed to report to his supervisor and had attended school on only 10 out of 32 days. He was due to leave school in another month, but the social worker requested the children's hearing to consider placing the boy in a 'List D' school as he had failed to comply with the supervision requirement. 'Don's' father had periods of unemployment due to illness and was said to be unable to control his family. His mother was described as capable but as having extreme difficulty in raising the family. There was also said to be marital tension. The social worker described 'Don' as 'intent on going his own way regardless of the consequences'. The hearing decided to place him in a 'List D' school because of 'the deliberate flouting of the supervision order', 'the aggressive attitude of the boy's mother' and 'his refusal to give an undertaking about his future behaviour'. Although 'Don' was due to leave school on the day of the hearing, the hearing felt that he 'must be brought to some awareness of responsibility and self-discipline'. The family appealed to the Sheriff who subsequently returned the case to the hearing for further consideration. The factors weighing with the Sheriff were that there was 'no offence of a criminal nature', that 'the supervision was a result of the boy's truancy and the boy had now reached the school-leaving age' and that a 'prolonged stay in a List D school was *more drastic than was justified or necessary*' (emphasis added). The hearing continued the supervision order.

Conflict, Compromise or Confusion?

These various criticisms or points of conflict reflect the different aims, ideologies and philosophies of the various groups involved in the operation of the children's hearing system. Indeed, in a sense, the different groups personalize the two approaches towards juvenile offenders which we mentioned in the first chapter: social welfare and criminal justice. Phyllida Parsloe has argued that the function of a juvenile justice system is to balance the different and, at times, conflicting approaches of criminal justice and social welfare. She wrote of the Scottish system: 'It is not a weakness of the system that it contains different approaches, but rather the very purpose for which it exists.'[20] This theme is commonly reiterated by administrators and, as we have shown, aspects of both approaches currently exist side by side in the Scottish system. But 'co-existence' is in direct opposition to what the Kilbrandon Committee intended or hoped for—it intended to resolve the conflict between the two approaches by getting rid of the characteristics in the juvenile court which seemed to it to have led in the past to a compromise between the two approaches. Theory has not been put into practice. Does this mean that compromise is unavoidable? The Scottish experience suggests that the conflict which the Kilbrandon Committee sought to resolve is an inherent and universal feature of the structure of any system dealing with children who offend. There is no essential difference between a juvenile court and a welfare tribunal. The fact that many of the general criticisms made against the Scottish system are almost identical to those made of the English juvenile court supports this suggestion. The main difference is that criticisms in England have been consistently voiced by various pressure groups; there is little difference in the content of these criticisms.

For example, the police in England feel that the 1969 Act has not prevented further increases in juvenile crime—they feel that, far from reducing juvenile crime, the legislation has created a hard core of criminals.[21] Many juvenile court magistrates have expressed concern over the number of children who are the subject of care orders but who continue to commit offences while living at home or while absconding from community homes.[22] There have also been complaints of the 'abrogation of the powers of the court' and of 'entrusting the lives and liberty of children to the discretion of the executive'.[23] The appointment of the House of Commons sub-committee in 1975 provided the various parties with an opportunity to state their case and to present their recommendations for the future. Overall the evidence submitted to the subcommittee fell into four categories, each of which highlights the divergent views held by those interested in juvenile delinquency. First there was the 'radical' view that the 1969 Act did not go far enough. The National Council for Civil Liberties, for example, felt that 'the roots of juvenile crime and thus measures to combat it are to be found in the social and physical environment.' Urgent attention, therefore, required to be focused on 'bad housing, poor planning, schools' and the 'lack of opportunities for acceptable achievements'.[24] The second view was that of 'crime control'—that the Act was based on unsound principles. The Justices' Clerks' Society, for example, said that the Act failed because it blurred the distinction between a child in need of care and a juvenile offender and because it deprived society of 'an important part of the criminal court's jurisdiction, namely to protect the public'.[25] The third view was the 'child care' view which accepted the broad principles of the Act and called for its full implementation. Thus the British Association of Social Workers suggested that the 'Act provides a legal structure for dealing with juvenile delinquency which is both enlightened and appropriate without substantial amendment'.[26] The final view was the 'crime control/child care' view (put forward by the Magistrates' Association) which suggested that children who offend might be susceptible to child care but that some required penal measures regardless of this susceptibility.[27]

Clearly, an agreed ideology or philosophy on the appropriate way of dealing with child offenders cannot be assumed to exist. As Cole writes:

> To speak of the system as a continuum may underplay the complexity and the flux of relationships within it; although the administration of criminal justice is composed of a set of subsystems, there are no formal provisions for the subordination of one unit to another. Each has its own clientele, goals and norms, yet the output of one constitutes the the inputs to another.[28]

The problem is an *operational* one of inter-agency communications but it is also an *ideological* issue of competing values and objectives. Each of the groups involved in the operation of the juvenile (or criminal) justice system has a specialist function. They perhaps share a common, long-term objective—the prevention of delinquent behaviour—but each group has its own more immediate and quite different objective. For example, the police are primarily concerned with the prevention and detection of crime; social work departments with the investigation of the needs of the client; and

panel members or magistrates with the determination of dispositions based on the need to control the child's behaviour. Individual
policies are developed to achieve these particular objectives and
these objectives may be in conflict with each other. For example the
Police Federation recently wrote: 'We are fundamentally concerned with the protection of the public, the prevention of crime,
and the detection of offenders. Our concern in the treatment of
offenders is therefore considered in the light of the above principles.'[29] This is, of course, what the public expect of the police. The
point is that it is not a view which is widely held by social workers.
Conflict between the two agencies is, accordingly, likely to arise.
(It is not, of course, always as clear cut as this. Strains may also
exist *within* the agencies concerned—for example, ambiguities in the
role of magistrates, panel members and social workers. These
internal strains aggravate the overall conflict.) Because of these
differing ideologies amongst key figures there is no way in which a
system of juvenile justice can be established which will not be
subject to criticisms by one or other of these groups; the basic value
dilemma cannot be eliminated. Consultation between the various
groups which operate the Children and Young Persons Act 1969
has been viewed as a solution to some of the Act's difficulties.[30]
But consultation cannot resolve these difficulties; there still remain
real differences of perception of objectives.

Lemert has suggested that all we can do is to clarify and specify
whose values are being represented in any particular system for
handling children who do offend. He argued that 'the salient problem of juvenile justice may be its confusion of purposes rather than
failure to move in the direction of satisfying a particular set of purposes.'[31] But moving in one particular direction does not resolve
these difficulties. The framework of the Social Work (Scotland)
Act 1968 and the Children and Young Persons Act 1969 represented
a clear preference for social welfare values. But agents who did not
give whole-hearted support to these values are still involved in the
operation of the new systems and continue to act on quite different
values. Juvenile court magistrates in England, for example, challenged the basic principles of the Children and Young Persons Act
from the outset[32] and the police in both countries have been critical
throughout. Explicit conflict has prevented the development of
'social welfare' in England; in Scotland explicit conflict is less
common but it exists. Conflict can only be avoided where groups

who do not give allegiance to the preferred value system are excluded from the operation of the system.

Although the police give social welfare values marginal allegiance, it is clearly not possible to exclude them from the operation of a system which deals primarily with children who offend. But it is possible to *minimize* their impact on the operation of such a system as in Scotland. The creation of the role of the reporter there led to a reduction in the number of children dealt with within a formal social control framework; the creation of juvenile bureaux in England did not achieve this. The fact that the police in Scotland did not support the values reflected in the new system had little impact. Value conflict can also be reduced by selecting a new group of people to do the new job where, for example, the intention is to move from one value preference to another. Juvenile court magistrates in England can remember 'the good old days' when the power of disposition lay solely in their hands; panel members, on the other hand, are new at their job, perhaps still unsure of themselves, and look to the 'expert' for support and guidance. Selection procedures and training can also ensure compliance with the chosen set of values. These values can thereby be applied more consistently.

If social welfare is the desired policy in any jurisdiction, we have outlined how this might be better achieved: minimize the role of the police and create agencies chosen for their receptivity to and trained in social welfare values. But we have also attempted to show in this book the consequences of implementing a social welfare approach for children who offend: the lives of children and their families are interfered with to a greater extent than in an explicit criminal justice system and its 'professional' strategies involve subjectivity and stereotyping in the guise of scientific objectivity and expert assessment. Social welfare is a technique of social control. Concealment of this leads to hypocrisy and injustice; acknowledgement leads to a reconsideration of recent trends in juvenile justice policy. Children who offend require protection from the 'humanitarianism' of social welfare.

Juvenile Justice Policy:
a reconsideration

We drew attention in the previous chapter to the consequences of a social welfare approach towards children who offend: high levels of intervention resulting from the re-emergence of the principle of the offence as the primary criterion of intervention supplemented and reinforced by a subjective and stereotypical image of the delinquent. It is always much easier to criticize than to construct but in this concluding chapter we put forward an alternative approach for consideration. We are primarily concerned with the principles which should underlie proposals for future action. What are we trying or hoping to achieve? What should be the basis of our juvenile justice system? Our aim is to raise issues for further discussion rather than to answer them.

First we must dismiss the view that the basic difficulties in social welfare (and hence in the practice of the juvenile court or children's hearings systems) stem from the lack of resources. Bruce and Spencer have argued of the children's hearings that 'to realize the hopes and expectations of those who laid the groundwork of this system requires a much better staffed and at the same time a more diversified range of treatment as well as of preventive services than at present exists.'[1] The same point has consistently been made in England by Directors of Social Service and the British Association of Social Work.[2] But what sort of resources? Methods of treatment have had very little effect on recidivism rates. Borstal, probation, approved schools, detention centres all have notoriously poor success rates. A recent survey of eighteen community homes showed that success rates were better in some schools than in others but the researchers concluded that 'it is difficult to establish a general conclusion about the effectiveness of junior, intermediate or senior schools, or of schools of particular styles, in preventing boys from getting into trouble with the law after release.'[3] American research on the size of case-loads in supervision suggests that success rates are not necessarily improved by a reduction in case-load size,[4] and doubts have recently been expressed over the apparent success rates of many pioneering schemes in America.[5]

Often, of course, resources mean quite different things to different groups, and as long as we deal in generalities this incongruity is concealed and harmony can be claimed. This enables participants to continue much the same as before whilst acknowledging to each other that 'things will get better once . . .' The sentence does not require completion for each group inserts its own preferences. This 'conspiracy' means that fundamental questions can be passed over. In the words of the House of Commons sub-committee: 'The Act itself or indeed any legislation that might conceivably be passed by Parliament has had and can have no significant effect on the general level of delinquency and general juvenile misbehaviour.'[6] The recent Government White Paper makes the same point. 'The underlying personal, social and environmental factors are too complex and too deep rooted to be readily susceptible to influence by legislative means.'[7] Whatever type of system is chosen—juvenile court or welfare tribunal—it is not likely to make more than a marginal contribution to the diminution of crime rates—juvenile justice policy cannot deal with the kinds of factors which underlie recorded delinquency.

If we cannot reduce crime through our juvenile justice system what then should its aim be? Which values should be met? We assume that *some* form of social control is necessary for *some* children. Edwin Schur has argued in favour of 'radical non intervention' i.e. 'leave kids alone wherever possible.'[8] He argues that socio-cultural change will reduce delinquency, that we must change the structure and values of our society rather than change its youth and that collective action programmes are necessary rather than programmes which single out specific individuals. Proponents of this approach favour voluntary treatment (there seems little logic in this), decriminalization and narrowing the scope of the jurisdiction of the juvenile court to exclude truants, runaways etc. But some of these aims cannot, in reality, be achieved. Few crimes can be decriminalized (and Schur gives us no information on the extent to which he feels this can occur). As Cohen states, crimes of property and personal violence cannot be dealt with by 'laissez-faire liberalism.'[9] Nor does Schur offer short as opposed to long term solutions.

Proponents of a radical perspective in Britain seem to favour, in the short term, community control of delinquency.[10] But this is inextricably tied up with their long term aims.[11] Community control can occur only where there is community agreement; there must be agreement both on which children are to be dealt with and on the mode of dealing with them. Currently this does not exist.

The report of the House of Commons subcommittee on the Children and Young Persons Act provides a useful starting point in answering the first part of this question: which children should be dealt with. It acknowledged that many, perhaps the majority of, children grew out of delinquency, that it was a normal phase of their development. But it also felt that 'some attempt must be made both to hasten the process in the case of certain offenders to deter others from embarking on criminal activities, to contain a hard core of persistent offenders and to punish some offenders.'[12] The subcommittee questioned the appropriateness of social welfare values for children who offend and suggested a new direction: 'that of satisfying society's wish to punish an offender and preventing him for a time from committing further offences at reasonable cost and in the most humane way.'[13]

In both the subcommittee's report and the subsequent White Paper there emerged a distinction between different categories of children, a distinction based on *behaviour*. The subcommittee described the major failing of the 1969 Act as follows:

> It is not wholly effective in differentiating between children who need care, welfare, better education and mere support from society and the small minority who need strict control and an element of punishment.[14]

This statement rejects the notion that the 'deprived' and the 'depraved' are one and the same, and suggests rather the existence of the 'acceptable depraved' and the 'unacceptable depraved'. The White Paper continued this theme.[15] What is suggested is the creation of two separate systems of dealing with juvenile offenders: one based on minor or inconsequential offending and the other based on serious or persistent offending. The response to the former group reflects social welfare values; the response to the latter reflects punitive values.

These statements of intent are responses to comments and criticisms on the 1969 Act made by magistrates and police. They accept the appropriateness of social welfare practice for some children but are concerned about a hard core of young offenders who, they claim, are committing crimes with impunity and with whom courts are powerless to deal. Their response to this group is primarily a punitive one; increased sanctions are necessary. Some social workers have reached the same conclusion (that a dual or two-tiered system is necessary), though from different reasoning. There have been suggestions recently that social workers should concentrate on younger, less sophisticated, delinquents, in the belief that therein lies the possibility of greater success.[16] The social work response to the 'unacceptable' group is one of abandonment; social work or social welfare is not appropriate.

We feel that the 'acceptable' group is, in fact, the group which could be 'abandoned'. Many of these children could be diverted from the juvenile justice system. Currently in England, most children appearing before the juvenile courts are fined or discharged.[17] We need to ask whether these children could not have been dealt with in some way other than an appearance before the juvenile court. We already know that public labelling increases the likelihood of further delinquent behaviour.[18] Are symbolic sanctions necessary? Is a court appearance *per se* constructive? We think not, and the Scottish experience successfully demonstrates this. The majority of children in our sample dealt with by the reporters as 'no action' dispositions did not re-enter the system within a 12 month follow-up period. What of the children currently placed under the supervision of a social worker? There is no research on the meaning of supervision (there are impressionistic accounts that it amounts to little), and, by definition, these children are seen as able to remain in the community. How many of these children could also be diverted from the juvenile justice system? Society can tolerate the majority of minor offending. The full weight (and expense) of the juvenile justice system is too heavy-nanded for the bulk of juvenile offending. It then becomes a question of balance: possible increased harm to society because of non-intervention versus known harm to society as a result of intervention. Juvenile courts and welfare tribunals should be measures of last resort used only when voluntary help on an informal basis has been offered to the child, when such measures have failed to correct his antisocial behaviour (or he has not grown out of it) and, in addition, the child has committed a serious offence. There are difficulties of definition here but they are not irresolvable. Wolfgang for example has developed a point system of seriousness[19] and others[20] are in the process of developing scales of seriousness.

As we mentioned in Chapter V, there are dangers in formal diversion. It may become just another tunnel which the child enters and from which he then emerges for the next stage in the process; old ideas may become re-cycled, social welfare may move back a stage (many schemes repeat the inadequacies of similar programmes offered by the juvenile courts[21]); social control may move back a stage (the question here is is there any real difference: does diversion reduce stigma? is the impact of labelling reduced?); and the process can become routine—the child is allowed an additional bite at the cherry, that's all. But diversion is a useful framework and is capable of development without a social welfare framework.

We raised previously the question of who should divert. We feel that this decision should lie with an independent assessor, something akin to the reporter in the Scottish system, uninfluenced by constraints of fellow professionals. (This is the major deficiency in the English police juvenile bureaux and in probation intake schemes in some American states.) This is not to suggest that the current role of the reporter is ideal. We drew attention, also in Chapter V, to the lack of criteria set out as guidelines for his action (and, consequently, to the subjectivity of many of the criteria used) and to the lack of review of the reporters' decisions. But these criticisms can be overcome—criteria for action can be set out (e.g. levels of seriousness in the circumstances surrounding the offence, the degree of involvement by the child etc.) and decisions to deal formally with the child can be challengeable. A basic rule should be that it would not be possible for greater intervention to occur at this stage than could occur if the child was referred to a juvenile court or welfare board.

Children should at all stages in the process have access to the advice of someone akin to the duty solicitors now appearing in many magistrates' courts in England. This is especially so for the children not diverted, the so-called 'hard core' because they will be, by definition, serious offenders. This may involve unsatisfactory consequences: plea bargaining, the entry of not guilty pleas where the child admits his guilt to the lawyer, the 'guilty' getting off on technicalities and so on. But this is part of courtroom 'games' and is no more unsatisfactory than what can happen now as a result of the lack of legal advice (e.g. the hearing or court may proceed to deal with the child on his own admission although subsequently the child in his account offers a defence). A question for discussion is the appropriate role for a lawyer in juvenile proceedings: to protect the child's legal rights or to act in the 'child's interests'? We prefer the former; the latter is a remnant of social welfare ideology and, as we have shown, is discriminatory.

What criteria should determine formal action? What standards should be applied once the child is before the court or tribunal? What options should be available to it? The subcommittee and the White Paper both concentrate on persistence as their criterion for movement between their two-tiered system. We feel that criteria for action should centre on the seriousness of the offence; persistence per se should be insufficient. The failure of preventive detention alerts us to the dangers of relying on persistence alone and recent research suggests that persistent violence in and absconding from institutions may be encouraged by something within *institutions* themselves rather than in their inmates.[22] Our current social reaction to many of these children may be misplaced. Action based on the number of referrals to official agencies is likely to do no more than reflect the beliefs of those operating the 'input' or 'labelling' machinery. The operation of police cautioning in England led to a widening of the net of control,[23] the very effect which we wish to avoid. It is difficult to determine how many children are likely to fall within this category. Estimates vary[24] and will depend on the tightness of the definitions chosen. We suggest two main criteria: nature of the offence and the degree of the child's involvement. These criteria dominate proceedings in criminal courts.

We see the role of a special juvenile tribunal as protecting society, protecting the offender from undue intervention and reasserting society's values. Punishment is society's and the child's right. In a practical context this means that formal action should be taken when the delinquent commits a serious offence, action should be proportionate to the offence and decisions should be manifestly fair and just. Notions of 'fairness' and 'justice' are complex. It might be argued that it is not 'just' to deprive a child of the 'care' he requires. We have tried in previous chapters, however, to show that 'care' involved subjective and individualized penalties and that we should not, therefore, premise future policy on such concepts. The little which we know about how children and parents view this process suggests that they are confused by dispositions which do not conform to retributive ideals.[25] Feelings of justice and fairness seem important to children. Matza has painted the picture of the child who appeared before an American juvenile court asking himself:

> Why should persons so important and so influential as the judge and his helpers lie to him regarding the true basis of disposition? Why should they insist, as they frequently do, that it is not what he did—which strikes delinquents and others as the sensible reason for intervention— but his underlying problems and difficulties that guide court action? Why do they say they are helping him when patently they are limiting his freedom of action and movement by putting him on probation or in prison? What on earth could they possibly be hiding that would lead them to such heights of deception?[26]

He also suggested that delinquents expect to be dealt with in accordance with certain standards.

> It is only fair that some steps be taken to ascertain whether I was really the wrong-doer; it is only fair that I be treated according to the same principles as others of my status; it is only fair that you who pass judgment on me sustain the right to do so; it is only fair that some relationship obtain between the magnitude of what I have done and what you propose to do to me; it is only fair that differences between the treatment of my status and others be reasonable and tenable.[27]

There is no place for concepts such as 'fairness' and 'justice' in a system based on social welfare ideology.[28] Cavenagh[29] has argued that social welfare is a part of fairness and justice, but this is not so— their standards differ. And yet if there is any value in referring children to courts or tribunals it may lie in such children being dealt with in accordance with these widely held values. Results of research[30] on the current juvenile courts in England suggest that the 'consumers' of the juvenile court process perceive the role of the court to be that of administering 'justice' in the traditional sense of the term: intervention justified on proof of the commission of an offence and the commensurability of sentence to offence. They expect a tariff of disposals founded in retributive ideals and it is on this basis that the efficacy of the juvenile court is measured. When deviation from these principles is observed (e.g. when an individualised disposition is made), a sense of injustice arises and with it alienation from the court's process and function. These comments raise a fundamental question for the future development of juvenile justice policy: the extent to which a policy of social welfare should be pursued. Not only do parents and children not seem to want the juvenile court to move away from doctrines of punishment—they seem censorious about any suggestion that it should do so. Parents may support and children may respect the juvenile court only for as long as it *maintains* a justice approach.[31]

'Justice' and 'fairness' are part of the notion of punishment. Punishment gets rid of individualized (i.e. discriminatory) penalties, indefinite periods of control and wide discretion. It limits action and, because of the inadequacy of our knowledge about human and delinquent behaviour, needs to be re-instated within the juvenile court or children's hearing framework. To some extent this has already happened. We drew attention in Chapters V and VI to the operation of a tariff system in the Scottish hearings. Priestley's research suggests that the same is true of the operation of the English juvenile courts.[32] But currently this is achieved covertly and, on occasions, on subjective criteria. Punishment requires objectivity and an open acknowledgement by those involved with child offenders that this is their primary orientation.

Acceptance of such principles does not mean the return to treadmills or to bread and water diets; there is a distinction between the aims of measures and their content and this is where consensus as to the *mode* of disposition is vital. It would mean an end to indeterminate orders; a movement towards a system of fixed penalties; the 'treatment' component of any order would become 'optional'; social background reports would not be presented and the relationship between social worker and client would be explicitly one of social control. Such a system of consistency between the scales of crime seriousness and sanctions may increase any deterrent value in sanctions and would reduce the injustice of disparity. A return towards the principles of punishment has already occurred in some American jurisdictions[33] with respect to adults and it is likely to be extended to juveniles.[34] Having gone this far, you might ask: why retain a separate tribunal for juveniles at all? We feel that there are advantages—the lack of publicity which currently surrounds the young people appearing before the juvenile court, the simplified and modified procedures and the safeguards against contamination. This is not to suggest that current tribunals do not require modification.[35]

We have not attempted definite proposals; it is too early for this. Our intention is to encourage further discussion. What we have stressed in these concluding chapters is the need to get rid of hypocrisy. Language has concealed the true state of affairs. We cannot assume that treatment works or may work some time in the future. Currently it does not. It can be argued that the case against treatment has not been proved,[36] that we must continue to develop programmes and to experiment. But where does the onus of proof lie? Because 'treatment' may be a harmful or stigmatizing experience, the onus of proving that 'treatment' works should lie with those seeking to retain social welfare practices. If success cannot be pointed to, we must protect the child from 'treatment'. Future policy debates must begin from that premise. The House of Commons subcommittee's trilogy of economy, humanity and punishment seems to us to offer a new direction and a reasonable starting point for future debates.

Appendix I

1974 Statistics

a. *Children referred to Reporter*   31,524
   Action by reporter:-

No action: Current S.R.	3,890	12·3%
Other	9,104	28·9%
Police warning or J.L.O. scheme	1,877	6·0%
Referral to S.W. Dept.	1,545	4·9%
Referral to hearing	15,108	47·9%

b. *Children referred to Reporter:*
           offence referrals   27,908
   Action by reporter:-

No action: Current S.R.	3,785	13·6%
Other	8,485	30·4%
Police warning or J.L.O. scheme	1,874	6·7%
Referral to S.W. Dept.	1,260	4·5%
Referral to hearing	12,504	44·8%

c. *Referrals to Children's Hearings*   15,108
   Initial disposal:

Supervision requirement: (non-residential)	7,181	47·5%
Supervision requirement: (residential)	1,592	10.5%
No supervision requirement	6,335	42·0%

   Offence referrals to Children's Hearings   11,015
   Initial disposal:

Supervision requirement: (non-residential)	5,438	49·4%
Supervision requirement: (residential)	1,301	11·8%
No supervision requirement	4,276	38·8%

Source: *Scottish Social Work Statistics, 1974*

Appendix II

1975 Statistics

1975 Statistics

At the time of going to press *Scottish Social Work Statistics, 1975* had not been published. The statistical section of Social Work Services Group are working on 1975 figures in two parts—pre- and post-regionalization. There is the added complication for 1976 that the Statistical Return completed by Reporters, on which published figures are based, was altered during the year and even when figures are published they will not be comparable with those given for the earlier years.

Provisional figures for Scotland as a whole for 1975 give the following picture:

a. *Reports to Reporter*   28,965
   Referred by Reporter to hearings   13,908   48.0%

b. *Offences referred to Reporter*   42,734
   of which dealt with at hearings   23,187   54.3%

c. *Referrals to Children's Hearings*   13,908
   Initial disposal:-
     Supervision requirement:
       (non-residential)   5,897   42.4%
     Supervision requirement:
       (residential)   1,868   13.4%
     No supervision requirement   6,143   44.2%

First returns for 1976 would appear to indicate a similar general picture to that in earlier years with some slight overall drop in the number of referrals.

Notes

Prologue

1. HOUSE OF COMMONS EXPENDITURE COMMITTEE, *Eleventh Report, Children and Young Persons Act 1969.* Vol. 1, London, H.M.S.O., 1975 (H.C. 534-i) para. 13.
2. HOME OFFICE, WELSH OFFICE, DEPARTMENT OF HEALTH AND SOCIAL SECURITY, DEPARTMENT OF EDUCATION AND SCIENCE, *Observations on the Eleventh Report from the Expenditure Committee.* London, H.M.S.O., 1976 (Cmnd. 6494), para. 3.
3. *Kent* v *U.S.* 383 U.S. 541., *In re Gault* 387 U.S. 1, *In re Winship* 397 U.S. 358, *McKeiver* v *Pennsylvania* 403 U.S. 528.
4. See SOSIN (Michael) and SARRI (Rosemary), "Due Process—Reality or Myth? in: SARRI (Rosemary) and HASENFELD (Yeheskel), eds., *Brought to Justice?* Ann Arbor, National Assessment of Juvenile Corrections, University of Michigan, 1976.
5. *McKeiver,* op. cit.
6. For example issues relating to admissibility of confessions and evidence procured during the investigatory process. These issues were decided for adults in *Mapp* v *Ohio* 367 U.S. 643 and *Miranda* v *Arizona* 384 U.S. 436.
7. FRIEDENBERG (Edgar), 'Adolescence as a Social Problem'. In: BECKER (Howard S.) ed., *Social Problems: A Modern Approach.* New York, John Wiley, 1966.
8. HOME OFFICE, *Criminal Statistics England and Wales 1975.* London, H.M.S.O., 1976 (Cmnd. 6566).
It is interesting to note that the proportion of detected crime assigned to juveniles in the U.S.A. is similar. *Uniform Crime Reports for the United States,* 1975, Washington, U.S. Government Printing Office.
9. LEMERT (Edwin M.), 'The Juvenile Court—Quest and Realities.' In: PRESIDENT'S COMMISSION ON LAW ENFORCEMENT AND ADMINISTRATION OF JUSTICE, *Task Force Report: Juvenile Delinquency and Youth Crime.* Washington, U.S. Government Printing Office, 1967.
10. The majority of juveniles dealt with by juvenile courts in England are fined or given conditional discharges; in America more than half are dealt with by discharge.
11. Jürgen Habermas has called this process the 'personalization' of public conflicts. *See* HABERMAS (Jürgen), *Towards a Rational Society.* London, Heinemann Educational Books, 1971.

12. BRUCE (Nigel) and SPENCER (John), *Face to Face with Families*. Loanhead, Macdonald, 1976, p. 23.

Chapter I

1. For a discussion of this *see* ARIES (P.), *Centuries of Childhood*. Harmondsworth, Penguin, 1962.

2. According to Hume, the Scots had not 'attained the same degree of maturity and precision' as England, and he seems uncertain of the position of 7- to 14-year-olds. Macdonald, on the other hand, is quite clear that the child over 7 had full responsibility.
   HUME (The Baron), *Commentories on the Law of Scotland respecting Crimes*. Vol. 1, Edinburgh, Bell and Bradfute, 1847, p. 13.
   MACDONALD (J.H.A.), WALKER (J.) and STEVENSON (D.) eds., *A practical treatise on the criminal law of Scotland*. Edinburgh, Green, 1948.

3. *See* PINCHBACK (I.) and HEWITT (M.), *Children in English Society*. Vol. II, London, Routledge and Kegan Paul, 1973. pp. 351–2. Capital punishment was incompetent in Scotland until the age of 14.

4. For a detailed account of these charges, *see* 'Summary of Parliamentary Action Regarding the Trial and Treatment of Delinquent Children 1828–1850, In: SANDERS (W. B.) ed., *Juvenile Offenders for A Thousand Years*. Chapel Hill, The University of North Carolina Press, 1970.

5. *See* SCOTT (Charles), 'What Changes are Desirable in the Mode of Dealing with Juvenile Delinquency?' Transactions of the National Association for the Promotion of Social Sciences (1880). In: SAUNDERS (W. B.), ed., op. cit.

6. For a discussion of this *see* LORD (D.), 'Changes in attitudes towards the treatment of juvenile offenders in Great Britain, 1823–1908,' *Australia and New Zealand Journal of Criminology*, 1968, 1, 4, 201–11.

7. *See* CARLEBACH (Julius), *Caring for Children in Trouble*. London, Routledge and Kegan Paul, 1970.
   Also THOMSON (A.), 'Social Evils: Their Causes and Cures', In: SANDERS (W. B.), ed., op. cit.

8. Children, however, had to serve 14 days in prison in expiation of their crimes before moving on to these schools.

9. The official policy of the prison system, for example, moved away from retribution towards reformation and deterrence.

10. Other changes during this period include the Probation of First Offenders Act 1887 (which introduced probation) and the Youthful Offenders Act 1901 (which gave courts the power to commit child offenders to the custody of a 'fit person' rather than send them to prison or reformatory schools). The Probation of Offenders Act 1907, though it applied to all offenders, was largely enacted as a result of the

interest of those concerned with child welfare and also enabled children to be kept out of institutions.

11. WAUGH (B.), *The Gaol Cradle: Who rocks it*. London, Daldy, Isbister, 1876.
    SCOTT (Charles), op. cit., outlined an alternative procedure for dealing with delinquent children in Scotland.
12. HOWARD ASSOCIATION, *Children, Courts and the Probation System*. London, Howard Association, 1904.
    Also by the HOWARD ASSOCIATION, *Special Courts for Children, Probation Officers and Parental Responsibility*. London, Howard Association, 1905.
13. *See* PINCHBECK (I.) and HEWITT (M.), op. cit., p. 492.
14. *See* HOWARD (John), *The State of Prisons in England and Wales*. London, Cadell and Conant, 1780. Also, BENTHAM (J.), *An Introduction to the Principles of Morals and Legislation*, Oxford, Clarendon Press, 1907.
15. The founding father, as it were, of positivist criminology is Cesare Lombroso who saw crime as a product or expression of constitutional factors in the individual. For an overview of this approach, *see* RADZINOWICZ (L.), *Ideology and Crime*. London, Heinemann, 1966. Ch. 2.
16. MATZA (D.), *Delinquency and Drift*. New York, John Wiley, 1964.
17. FLINN (M. W.) ed., Introduction to CHADWICK (E.), *Poor Law Commissioners' Report on the sanitary condition of the labouring population of Great Britain*. Edinburgh, Edinburgh University Press, 1964.
18. FLINN (M. W.), 'Social Theory and the Industrial Revolution,' In: BURNS (T.) and SAUL (S. B.), eds., *Social Theory and Economic Change*. London, Tavistock, 1967.
19. ibid.
20. WILLIAMS (R.), *The Long Revolution*. Harmondsworth, Pelican Books, 1965, p. 156.
21. Referred to by ROOLF (M.), *Voluntary Societies and Social Policy*. London, Routledge and Kegan Paul, 1957, p. 87.
22. *See*, for example, SELECT COMMITTEE ON REFORMATORY AND INDUSTRIAL SCHOOLS, *Report*. London, H.M.S.O., 1896 (Cmnd. 8204).
23. In particular the direction was towards Protestantism. This was a pattern which also developed in the United States. *See* FOX (S.), 'Juvenile Justice Reform: an historical perspective,' *Stanford Law Review*, 1970, **20**, 6, 1187–1239.
24. THOMPSON (A.), 'Social Evils: Their Causes and Their Cures,' In: SAUNDERS (W. B.), ed., op. cit. This description is of the Institution for Juvenile Offenders at Aberdeen, 1841.
25. Referred to by CARLEBACH (J.), op. cit.
    A similar process occurred in the United States: *see* Fox (S.), op. cit.
26. Platt suggests that the extension of the housewife role to that of social worker was a natural step in the emancipation of women. Far from

being the sign of a feminist revolution, these initial steps clearly show that emancipation of women was restricted to well-defined and stereotyped boundaries of women's role in society. See PLATT(A.), *The Child Savers*. Chicago, University Press, 1969.

27. In Scotland, after the 1908 Act, there were two courts with concurrent jurisdiction: the sheriff court and the justice of the peace court (in the counties) or the burgh court (in the burghs).
28. PLATT (A.), op. cit.
29. DAHL (T. Stang), 'The Emergence of the Norwegian Child Welfare Law', in: CHRISTIE (Nils), ed., *Scandinavian Studies in Criminology*, Vol. 5, London, Martin Robertson, 1974, p. 85.
30. MACK (J. W.), 'The Juvenile Court,' *Harvard Law Review*, 1909, 23, 104.
31. ibid.
32. For a more detailed outline, see VAN WATERS (M.), 'The Socialization of Juvenile Court Procedure', *Journal of the American Institute of Criminal Law and Criminology*, 1922, 13, 61.
33. NYQUIST (O.), *Juvenile Justice*. Cambridge Studies in Criminology, Vol. 12, London, Macmillan, 1960.
    For an outline of the current system in Sweden see:
    TEMKIN (J.), 'The Child, The Family and the Young Offender—Swedish Style', *Modern Law Review*, 1973, 36, 6, 569–86.
34. MORRIS (N.) and HAWKINS (G.), *The Honest Politician's Guide to Crime Control*. Chicago, University of Chicago Press, 1970.
35. CLARKE HALL (Sir William), *Children's Courts*. London, George Allen and Unwin, 1926, p. 64.
36. *H.C. Deb.*, Vol. 183, col. 1435–6.
37. DEPARTMENTAL COMMITTEE ON THE TREATMENT OF YOUNG OFFENDERS, *Report*. London, H.M.S.O. 1927 (Cmd. 2831). (Hereinafter referred to as The Molony Committee.)
38. DEPARTMENTAL COMMITTEE ON PROTECTION AND TRAINING (SCOTLAND), *Report*. London, H.M.S.O., 1928 (49–192). (Hereinafter referred to as The Morton Committee.)
39. The Molony Committee, op. cit. The Morton Committee, op. cit., made much the same point. It felt that the replacement of the juvenile court by a welfare or educational board 'would give judicial authority to a body not primarily elected for that purpose,' (p. 39).
40. The Molony Committee, op. cit., p. 20. See also the Morton Committee, op. cit., p. 43.
41. The Morton Committee , op. cit., p. 42.
42. The Molony Committee, op. cit., p. 25.
43. The Morton Committee, op. cit., p. 43.
44. The Molony Committee, op. cit., pp. 20–21. The Morton Committee, op. cit., pp. 44–5.
45. The Molony Committee, op. cit., p. 43.

46. ibid., p. 48.

47. There are no obvious reasons for the development of special juvenile courts in these areas. It was not a response to the high crime rates.

48. COMMITTEE ON CHILDREN AND YOUNG PERSONS, *Report*. London, H.M.S.O., 1960 (Cmnd. 1191). Chairman: The Rt. Hon. The Viscount Ingleby. (Hereinafter referred to as the Ingleby Committee.)

49. COMMITTEE ON CHILDREN AND YOUNG PERSONS (SCOTLAND), *Report*. Edinburgh, H.M.S.O., 1964 (Cmnd. 2306). Chairman: The Hon. Lord Kilbrandon. (Hereinafter referred to as The Kilbrandon Committee.)

50. ROBSON (W. A.), *Welfare State and Welfare Society: Illusion and Reality*. London, George Allen and Unwin, 1976.

51. *See*, for example, GEORGE (V.) and WILDING (P.), *Ideology and Social Welfare*. London, Routledge and Kegan Paul, 1976.

52. LOCKWOOD (D.), 'Some Remarks on "The Social System,"' *British Journal of Sociology*, 1956, **7**, 2, 134–46.

53. THE CARE OF CHILDREN COMMITTEE, *Report*. London, H.M.S.O., 1946 (Cmnd. 6922). Chairman: Miss M. Curtis, C.B.E. (Hereinafter referred to as The Curtis Committee.)

54. The Committee clearly had some reservations about this for it likened the delinquent to 'the *really* difficult or unruly child and the child who has been exposed to *very* deprived influences' (emphasis added).

55. BOWLBY (J.), *Forty-Four Juvenile Thieves*. London, Baillière, Tindall and Cox, 1946.
BOWLBY (J.), *Maternal Care and Mental Health*. Geneva, World Health Organization, 1952.

56. The Ingleby Committee, op. cit., para. 60.

57. ibid., para. 66.

58. ibid., para. 76.

59. ibid., para. 341.

60. *The Times*, 28 October 1960.

61. CAVENAGH (W.), 'Justice and Welfare in the Juvenile Courts', *British Journal of Delinquency*, 1957, **7**, 3, 196–205.

62. CAVENAGH (W.), 'A comment on the Ingleby Report', *British Journal of Criminology*, 1961–2, **2**, 1, 54–67 at 57.

63. *See*, for example, 'Notes of the Week', *Justice of the Peace*, 1960, Vol. 124, 712.

64. YOUNGHUSBAND (E.), 'The Juvenile Court and the Child', *British Journal of Delinquency*, 1957, **7**, 3, 181–95.

65. For a detailed discussion of this *see* BOTTOMS (A. E.), 'On the decriminalization of the English Juvenile Courts. In: HOOD (R. G.), ed., *Crime, Criminology and Public Policy*. London, Heinemann Educational Books, 1974.

66. The age of criminal responsibility was raised in England from seven to eight in the Children and Young Persons Act 1933, S.50.

67. BROOKE (The Rt. Hon. Henry), Foreword to HOME OFFICE, *Report on the work of the Children's Department 1961–1963*. London, H.M.S.O. 1964 (H.C. 155), p. viii.

68. LABOUR PARTY STUDY GROUP, *Crime—A Challenge to Us All*. London Transport House, 1964.

69. CROSLAND (C. A. R.), *The future of Socialism*. London, Cape, 1961, p. 113.

70. HOME OFFICE, *The Child, the Family and the Young Offender*. London, H.M.S.O., 1965 (Cmnd. 2742).

71. WOOTTON (B.). 'White Paper on Children in Trouble', *Criminal Law Review*, 1968, 465–73.

72. CAVENAGH (W.), 'What kind of Court or Committee?', *British Journal of Criminology*, 1966, **6**, 2, 123–38.

73. DOWNEY (B.), 'White Paper: The Child, the Family and the Young Offender', *Modern Law Review*, 1966, **29**, 409.

74. FITZGERALD, (P.), 'The Child, the White Paper and the Criminal Law: Some Reflections', *Criminal Law Review*, 1966, 607–12.

75. KAHAN (B.), 'The Child, the Family and the Young Offender: Revolutionary or Evolutionary?', *British Journal of Criminology*, 1966, **6**, 2, 159–69.

76. SCOTT (P.), 'The Child, the Family and the Young Offender', *British Journal of Criminology*, 1966, **6**, 2, 105–11.

77. HOME OFFICE, *Children in Trouble*. London, H.M.S.O., 1968 (Cmnd. 3601), para. 33.

78. BOTTOMS (A. E.), op. cit.

79. HOME OFFICE, *Children in Trouble*, op. cit., para. 33.

80. ibid., para. 20.

81. The Kilbrandon Committee, op. cit.

82. ibid., para. 13.

83. ibid., para. 11.

84. ibid., para. 14.

85. ibid., para. 14.

86. KILBRANDON (The Hon. Lord), 'The Scottish Reforms. The Impact on the Public', *British Journal of Criminology*, 1968, **8**, 3, 235–41.

87. The Kilbrandon Committee, op. cit., para. 87.

88. ibid., para. 86.

89. ibid., para. 12.

90. ibid., para. 78.

91. ibid., para. 73.

Chapter II

1. *See* PLATT (A.), *The Child Savers*. Chicago, University of Chicago Press, 1969.

LEMERT (E. M.), *Social Action and Legal Change. Revolution within the Juvenile Court.* Chicago, Aldine, 1970.

DAHL (T. Stang), *The Emergence of the Norwegian Child Welfare Law.* In: CHRISTIE (Nils), ed., *Scandinavian Studies in Criminology* Vol. 5, London, Martin Robertson, 1974.

BOTTOMS (A. E.), 'On the decriminalization of the English Juvenile Courts'. In: HOOD (R. G.), ed., *Crime, Criminology, and Public Policy,* London, Heinemann Educational Books, 1974.

2. We had access to copies of most, though not all, of the memoranda submitted to the Kilbrandon Committee.

3. Suggested by the Approved Schools Association in its memorandum to the Committee.

4. Suggested by the Church of Scotland Committee on Social Services in its memorandum to the Committee.

5. Suggested, for example, in the memorandum of the Procurators Fiscal Society.

6. SMITH (E.) and STOCKMAN (N.), 'Some suggestions for a sociological approach to the study of Government Reports', *Sociological Review,* 1972, **20**, 59.

7. PRESIDENT'S COMMISSION ON LAW ENFORCEMENT AND ADMINISTRATION OF JUSTICE, *The Challenge of Crime in a Free Society.* Washington, U.S. Government Printing Office, 1967.

8. *See* a fuller discussion of this point by WOOTTON (The Baroness), 'Official advisory bodies'. In: WALKER (Nigel) with the assistance of GILLER (Henri), eds., *Penal Policy-Making in England.* Cambridge, Institute of Criminology, 1977.

9. Quoted in *The Scotsman,* 23 April 1964.

10. Memorandum of the School Welfare Officers' Service, Glasgow, on the recommendation of the Kilbrandon Committee Report, p. 1.

11. *See* the memorandum of the Association of Child Care Officers (Scottish Region) on the recommendations of the Kilbrandon Committee Report.

12. The Committee stated in para. 35 that 'such a process of education in a social context ... essentially involves the application of social and family casework.'

13. Memorandum of the Sheriff Substitutes Association on the recommendations of the Kilbrandon Committee Report at p. 1.

14. COMMITTEE ON CHILDREN AND YOUNG PERSONS, SCOTLAND, *Report.* Edinburgh, H.M.S.O., 1964 (Cmnd. 2306). Chairman: The Hon. Lord Kilbrandon. para. 143. (Hereinafter referred to as the Kilbrandon Committee.)

15. Quoted in the *Scottish Daily Express,* 23 April 1964.

16. *The Scotsman,* 23 April 1964.

17. *The Glasgow Herald,* 23 April 1964.

18. SCOTTISH EDUCATION DEPARTMENT, SCOTTISH HOME AND HEALTH DEPARTMENT, *Social Work and the Community*. Edinburgh, H.M.S.O., 1966 (Cmnd. 3065).
19. These proposals did not fall completely outside the spirit of the Kilbrandon Committee recommendations. The Committee saw its recommendations as forming the centre 'core' of a wider service in the future which might cater for the needs of adults and of all ages as well as those of the children in the family.
20. MACK (J.), 'The Scottish White Paper—"*Social Work and the Community*"', *British Journal of Criminology*, 1967, **7**, 3, 336–9.
21. Memorandum of the British Psychological Society (Scottish Section) on the White Paper, para. 4.
22. Letter by G. A. Dell in: *British Journal of Criminology*, 1967, 7, 4, 478–9.
23. DEPARTMENTAL COMMITTEE ON THE PROBATION SERVICE, *Report*. London, H.M.S.O., 1962. Chairman: Mr R. P. Morison Q.C. (Hereinafter referred to as the Morison Report.)
24. We are not suggesting that the merger was wrong, only that it is odd to have different systems within Great Britain. The main explanation for the difference seems to lie in the political strength of the probation service in England. The terms of reference of the Seebohm Committee* which considered the structure of social services in England were framed in such a way that consideration of the probation service was prevented. This was a consequence of pressure from the National Association of Probation Officers.

   * COMMITTEE ON LOCAL AUTHORITY AND ALLIED PERSONAL SOCIAL SERVICES, *Report*. London, H.M.S.O., 1968 (Cmnd. 3703). Chairman: Frederic Seebohm Esq.
25. A number of individual commentators remained critical of the second White Paper—their common ground was the rejection of a social welfare approach and a preference for what might be called a 'criminal justice' approach. Sparks, for example, foresaw a reduced protection of children's rights; Napley argued that procedures in the juvenile court should be tightened up rather than relaxed and that informal procedures provided insufficient protection for the child. Similar criticisms were made by Ratcliffe. He felt that the proposals 'would create serious inroads into, and radical changes in, some of our long-established and cherished legal and "philosophical" concepts of justice and freedom of the individual'. *See* SPARKS (R.), 'Children in Trouble Attacked', *New Society*, 1968, **12**, 449.

   NAPLEY (D.), 'A Comment', *Criminal Law Review*, 1968, 474–7.
   RATCLIFFE (T.), 'Children in Trouble', *The Criminologist*, 1968, **3**, (10), 90–96.
26. BOTTOMS (A. E.), 'On the decriminalization of the English Juvenile Court', op. cit.
27. This is a difficult argument to sustain. The Bill was a product of the

reactions to the two White Papers, the first published some four years previously.

28. This argument that the Bill was biased against working-class children proved to be the most difficult for Labour ministers to counteract. James Callaghan, for example, drew the distinction between equality and uniformity and claimed that the Bill would 'ensure as nearly as we can real equality for all children of all classes and backgrounds', *H.C. Deb.*, Vol. 779, cols. 1776–7.

29. *H. C. Deb.* Vol. 787 col. 1290.

30. The juvenile panels referred to by the Kilbrandon Committee became 'children's hearings' in the Social Work (Scotland) Bill. The term 'panel' became the collective name for the members of these hearings.

31. *H. C. Deb.*, Vol. 764, col. 114.

32. ibid., col. 120.

33. Winifred Ewing, a Scottish Nationalist M.P. and solicitor, expressed similar concerns. She felt that legal aid should be available to the child and/or his parents to enable legal representation at the hearing because of the considerable powers of disposal which the hearing would have. Indeed, Mrs Ewing was not in favour of a lay panel at all. 'The most refined activity in social work is the power to dispose of a person's liberty or future, and for this I want a professional person.' She argued, somewhat inconsistently with this statement, for the implementation of the 1937 Children and Young Persons (Scotland) Act— the Act which provided for the creation of special juvenile courts.

34. ibid., col. 127.

35. ibid., col. 59.

36. ibid., col. 67.

37. ibid., col. 142.

38. Reorganization of the personal social services in England and Wales took place in 1971 after the passing of the Local Authority Social Services Act 1971. The probation service was excluded from this Act.

39. Social Work (Scotland) Bill, third reading: *H.C. Deb.*, Vol. 768, col. 1587.

40. These are S.4 which prohibits criminal proceedings for offences by children under fourteen; S.5 which restricts criminal proceedings for offences by young persons under seventeen; and S.7 which raises the minimum age for qualification for a borstal sentence from fifteen to seventeen and which planned the phasing out of detention centres as intermediate treatment facilities became available.

Chapter III

1. *See* for example ALLEN (F.), *The Borderland of Criminal Justice.* Chicago, University of Chicago Press, 1964.

TAPPAN (P.), *Juvenile Delinquency*. New York, McGraw-Hill, 1969.

2. PLATT (A.), *The Child Savers*. Chicago, Chicago University Press, 1969.

3. *See* for example The Kilbrandon Committee, op. cit., paras. 13 and 86.

4. ibid., para. 54.

5. WALKER (N.), 'A century of causal theory'. In: KLARE (H.) and HAXBY (D.), eds., *Frontiers of Criminology*, Oxford, Pergamon Press, 1967.

6. MATZA (D.), *Delinquency and Drift*. New York, John Wiley, 1964.

7. The Kilbrandon Committee Report reflects the state of criminology in Britain in the early 1960s when the discipline was dominated by the contributions of psychologists and psychiatrists. There was little reference in the Report to the work of sociological criminologists— writers who stressed the cultural normality of certain kinds of delinquency. Indeed the relevance of this kind of approach was explicitly questioned in para. 77.

8. The Kilbrandon Committee, op. cit., para. 35.

9. ibid., para. 17.

10. SOCIAL WORK SERVICES GROUP, *Children's Hearings: Questions and Answers*. Edinburgh, H.M.S.O., 1971.

11. *See* SCHUR (E.), *Radical Nonintervention*. Englewood Cliffs, Prentice-Hall, 1973, Ch. 1, for a review of the literature.

12. BELSON (W.), *Juvenile Theft, the causal factors*. London, Harper and Row, 1975.

13. *See*, for example, RUTTER (M.), *Maternal Deprivation Reassessed*. Harmondsworth, Penguin Books, 1972.
MOREAN (P.), *Child Care, Sense and Fable*. London, Temple Smith, 1975.

14. POWER (M.), ASH (P.), SHOENBERY (E.), and SIREY (E.), 'Delinquency and the Family', *British Journal of Social Work*, 1974, **4**, 1, 13–38.

15. PRESIDENT'S COMMISSION ON LAW ENFORCEMENT AND ADMINISTRATION OF JUSTICE, *Task Force Report: Juvenile Delinquency and Youth Crime*. Washington, U.S. Government Printing Office, 1974, p. 8.

16. ibid.

17. For attempts to view adolescent behaviour in this wider context *see* *Resistance through rituals*. Working papers on Cultural Studies 7 and 8, Birmingham, Centre for Contemporary Cultural Studies, 1975.
Also, MUNGHAM (G.) and PEARSON (G.), *Working Class Youth Culture*. London, Routledge and Kegan Paul, 1976.

18. MILLHAM (S.), BULLOCK (R.) and CHERRETT (P.), 'Can we legislate for care?', *Community Schools Gazette*, 1974, **67**, 11, 622–9 at 629.

19. *See* for example CLARKE (R.) and CORNISH (D.), *Residential Treatment and Effects on Delinquency*. Home Office Research Unit Studies No. 32. London, H.M.S.O., 1975.

Where differences are reveale[...]
grammes are more effective a[...]
Programmes described as 'bette[...]
beneficial effects and those describe[...]
chances of recidivism.

20. *See* for example ARMSTRONG (G.) and [...]
    and Deviancy Amplification'. In: TAYLOR (I.[...]
    Politics and Deviance. Harmondsworth, Penguin[...]
    BUIKHUSEN (W.) and DIJKSTERHUIS (F.), 'Delinq[...]
    zation,' *British Journal of Criminology*, 1971, **11**, 2, [...]

21. AGETON (S.) and ELLIOT (D.), 'The effect of legal[...]
    delinquent orientations, *Social Problems*, 1974, **22**, 1, 87–[...]

22. FARRINGTON (D.), 'The effects of public labelling', *British Journal
    of Criminology*, 1977, **17**, 2, 112–25.

23. *See* for example GOLD (M.), 'Undetected Delinquent Behaviour',
    Journal of Research in Crime and Delinquency, 1966, **3**, 1, 27–46.
    CLARK (J. P.) and WENNINGER (E.), 'Socio-Economic class and area as
    correlates of illegal behaviour among juveniles', *American Sociological
    Review*, 1962, **27**, 6, 826–34.
    REISS (A.) and RHODES (A.), 'The distribution of juvenile delin-
    quency in the social class structure', *American Sociological Review*,
    1961, **26**, 5, 720–32.

24. CICOUREL (A.), *The Social Organization of Juvenile Justice.* 2nd ed.,
    London, Heinemann, 1977.

25. *See* for example PILIAVIN (I.) and BRIAR (S.), 'Police encounters
    with juveniles', *American Journal of Sociology*, 1964, **70**, 2, 206–14.
    WILSON (J. Q.), 'The Police and the delinquent in two cities.' In:
    GARABEDIAN (P.) and GIBBONS (D.), eds., *Becoming Delinquent.*
    Chicago, Aldine, 1970.
    CICOUREL (A.), ibid., chs. 3 and 5.

26. HOUSE OF COMMONS EXPENDITURE COMMITTEE, *Eleventh Report,
    Children and Young Persons Act 1969.* Vol. II. Minutes of Evidence.
    London, H.M.S.O., 1974 (HC 534–ii).

27. *Case Con.*, Autumn 1974, **17**, editorial.

28. RYAN (W.), *Blaming the Victim.* New York, Pantheon, 1971.

29. A more directly political form of analysis is found in Jürgen Habermas'
    writings. He suggests that public conflicts become 'personalized' in
    order to remove legitimacy from the conflicts. 'Previously, revolutions,
    and especially pseudo-revolutionary youth movements, have always
    incorporated motives of deviant behaviour, in other words clinical
    potential.'
    HABERMAS (J.), *Towards a Rational Society.* London, Heinemann
    Educational Books, 1971, p. 42.

30. SCOTT (P.), 'The Child, the Family and the Young Offender', *British
    Journal of Criminology*, 1966, **6**, 2, 105–111.

nd SPARKS (R.), eds., *Community homes and the approved
tem*. Papers presented to the Cropwood Round-Table Con-
e, Cambridge, Institute of Criminology, 1969.

ILLIP (A.), and McCULLOCH (J.), 'Uses of social indicators in psychiatric epidemiology, *British Journal of Preventive Social Medicine*,
1966, **20**, 122.

33. McALLISTER (J.) and MASON (A.), 'A comparison of juvenile delinquency and children in care—an analysis of socio-economic factors,'
British Journal of Criminology, 1972, **12**, 3, 280–86.

34. In Scotland orphaned children are dealt with in Part II of the Social
Work (Scotland) Act 1968 and in England in Part II of the Children
and Young Persons Act 1969; delinquent children are dealt with in Part
III of the Scottish Act and Part I of the English Act.

35. In Scotland the reporter has a statutory duty to refer children to the
hearing only where 'compulsory measures of care' may be necessary
(S.32 (9) and S.39 (3) of the Social Work (Scotland) Act 1968), but he
need satisfy no-one that voluntary measures have failed, or indeed,
have been tried. In England there exists the double-barrelled test (S.1
(2) of the Children and Young Persons Act 1969) but it seems that the
offence itself can indicate the need for measures of care. In the U.S.A.
about half of the referrals to the juvenile courts are for offences.

36. ERIKSON (E.), 'Notes on the Sociology of Deviance'. In: BECKER
(H.), *The Other Side*. New York, New York Free Press, 1967.
GARFINKEL (H.), 'Conditions of successful degradation ceremonies',
American Journal of Sociology, 1956, **61**.
COSER (L.), 'Some functions of deviant behaviour and normative
flexibility', *American Journal of Sociology*, 1962, *68* (2) 172–181.

37. ALLEN (F.), op. cit.

38. ibid. Some jurisdictions made token changes in language. S.59 of the
Children and Young Persons Act 1933 refers to 'findings of guilt' instead of convictions and to 'order upon such finding' instead of
sentence.

39. *See* for example S.43 (1) and S.47 (1), Social Work (Scotland) Act 1968.

40. *See* S.41 (2), Social Work (Scotland) Act 1968.

41. ALLEN (F.), op. cit.

42. SCOTT (P.), 'Juvenile Courts: The Juvenile Point of View', *British
Journal of Delinquency*, 1958–59, **9**, 3, 200–210.

43. MORRIS (A.) and GILLER (H.), 'The Juvenile Court—The Client's
Perspective', *Criminal Law Review*, 1977, 198–205.

44. For a discussion of this point in an English context *see* 'The Welfare
principle', *The Community Schools Gazette*, 1976, **70**, 8, 380–3.

45. The demand for additional secure places is a response to continued
offending by children rather than a response to their needs. There is
no suggestion that such institutions improve recidivism rates. Indeed
what evidence there is points in the opposite direction.

MILLHAM (S.) *et al.*, forthcoming work on secure accommodation.

46. The Kilbrandon Committee, op. cit., para. 17.

47. S.32 (3) Social Work (Scotland) Act 1968.

48. S.31 (1) Social Work (Scotland) Act 1968. Similar powers exist in England and Wales.

49. The Kilbrandon Committee, op. cit., para. 125.

50. S.38 (2) Social Work (Scotland) Act 1968.

51. RUSHFORTH (M.), 'Two Systems of Committal to Residential Training: A Scottish Case Study'. In: Home Office Research Unit, *Research Bulletin No. 3.* London, H.M.S.O., 1976.

52. WOOTTON (B.), 'The Juvenile Courts', *Criminal Law Review*, 1961, 669–77 at 673.

53. KILBRANDON (The Hon. Lord), 'The Scottish Reforms I: The Impact on the Public', *British Journal of Criminology*, 1968, **8**, 3, 235–41.

54. *In the Interests of Carlo*, 48, NJ, 224 at 245–6.

55. *Kent* v. *U.S.*, 583, U.S. 541.

56. *Gault* v. *U.S.*, 387, U.S. 1.

57. Juveniles were also given the right to have written notice of the charge or of the allegations, to confront and cross-examine witnesses and to be advised that they did not have to testify or make a statement. The court did not, however, extend all the procedural guarantees available in the case of an adult charged with a crime (e.g. the right to jury trial).

58. Where the child cannot be brought immediately before a sheriff summary court, the police are bound to liberate the child (on an obligation that he will attend the subsequent hearing or on bail) unless the charge is one of homicide or other 'grave crime', unless it is necessary in the interests of the child to remove him from association with any convicted criminal or prostitute, or unless the police have reason to believe that the child's liberation would defeat the ends of justice.

59. S.37 (2), Social Work (Scotland) Act, 1968.

60. The reporter must, wherever practicable, arrange a children's hearing to sit no later than the first day after the commencement of the child's detention to consider the case, or at least within seven days. If the hearing is unable to dispose of the case that day and is satisfied that further detention is necessary in the child's interest, or has reason to believe that he would run away during the investigation of the case, the hearing may issue a warrant requiring the child to be detained for 21 days (*see* S.40C7), Social Work (Scotland) Act, 1968). The Children Act 1975 has made some changes in the warrant rules to enable detention for a longer period.

61. SOCIAL WORK SERVICES GROUP. SCOTTISH EDUCATION DEPARTMENT, *Scottish Social Work Statistics, 1973*. Edinburgh, H.M.S.O., 1975. More than one report can relate to a single child and so this figure is likely to be an overestimate.

62. Children's Hearings (Scotland) Rules, 1971, rule 17 (2). Similar rules govern the operation of the English juvenile courts.

63. SOCIAL WORK SERVICES GROUP, SCOTTISH EDUCATION DEPART-MENT, op. cit. It is interesting to note the direction of this variation: 17% of the supervision requirements were varied from residential to non-residential; 9% from non-residential to residential.

64. GOODWIN (C.), 'The Rules of Procedure'. In: MARTIN (F.) and MURRAY (K.), eds., Children's Hearings. Edinburgh, Scottish Academic Press, 1976.

65. The Kilbrandon Committee, op. cit., para. 70.

66. SOCIAL WORK SERVICES GROUP, SCOTTISH EDUCATION DEPART-MENT, op. cit.

67. GORDON (G.), 'The Role of The Courts'. In: MARTIN(F.) and MURRAY (K.), eds., op. cit.

68. GOODWIN (C.), op. cit.

69. The Kilbrandon Committee, op. cit., para. 71.

70. ibid., para. 111.

71. D. v. Sinclair, 1973, S.L.T. (Sh. Ct.) 47.

72. GRANT (J. P.), 'Protecting The Rights Of The Child'. In: MARTIN (F.) and MURRAY (K.), eds., op. cit.

73. See S.49 (6), Social Work (Scotland) Act, 1968.

74. SOCIAL WORK SERVICES GROUP, Scottish Education Department, op. cit.

Chapter IV

1. COMMITTEE ON CHILDREN AND YOUNG PERSONS (SCOTLAND), Report. Edinburgh, H.M.S.O., 1964 (Cmnd. 2306). Chairman: The Hon. Lord Kilbrandon (Hereinafter referred to as The Kilbrandon Committee.) para. 98.

2. ibid., para. 75.

3. ibid., para. 76.

4. ibid., para. 43.

5. WORKING PARTY ON POLICE PROCEDURES UNDER THE SOCIAL WORK (SCOTLAND) ACT, Report. Edinburgh, H.M.S.O., 1970, para. 7.

6. SCOTTISH HOME AND HEALTH DEPARTMENT, Criminal Statistics Scotland, 1973. Edinburgh, H.M.S.O., 1974 (Cmnd. 5640).

7. SOCIAL WORK SERVICES GROUP. SCOTTISH EDUCATION DEPART-MENT, Scottish Social Work Statistics, 1973. Edinburgh, H.M.S.O., 1975.

8. ibid., table 2.55.

9. ibid., p. 30.

10. ibid., table 2.60.

11. ibid.

12. SCOTTISH HOME AND HEALTH DEPARTMENT, Criminal Statistics

Scotland, 1969. Edinburgh, H.M.S.O., 1970 (Cmnd. 4423).

13. SCOTTISH HOME AND HEALTH DEPARTMENT, *Criminal Statistics Scotland, 1973*, Edinburgh, H.M.S.O., 1974 (Cmnd. 5640).

14. HOME OFFICE, *Criminal Statistics England and Wales, 1973.* London, H.M.S.O., 1974 (Cmnd. 5677). The increase between 1969 and 1975 is also 4%.

15. SOCIAL WORK SERVICES GROUP, Scottish Education Department, op. cit.

16. ibid., table 2.63. There is no explanation presented for the difference between this figure and that presented in table 2.60. (*See* diagram II and footnote 10 above.)

17. The former juvenile courts could fine the child or the parent, place the child on probation, place him on a fit person or approved school order, send him to borstal (where the child was 16 or over and where he appeared in the sheriff juvenile court) or remand home, or admonish or discharge him.

18. SCOTTISH HOME AND HEALTH DEPARTMENT, *Criminal Statistics Scotland, 1970.* Edinburgh, H.M.S.O., 1971, (Cmnd. 4707).

19. In 1973, 18% of those found guilty of indictable offences in the 14 to 17 age group were placed on supervision by the juvenile court and only 5% of those found guilty of non-indictable offences. In the 10 to 14 group, 25% of those found guilty of indictable offences and 11% of those found guilty of non-indictable offences were placed on supervision. These are startling figure in view of a major aim of the Children and Young Persons Act—to deal with the child offender as much as possible in the community. The most commonly used measure in England is the fine—a measure not available to the children's hearings. In the 14 to 17 age-group 40% of those found guilty of indictable offences and 75% of those found guilty of non-indictable offences were fined; the percentage for the 10 to 14 age-group were 23% and 48% respectively (HOME OFFICE, op. cit.).

20. DUNCAN (J.) and ARNOTT (A.), Unpublished research on the juvenile courts. University of Edinburgh.

21. The Kilbrandon Committee, op. cit., para. 140.

22. i.e. former approved schools.

23. i.e. former remand homes.

24. SCOTTISH HOME AND HEALTH DEPARTMENT, *Criminal Statistics Scotland, 1970,* op. cit., note 18.

25. SCOTTISH HOME AND HEALTH DEPARTMENT, *Criminal Statistics Scotland, 1973,* op. cit., note 6.

26. Care orders, though imposed by juvenile court magistrates, are implemented by social workers—magistrates cannot commit directly to community homes—and this explains the fall in numbers. The *use* of care orders by the juvenile courts, however, has increased slightly over this period—from 8% in 1969 to 10% in 1973. English magistrates,

unlike panel members, also have the power to send children to detention centres and to remit them to Crown Courts for sentence. Sentences to detention centres rose by 67% from 1969 to 1973 and sentences
to borstal training for 15- to 17-year-olds doubled over the same
period. In 1973 just over 3,000 children were sent to detention centres
by juvenile court magistrates. Of those remitted from the magistrates'
court to the Crown Court for sentence, 62% were sentenced to borstal
and 20% to detention centres.

27. In 1973, 19% of 14- to 17-year-olds found guilty of indictable offences
    were discharged, and 12% of those found guilty of non-indictable
    offences were discharged. The figures are higher for those under 14:
    27% of those found guilty of indictable offences and 29% of those
    found guilty of non-indictable offences. HOME OFFICE, op. cit.

28. SCOTTISH HOME AND HEALTH DEPARTMENT, *Criminal Statistics
    Scotland, 1973*, op. cit., note 6.

29. The Kilbrandon Committee, op. cit.

30. *H. C. Deb.* vol. 10.

31. There is currently discussion over whether these powers should be
    given to the hearings.

32. GORDON (G.), 'The Role of the Courts', In: MARTIN (F.) and
    MURRAY (K.), eds., *Children's Hearings*. Edinburgh, Scottish Acade-
    mic Press, 1976.

33. SCOTTISH HOME AND HEALTH DEPARTMENT, *Criminal Statistics
    Scotland, 1973*, op. cit., note 6.

34. ibid.

35. In 1975, 2,262 persons under 16 were proceeded against in Scottish
    courts. *See* table 17, SCOTTISH HOME AND HEALTH DEPARTMENT,
    Criminal Statistics Scotland, 1975. Edinburgh, H.M.S.O., 1976
    (Cmnd. 6631).

36. 135 out of 175 children referred by the police to the fiscals in the survey
    city were referred by them to the reporters. 13 were not proceeded
    against; only 27 were referred to a court (and only 7 of these were dealt
    with by the sheriff without the advice of the hearing).

37. *See*, for example, GORDON (G.), op. cit.

38. DUNCAN (J.) and ARNOTT (A.), op. cit. This project examined how
    two different systems for dealing with juveniles were working before
    the proposals of the Kilbrandon Committee were implemented. One
    area dealt with juveniles by the usual practice, that is a modified ver-
    sion of the adult criminal court, and the other had a special juvenile
    court. Information from police, probation and court reports was col-
    lected on 300 children referred to the police in 1967 in each of these
    areas. The material gathered fell into two main categories: in-
    formation about the children themselves, their delinquencies,
    general characteristics and the like; and information on the way in

which the administration of justice worked in relation to these children.

39. *See*, for example, WEST (D.) and FARRINGTON (D.), *Who Becomes Delinquent?* London, Heinemann Educational Books, 1973.

Chapter V

1. SOCIAL WORK SERVICES GROUP, SCOTTISH EDUCATION DEPARTMENT, *Scottish Social Work Statistics, 1973.* Edinburgh, H.M.S.O., 1975.

2. SCOTTISH HOME AND HEALTH DEPARTMENT, *Criminal Statistics Scotland, 1973.* Edinburgh, H.M.S.O., 1974 (Cmnd. 5640).

3. A community relations branch was subsequently set up in the city in 1975.

4. A liaison officer was subsequently appointed in the county in 1972 and became operative in the summer of 1973.

5. The authorized strength in the city in 1973 was 1,269, actual strength was 1,236; the county numbers were 643 and 634 respectively. Annual Reports of the Chief Constables in the two research areas, 1973.

6. ibid.

7. The rate per 1,000 population for Scotland as a whole was 97.0.

8. Annual Report of the Chief Constable, 1973.

9. This description excludes cases referred during this period by the police to the procurator fiscal—arguably the most serious cases. But most of these referrals were, in fact, for technical or procedural reasons. For example, only 17 out of the 171 children referred to the city procurators fiscal for consideration of prosecution were dealt with by the sheriff court. It is unlikely that these cases alter the overall picture of juvenile crime.

10. Annual Report of the Chief Constable (city), 1968 and 1969.

11. Annual Report of the Chief Constable (county), 1969.

12. Annual Report of the Chief Constable (county), 1973.

13. SCOTTISH ADVISORY COUNCIL ON TREATMENT AND REHABILITATION OF OFFENDERS, *Police warnings: Report.* Edinburgh, H.M.S.O., 1945.

14. DUNCAN (J.) and ARNOTT (A.), Unpublished research on the juvenile court. University of Edinburgh.

15. MACK (J.) and RITCHIE (M.), *Police Warnings.* Glasgow, University of Glasgow, 1974.

16. SCOTTISH HOME AND HEALTH DEPARTMENT, *Criminal Statistics Scotland, 1969.* Edinburgh, H.M.S.O., 1970 (Cmnd. 4423).

17. SCOTTISH HOME AND HEALTH DEPARTMENT, *Criminal Statistics Scotland,* 1969, op. cit.

18. SCOTTISH HOME AND HEALTH DEPARTMENT, *Criminal Statistics Scotland 1973,* op. cit., note 2.

19. SCOTTISH HOME AND HEALTH DEPARTMENT, *Criminal Statistics Scotland, 1969*, op. cit. note 16.
20. SCOTTISH HOME AND HEALTH DEPARTMENT, *Criminal Statistics Scotland, 1973*, op. cit., note 2.
21. *See*, for example HOWLETT (P. W.), 'Is the Y.S.B. all it's cracked up to be?' *Crime and Delinquency*, 1973, **19**, 4, 485–92.
22. TAYLOR (M.), *Study of the Juvenile Liaison Scheme in West Ham, 1961–65.* Home Office Research Studies No. 8. London, H.M.S.O., 1971.
23. DITCHFIELD (J.), *Police Cautioning in England and Wales.* Home Office Research Study No. 37. London, H.M.S.O., 1976.
24. MACK (J.) and RITCHIE (M.), op. cit.
25. SOCIAL WORK SERVICES GROUP, SCOTTISH EDUCATION DEPARTMENT, op. cit.
26. Practice has changed since this research but the general point remains valid.
27. Memorandum of the General Purposes Committee of the Association of Chief Police Officers, 1974.
28. Referred to by MACK (J.) and RITCHIE (M.), op. cit., p. 33.
29. COMMITTEE ON CHILDREN AND YOUNG PERSONS (SCOTLAND), *Report.* Edinburgh, H.M.S.O., 1964, (Cmnd. 2306). Chairman: The Hon. Lord Kilbrandon (Hereinafter referred to as the Kilbrandon Committee.) para. 138.
30. S. 37(1) and S. 39(2), Social Work (Scotland) Act, 1968.
31. The Kilbrandon Committee, op. cit.
32. ibid., para. 152.
33. There was little criticism by the police of what we could call the 'no action rate of the juvenile courts. The juvenile courts discharged, on average, one third of those dealt with by them. The difference is that the child appeared before a court and this had symbolic importance.
34. op. cit., note 26.
35. Quoted in *Justice of the Peace*, 12 September 1972.
36. The Kilbrandon Committee, op. cit., para. 146.
37. *See*, for example, FARRINGTON (D.), 'The effects of public labelling,' *British Journal of Criminology*, 1977. **17**, 2, 112–25.
38. The Kilbrandon Committee, op. cit., para. 13.
39. SCOTTISH HOME AND HEALTH DEPARTMENT, *Report of the Working Party on Police Procedure arising from the Social Work (Scotland) Act, 1968.* Edinburgh, H.M.S.O., 1970.
40. The Kilbrandon Committee, op. cit., para. 146.
41. The seriousness of the offence does, however, indicate the seriousness of society's concern about the offence.
42. Such stereotypes are likely to be maintained as long as certain assumptions are made about delinquent behaviour, and we discuss this in subsequent chapters.

Chapter VI

1. LEMERT (Edwin M.), 'The Juvenile Court'—Quest and Realities'. In: PRESIDENT'S COMMISSION ON LAW ENFORCEMENT AND ADMINISTRATION OF JUSTICE, *Task force Report: Juvenile Delinquency and Youth Crime*. Washington, U.S. Government Printing Office, 1967.
2. The labelling perspective suggests that the process of arrest, trial and conviction changes the self-image of the juvenile. He increasingly sees himself as delinquent, acts *as if* delinquent, and others respond to him as if he *always was* delinquent. *See* LEMERT (Edwin M.), *Human Deviance, social problems and social control*. Englewood Cliffs, Prentice Hall, 1972.
3. Differential association theory suggests that criminal behaviour occurs when individuals have more contact with those with delinquent than with those with non-delinquent attitudes. *See* SUTHERLAND (E.) and CRESSEY (D.), *Principles of Criminology*. 8th ed. Philadelphia, Lippincott, 1970, pp. 72–91.
4. *See*, for example, FARRINGTON (D.), 'The effects of public labelling', *British Journal of Criminology*, 1977, **17**, 2, 112–25.
5. CRESSEY (D.) and MCDERMOT (R.), *Diversion from the Juvenile Justice System*. Michigan, University of Michigan, 1973.
6. S.39(3), Social Work (Scotland) Act 1968.
7. COMMITTEE ON CHILDREN AND YOUNG PERSONS (SCOTLAND), *Report*. Edinburgh H.M.S.O., 1964 (Cmnd. 2306). Chairman: The Hon. Lord Kilbrandon (Hereinafter referred to as the Kilbrandon Committee), para. 98.
8. After local government reorganization in 1975, social workers became the dominant professional group amongst reporters.
9. SOCIAL WORK SERVICES GROUP, SCOTTISH EDUCATION DEPARTMENT, *Scottish Social Work Statistics*, 1973. Edinburgh, H.M.S.O. 1975.
10. DUNCAN (J.) and ARNOTT (A.), Unpublished research on the juvenile courts. University of Edinburgh.
11. The Kilbrandon Committee, op. cit. para. 78.
12. EMERSON (R.), *Judging Delinquents*. Chicago, Aldine, 1970.

Chapter VII

1. COMMITTEE ON CHILDREN AND YOUNG PERSONS (SCOTLAND), *Report*. Edinburgh, H.M.S.O., 1964 (Cmnd. 2306). Chairman The Hon. Lord Kilbrandon (Hereinafter referred to as the Kilbrandon Committee), para. 92.
2. In some areas magistrates are appointed directly to the juvenile bench but this is the exception rather than the rule.
3. English juvenile magistrates appear influenced by their work as magistrates in the adult courts in their work on the juvenile bench.

Cavenagh, for example, wrote that juvenile courts were 'closely integrated in the general system of the administration of justice, and there is to some extent a two-way flow of ideas and attitudes between the juvenile courts and adult courts.' She also wrote 'the sorts of personal qualities, attitudes and capacities desirable for service in the juvenile court are probably equally desired in the adult court.' CAVENAGH (W.E.), *Juvenile Courts, the Child and the Law.* Harmondsworth, Pelican Books, 1967, p. 13.

4. *Criteria for Selection.* Paper 5 of a series of papers presented to Children's Panel Advisory Committees.

5. SCOTTISH EDUCATION DEPARTMENT, SCOTTISH HOME AND HEALTH DEPARTMENT, *Social Work and the Community.* Edinburgh, H.M.S.O., 1966 (Cmnd. 3065), para. 81.

6. SOCIAL WORK SERVICES GROUP, Appendix A. Circular No. SW7/1969.

7. ibid., para. 1.

8. MAPSTONE (E.), 'The Selection of the Children's Panels for the County of Fife', *British Journal of Social Work*, 1972, **2**, 4, 445–69.

9. ROWE (A.), *Initial Selection for Children's Panels in Scotland.* London, Bookstall Publications, 1972.

10. HIGGINS (L. W.), Unpublished research on the characteristics of panel members. University of Glasgow, 1974.

11. MAPSTONE (E.), op. cit.

12. CAVENAGH (W.), Unpublished report to a conference of juvenile court magistrates, Paris, 1973.

13. It is interesting to note that magistrates in England are trained primarily by fellow magistrates and clerks to the justices. This means that they are likely to be receptive to legal or criminal justice values.

14. SOCIAL WORK SERVICES GROUP, *Assessment of Children.* Report of a study group set up by the Chief Social Work Adviser. Edinburgh, H.M.S.O., 1971.

15. PRIESTLEY (P.), *In the Interests of the Child.* Unpublished research report. University of Bristol, 1975.

16. Cf. the view of the Morison Committee: 'Probation Officers are not now equipped by their experience, and research cannot yet equip them, to assume a general function of expressing opinions to the courts about the likely effects of sentences.' The same is true of social workers and of research today. Most recommendations are based on experience of what the court or hearing is likely to do. *See* DEPARTMENTAL COMMITTEE ON THE PROBATION SERVICE, *Report.* London, H.M.S.O., 1962 (Cmnd. 1650). para. 41.

17. PATERSON (L.), 'Lay Bodies and Social Workers', SOCIAL WORK TODAY, 1972, **3**, (2) 13–14.

18. SOCIAL WORK SERVICES GROUP, SCOTTISH EDUCATION DEPARTMENT, *Scottish Social Work Statistics, 1973.* Edinburgh, H.M.S.O., 1975.

19. In 1973, 18% of referrals in the city were discharged compared with 6% in the county. 17% in the city were given supervision with a residential requirement compared with 20% in the county and 66% in the city were given a non-residential order comparable with 74% in the county.

20. The Kilbrandon Committee, op. cit., para. 88.

21. Duncan and Arnott found that the child's previous record was more important than his current offence in the decision to remove him from home.
  DUNCAN (J.) and ARNOTT (A.), Unpublished research on the juvenile courts. University of Edinburgh.

22. Panel members in area A emphasized the child whereas panel members from area Z emphasized society's interests. See BRUCE (N.) and SPENCER (J.), *Face to Face with Families*. Edinburgh, Macdonald, 1976, p. 140.

23. The Kilbrandon Committee, op. cit., para. 109.

24. EMERSON (R.), *Judging Delinquents*. Chicago, Aldine, 1969, Part II.

25. ibid., p. 108.
  'Typical delinquencies also identify the kind of typical actor in terms of moral character because they include a picture of the kind of youth who is apt to be involved in this kind of performance.'

26. MATZA (D.), *Delinquency and Drift*. New York, John Wiley, 1964.

27. ibid., p. 125.

28. CICOUREL (A.), *The Social Organisation of Juvenile Justice*. 2nd edition. London, Heinemann Educational Books, 1976, p. 243.

29. EMERSON (R.), op. cit., p. 131. Emerson, in fact, borrows Matza's distinction. See MATZA (D.), 'The disreputable poor.' In: BENDIX (R.) and LIPSTEIN (S.), eds., *Class, Status and Power*. New York, Free Press, 1966.

30. *See*, for example, ROWE (A.), op. cit. Reporters, because of their previous professional background and current social and economic status, are also middle-class, as are social workers—the main presenters of information to the hearings.

31. DAVIES (M.), 'Social Inquiry for the Courts', *British Journal of Criminology*, 1974, **14** 1, 18–33.

32. EMERSON (R.), op. cit.

33. LEMERT (E.), 'Choice and change in juvenile justice,' *British Journal of Law and Society*, 1976, **3**, 1, 59–75.

34. We were able to make some comparisons between offenders in our sample and those in the earlier 1967 sample. Offenders in the 1972/3 samples committed more offences than those in the 1967 samples. Around one third of the 1967 samples had committed two or more offences compared with almost half of the 1972/3 samples. This latter figure increased to almost two thirds in the city and to three quarters in the county where the comparison was made with the 1972/3 'children's

hearing' sample rather than the 'reporter' sample. The 1972/3 samples also stole property of slightly higher value than the 1967 sample—this could, of course, reflect no more than changes in police recording practices and inflation! There was no difference in the indication of 'problems' between the 1967 city sample and those referred to the city reporters (and to the city's children's hearings) in 1972/3—just over 60% of the children in both samples were described as presenting some indication of 'problems'. There was, however, some difference between the county samples. About half of the 1972/3 children's hearing sample were described as presenting 'problems' compared with one third in the 1967 sample. But, overall, we cannot make any firm conclusions—the comparability of the data is suspect and any apparent changes must be treated with caution.

35. At a recent conference it was suggested that 40% of children in 'List D' schools did not need to be there.

Chapter VIII

1. 'Children's Panels—a costly failure,' *Glasgow Herald*, 8 March 1975.
2. ibid.
3. Letter by B. Dickson in *Glasgow Herald*, 7 March 1975.
4. Letter by E. Thompson in *The Scotsman*, 10 August 1974.
5. 'Children's Panels—a costly failure', op. cit.
6. SCOTTISH HOME AND HEALTH DEPARTMENT, *Criminal Statistics Scotland, 1969*. Edinburgh, H.M.S.O., 1970, (Cmnd. 4423).
7. SCOTTISH HOME AND HEALTH DEPARTMENT, *Criminal Statistics Scotland, 1973*. Edinburgh, H.M.S.O., 1974 (Cmnd. 5640).
8. *See*, for example, MCCLINTOCK (F. H.), *Crimes of Violence*. Cambridge Studies in Criminology, Vol. 18. London, Macmillan, 1963.
9. WILSON (J. Q.), 'The police and the delinquent in two cities.' In: GARABEDIAN (P.) and GIBBONS (D.), eds., *Becoming Delinquent*. Chicago, Aldine, 1970.
10. COMMITTEE ON CHILDREN AND YOUNG PERSONS SCOTLAND, *Report*. Edinburgh, H.M.S.O., 1964 (Cmnd. 2306). Chairman: The Hon. Lord Kilbrandon, para. 28.
11. Letter by E. Thompson, op. cit.
12. A recent circular from the Scottish Home and Health Department canvassed the idea that panels should have the power to fine.
13. DONE (K.), 'Judiciary condemn some aspects of social work legislation', *The Scotsman*, 19 March 1975.
14. WILLOCK (I.), 'Children's Panels after a year,' *The Scotsman*, 15 April 1972.
15. 'Children's Panels—a costly failure', op. cit.
16. ibid.
17. ibid.

18. BRUCE (N.), 'Children's Hearings: promise not yet fulfilled,' *The Times Educational Supplement*, Scotland, 23 May 1975.
19. *K v Finlayson* S.L.T. 1974 (Sher. Ct.), 51.
20. PARSLOE (P.), 'The boundaries between legal and social work concerns in the hearing system.' In: HOUSTON (D.), ed., *Social Work in the Children's Hearing System*. Edinburgh, Glasgow and Edinburgh Joint Committee for further and Advanced Training, 1975.
21. Letter by J. Boddycombe in *Observer*, 7 July 1972.
See also the evidence of the Police Federation to the Subcommittee of the House of Commons Expenditure Committee investigating the Children and Young Persons Act 1969. In: HOUSE OF COMMONS EXPENDITURE COMMITTEE, *Eleventh Report. Children and Young Persons Act 1969*. Vol. II. London, H.M.S.O., 1975 (H.C. 534–ii).
22. *See* evidence of the Magistrates' Association, ibid.
23. Letter by J. Watson in *The Times*, 8 July 1972.
24. Evidence of the National Council for Civil Liberties. In: HOUSE OF COMMONS EXPENDITURE COMMITTEE, op. cit., p. 274.
25. Evidence of the Justices' Clerks' Society, ibid., p. 303.
26. Evidence of the British Association of Social Workers, ibid., p. 222.
27. Evidence of the Magistrates' Association, ibid.
28. COLE (E.), *Politics and the Administration of Justice*. New York, Sage, 1973.
29. Evidence of the Police Federation, HOUSE OF COMMONS EXPENDITURE COMMITTEE, op. cit.
30. The recent White Paper on the 1969 Act recommends the establishment of a National Advisory Council 'providing a forum for the provision of advice to Ministers ... the encouragement of the local liaison arrangements ... and the formulation of advice regarding the forms that these might best take'. HOME OFFICE, WELSH OFFICE, DEPARTMENT OF HEALTH AND SOCIAL SECURITY, DEPARTMENT OF EDUCATION AND SCIENCE, *Observations on the Eleventh Report from the Expenditure Committee*. London, H.M.S.O., 1976 (Cmnd. 6494), para. 81.
31. LEMERT (E.), 'Choice and change in juvenile justice', *British Journal of Law and Society*, 1976, 3, 1, 59–75.
32. *See*, for example, 'The Children and Young Persons Bill,' *The Magistrate*, 1969, **25**, 4, 48–50.
'Resolutions of the Annual General Meeting of the Magistrates' Association,' *The Magistrate*, 1972, **28**, 11, 181–5.

Epilogue

1. BRUCE (N.) and SPENCER (J.), 'Children's Hearings and the Scottish Courts.' In: JONES (K.), ed., *Yearbook of Social Policy in Britain 1973*. London, Routledge and Kegan Paul, 1974.

2. *See*, for example, the evidence of these groups to the House of Commons Expenditure Committee. HOUSE OF COMMONS EXPENDITURE COMMITTEE, *Eleventh Report, Children and Young Persons Act 1969*. Vol. II. London, H.M.S.O., 1975 (H.C. 534-ii).

3. MILLHAM (S.), BULLOCK (R.) and CHERRITT (P.), *After Grace—Teeth*. London, Human Context Books, 1975.

4. ADAMS (S.), 'Corrections and Caseloads.' In: JOHNSON (N.) *et al.*, *Sociology of Punishment and Corrections*. New York. John Wiley, 1970.

5. LERMAN (P.), *Community Treatment and Social Control*. Chicago, University Press, 1975.

6. HOUSE OF COMMONS EXPENDITURE COMMITTEE, op. cit., Vol. 1, para. 167.

7. HOME OFFICE, WELSH OFFICE, DEPARTMENT OF HEALTH AND SOCIAL SECURITY, DEPARTMENT OF EDUCATION AND SCIENCE, *Observations on the Eleventh Report from the Expenditure Committee*. London, H.M.S.O., 1976 (Cmnd. 6494), para. 2.

8. SCHUR (E.), *Radical Nonintervention*. Englewood Cliffs, Prentice-Hall, 1973.

9. COHEN (S.), 'It's All Right for You to Talk: Political and Sociological Manifestos for Social Work Action,' In: BAILEY (R.) and BRAKE (M.), eds., *Radical Social Work*. London, Edward Arnold, 1975.

10. Jock Young, for example, writes: 'We have to argue, therefore, strategically, for the exercise of social control, but also to argue that such control must be exercised within the working class community and not by external policing agencies. The control of crime on the streets, like the control of rate-busting on the factory floor, can only be achieved *effectively* by the community immediately involved,' (author's emphasis).
YOUNG (J.), 'Working-class criminology.' In: TAYLOR (I.), WALTON (P.) and YOUNG (J.), eds., *Critical Criminology*. London, Routledge and Kegan Paul, 1975.

11. 'The task we have set ourselves, and other criminologists, is the attempt to create the kind of society in which the facts of human diversity are not subject to the power to criminalize.' *See* TAYLOR (I.), WALTON (P.) and YOUNG (J.), eds., op. cit. p. 44.

12. HOUSE OF COMMONS EXPENDITURE COMMITTEE, op. cit., Vol. 1, para. 17.

13. ibid., para. 13. The Committee's specific recommendations based on this approach were the creation of secure care orders, a return to probation in favour of supervision orders, the development of attendance centres and the retention and expansion of the detention centre system.

14. ibid., para. 167.

15. HOME OFFICE *et al.*, op. cit., para. 3.

16. *See* a discussion of the London Borough of Islington's policy, 'The Youngsters Who'll be Left in the Cold,' *Community Care*, 17 November 1976.

17. In 1975, 48% of those under 14 years and 74% of those between 14 and 17 years who committed non-indictable offences were fined: for indictable offences the figures were 21% and 39% respectively (a further 30% and 18% were given conditional discharges).

18. FARRINGTON (D.), 'The effects of public labelling,' *British Journal of Criminology*, 1977, **17**, 2, 112–25.

19. WOLFGANG (M.), 'Seriousness of crime and a policy of juvenile justice', In: SLORT (J.F.), ed., *Delinquency, Crime and Society*. The University of Chicago Press, 1976.

20. e.g. current research by N. Walker. Institute of Criminology, Cambridge.

21. Intermediate treatment schemes are increasingly being extended to what are seen as *potentially* delinquent children.

22. *See*, for example, MILLHAM (S.), BULLOCK (R.) and HOSIE (K.), 'On Violence in Community Homes.' In: TUTT (N.), ed., *Violence*. London, H.M.S.O. 1976. Also, CLARKE (R.V.G.) and MARTIN (D.N.), *Absconding From Approved Schools*. Home Office Research Study No. 12. London H.M.S.O., 1971.

23. DITCHFIELD (J.A.), *Police Cautioning in England and Wales*. Home Office Research Study No. 37. London, H.M.S.O., 1976.

24. Berlins and Wansell write: 'As a purely working estimate we would like to venture that something in the order of 4 per cent of all the children under seventeen who appear before the courts on indictable offences in any single year may pose extreme difficulties. In bleak terms this could mean that more than 2,500 children would fall into this group. . . .'
    BERLINS (M.) and WANSELL (G.), *Caught in the Act*. Harmondsworth, Penguin Books, 1974, p. 104.

25. *See* SCOTT (P.), 'Juvenile Courts: The Juveniles' Point of View,' *British Journal of Delinquency*, 1959, **9**, 3, 200–210. LIPSETT (P.), 'The Juvenile Offender's Perception,' *Crime and Delinquency*, 1968, **14**, 1, 49–62.

26. MATZA (D.), *Delinquency and Drift*. New York, John Wiley, 1964, pp. 133–4.

27. ibid.

28. Matza, ibid., distinguishes between principles (such as individualized justice) and doctrines (such as equity) in the foundation and the operation of the juvenile court. Here we are considering only the ideological principles which form the basis of the court.

29. CAVENAGH (W.), Unpublished report to a conference of juvenile court magistrates. Paris, 1973.

30. MORRIS (A.) and GILLER (H.), 'The Juvenile Court—The Client's Perspective,' *Criminal Law Review*, 1977, 198–205.

31. MORRIS (A.) and GILLER (H.), op. cit. Such results give support to Matza's contention that the sense of injustice produced when these standards are not maintained by the court may well aid the child's drift into delinquency.
32. PRIESTLEY (P.), *In the interest of the child.* Unpublished research report. University of Bristol, 1975.
33. For example in California and Maine elements of indeterminacy in sentence for adults have been removed. This means that mechanisms such as parole have been expunged.
34. Fox (S.), 'Philosophy and the Principles of Punishmént in the Juvenile Court', *Family Law Quarterly*, 1974, **8**, 373–84. According to Fox, in a paper to the British Society of Criminology in February 1977, the American Bar Association is currently developing a sentencing code for juveniles based on similar principles.
35. MORRIS (A.) and GILLER (H.), op. cit., give some examples of parents' views of improvements. There are also often gaps between theory and practice. American experience shows that judicial statements of the child's legal rights are not enough to ensure their implementation in practice.
36. LIPTON (D.), MARTINSON (R.) and WILKS (J.), *The Effectiveness of Correctional Treatment.* A Survey of Treatment Evaluation Studies. New York, Prager, 1975.
Howevef others, such as Brody, have written:

> This apparent failure of research to demonstrate the corrective value of rehabilitation as a sentencing aim has nevertheless had one refreshing consequence. It has seen the rejection of reconviction as the sole criterion of success, and a growing concern for evaluation according to other standards. A noticeable trend has been a readiness to justify non-custodial or semi-custodial sentences in preference to imprisonment or incarceration, on the grounds that they cost very much less to implement, and decrease at the same time the risk of psychological and practical harm to the offender. As 'softer' sentences have apparently no worse effect on recidivism and still offer the chance of less tangible if as yet unknown advantages, they are seen as preferable by all schools of thought except perhaps the retributivist.
>
> But is this a pessimistic outlook entirely substantiated by the results of research? To the researcher, the subject is by no means closed. Just as methodological deficiencies and flaws in carrying out experiments make any results dubious—so they make unacceptable any assurances that corrective changes cannot be induced.'

BRODY (S.R.), *The Effectiveness of Sentencing.* Home Office Research Study No. 35. London, H.M.S.O., 1976.

Index

appeals, 27, 65–9, 141–3
approved schools, 19, 20, 25, 51, 74, 76, 148
attendance centres, 16, 25

borstal, 51, 77, 131, 148

care proceedings, 18–20, 24–5, 56, 58–62, 65–6
Child, the Family and the Young Offender, The, 22–3, 42, 47, 55
Children Act (1908), 4, 9–10
Children Act (1948), 16
Children and Young Persons Act (1932), 13
Children and Young Persons Act (1933), 13, 114
Children and Young Persons Act (1963), 21
Children and Young Persons Act (1969), 23, 30, 32, 46, 53, 76, 87, 114, 144–6, 149–50
Children and Young Persons Bill (1969), 43–4
Children and Young Persons (Scotland) Act (1932), 13
Children and Young Persons (Scotland) Act (1937), 13, 25, 36
Children in Trouble, 23–5, 30, 42–3
children's hearings, 44, 56–8, 65–9, 71–7, 81, 89–90, 97, 118–36, 139–44, 155
community homes, 25, 148

see also approved schools; List D schools
criminal proceedings, 1–4, 6, 18–21, 25, 60–7

delinquency, 4–5, 7, 16–17, 21–4, 26, 33–4, 38, 43, 48–57, 61, 91–2, 128, 149, 151
detention centres, 16, 25, 51, 77, 131, 148
discharges, 76, 118–19, 121–4, 130–32

fines, 75, 139, 151

House of Commons Expenditure Committee, 53, 144, 149–51, 153, 156

Ingleby Committee (1960), 14, 17–21, 25, 36
intermediate treatment, 25

juvenile courts, 57–8, 94–5, 151–6
in England, 4, 6, 8–14, 17–25, 30, 42–4, 58–9, 62, 73, 76, 144–7, 151, 154–5
in Scotland, 11–14, 25–31, 32–7, 71, 73, 75, 84, 86, 110, 119
in USA, 4, 9, 57, 62–4, 127, 154

Kilbrandon Committee (1964), 14, 26–30, 32–9, 42, 49, 53, 56, 59–61, 67–9, 71, 75–6, 89–92, 96, 110–11, 114, 119, 122, 128, 136, 139, 142–4